February 23–24, 2016
St. Augustine, FL, USA

I0053555

**Association for
Computing Machinery**

Advancing Computing as a Science & Profession

HotMobile'16

Proceedings of the 17th International Workshop on
Mobile Computing Systems and Applications

Sponsored by:
ACM SIGMOBILE

Supported by:
Microsoft Research, Google, HP, IBM, and Facebook

**Association for
Computing Machinery**

Advancing Computing as a Science & Profession

The Association for Computing Machinery
2 Penn Plaza, Suite 701
New York, New York 10121-0701

ISBN: 978-1-4503-4500-2

ACM Order No: 103160

Additional copies may be ordered prepaid from:

ACM Order Department
PO Box 30777
New York, NY 10087-0777, USA

Phone: 1-800-342-6626 (USA and Canada)
+1-212-626-0500 (Global)
Fax: +1-212-944-1318
E-mail: acmhelp@acm.org
Hours of Operation: 8:30 am – 4:30 pm ET

Printed in the USA

Welcome to ACM HotMobile 2016

It is our great pleasure to welcome you to *the Seventeenth Workshop on Mobile Computing Systems and Applications – HotMobile'16.* This year's workshop continues the series of highly selective, interactive workshops focused on mobile applications, systems, and environments, as well as their underlying state-of-the-art technologies. HotMobile's small workshop format makes it ideal for processing and discussing new directions or controversial approaches.

The call for papers attracted submissions from Asia, Europe, and the United States. The program committee reviewed and accepted 18 papers out of 55 submissions (acceptance rate 32%).

We also encourage attendees to attend the keynote and invited talk presentations. These valuable and insightful talks can and will guide us to a better understanding of the future:

- *Keynote: **Hot or Not? Moving forward from Weiser's vision of ubiquitous computing***

  *Speaker: **Gregory D. Abowd (School of Interactive Computing, Georgia Tech)***

Putting together *HotMobile'16* was a team effort. We first thank the authors for providing the content of the program. We are grateful to the program committee and the steering committee, who worked very hard in reviewing papers and providing feedback for authors. Finally, we thank our sponsor, ACM SIGMOBILE, and our generous corporate supporters, Google, Microsoft, Facebook, IBM and HP. We hope that you will find this program interesting and thought-provoking and that the workshop will provide you with a valuable opportunity to share ideas with other researchers and practitioners from institutions around the world.

David Chu
HotMobile'16 General Chair
Microsoft Research, Redmond, USA

Prabal Dutta
HotMobile'16 Program Chair
University of Michigan, USA

Table of Contents

Session 5: Wireless Sensing

Session Chair: Chunyi Peng *(Ohio State University, USA)*

Session 6: For Fun and Performance

Session Chair: Geoff Challen *(University at Buffalo, USA)*

Session 7: Private, Please

Session Chair: Robin Kravets *(University of Illinois, USA)*

HotMobile 2016 Workshop Organization

General Chairs: David Chu *(Microsoft Research - Redmond WA, USA)*

Program Chair: Prabal Dutta *(University of Michigan, USA)*

Demo and Poster Chair: Eduardo Cuervo *(Microsoft Research - Redmond WA, USA)*

Sponsorship Chair: Shivacant Mishra *(University of Colorado Boulder, USA)*

Publicity Chair: Wenjun Hu *(Yale University, USA)*
Sarah Clinch *(Lancaster University, UK)*

Publication Chair: Xuan Bao *(Google, USA)*

Local Arrangements Chair: Ted Tsung-Te Lai *(University of Illinois at Urbana-Champaign, USA)*

Registration Chair: Taiwoo Park *(Michigan State University, USA)*

Web Chair: Jeremy Gummeson *(Disney Research Pittsburgh, USA)*

Steering Committee Chair: Nigel Davies *(Lancaster University, UK)*

Steering Committee: Ramón Cáceres *(Rutgers Institute, USA)*
Mahadev Satyanarayanan *(Carnegie Mellon University, USA)*
Roy Want *(Google, USA)*
Matt Welsh *(Google, USA)*
Stefan Saroiu *(Microsoft Research, USA)*
Justin Manweiler *(IBM T.J. Watson Research Center, USA)*
Romit Roy Choudhury *(University of Illinois at Urbana Champaign, USA)*

Program Committee: Aruna Balasubramanian *(Stony Brook University, USA)*
Nilanjan Banerjee *(University of Maryland, Baltimore County, USA)*
Geoff Challen *(University at Buffalo, USA)*
Landon Cox *(Duke University, USA)*
Rodrigo Fonseca *(Brown University, USA)*
Roxana Geambasu *(Columbia University, USA)*
Ben Greenstein *(Google, USA)*
Kurtis Heimerl *(University of Washington & Facebook, USA)*
Xiaofan Jiang *(Columbia University, USA)*
Robin Kravets *(University of Illinois, USA)*

Program Committee
(continued) :

Nic Lane *(Bell Labs, UK)*
Youngki Lee *(Singapore Management University, Singapore)*
Tamer Nadeem *(Old Dominion University, USA)*
Chunyi Peng *(Ohio State University, USA)*
Andrew Rice *(Cambridge University, UK)*
Anthony Rowe *(Carnegie Mellon University, USA)*
Aaron Schulman *(Stanford University, USA)*
Kannan Srinivasan *(Ohio State University, USA)*
Kaushik Veeraraghavan *(Facebook, USA)*
Roy Want *(Google, USA)*
Guoliang Xing *(Michigan State University, USA)*
Pei Zhang *(Carnegie Mellon University, USA)*

Sponsor:

Supporters:

Microsoft **Research**   Google

Hot or Not? Moving Forward from Weiser's Vision of Ubiquitous Computing

Gregory D. Abowd
School of Interactive Computing
Georgia Tech

Abstract

I read Mark Weiser's inspiring vision of ubiquitous computing, or ubicomp, when I joined the faculty in the College of Computing in 1994, and have been pursuing applications of ubicomp ever since. While the grand idea of ubiquitous computing can still inspire lots of research, there are several new technologies that Weiser did not discuss that can and will influence computing research and its application in the coming years. Weiser described a 3rd generation of computing; I will describe both a 4th generation which has already emerged over the past decade, and a 5th generation that may soon emerge. I will highlight some interaction and applications challenges for these new generations of computing.

Keywords

Wearable computing; Future of computing

Bio

Gregory D. Abowd is a Regents' and Distinguished Professor in the School of Interactive Computing at Georgia Tech, where he has been on the faculty since 1994. His research interests concern how the advanced information technologies of ubiquitous computing (or ubicomp) impact our everyday lives when they are seamlessly integrated into our living spaces. Dr. Abowd's work has involved schools (Classroom 2000) and homes (The Aware Home), with a recent focus on health and particularly autism. Dr. Abowd received the degree of B.S. in Honors Mathematics in 1986 from the University of Notre Dame. He then attended the University of Oxford in the United Kingdom as a Rhodes Scholar, earning the degrees of M.Sc. (1987) and D.Phil. (1991) in Computation. From 1989-1992 he was a Research Associate/Postdoc with the Human-Computer Interaction Group in the Department of Computer Science at the University of York in England. From 1992-1994, he was a Postdoctoral Research Associate with the Software Engineering Institute and the Computer Science Department at Carnegie Mellon University. He has graduated 23 PhD students who have gone on to a variety of successful careers in academia and industry He is an ACM Fellow, a member of the CHI Academy and recipient of the SIGCHI Social Impact Award and ACM Eugene Lawler Humanitarian Award. He is also the founding President of the Atlanta Autism Consortium, a non-profit dedicated to enhancing communication and understanding across the varied stakeholder communities connected to autism.

HotMobile'16, Feb. 23–24, 2016, St. Augustine, FL, USA.
ACM ISBN: 978-1-4503-4145-5/16/02.
DOI: http://dx.doi.org/10.1145/2873587.2873606

VoLTE*: A Lightweight Voice Solution to 4G LTE Networks

Guan-Hua Tu†*, Chi-Yu Li†*, Chunyi Peng‡, Zengwen Yuan†, Yuanjie Li†, Xiaohu Zhao‡, Songwu Lu†

† Department of Computer Science, University of California, Los Angeles, Los Angeles, CA 90095
‡ Department of Computer Science and Engineering, The Ohio State University, Columbus, OH 43210
{ghtu,lichiyu,zyuan,yuanjie.li,slu}@cs.ucla.edu, {peng.377,zhao.1722}@osu.edu

ABSTRACT

VoLTE is the designated voice solution to the LTE network. Its early deployment is ongoing worldwide. In this work, we report an assessment on VoLTE. We show that VoLTE offers no categorically better quality than popular VoIP applications in all tested scenarios except some congested scenarios. Given the high cost on infrastructure upgrade, we argue that VoLTE, in its current form, might not warrant the deployment effort. We sketch VoLTE*, a lightweight voice solution from which all parties of users, LTE carriers, and VoIP service providers may benefit.

Keywords

Cellular Networks; Voice; VoLTE*

1. INTRODUCTION

Voice is a simple, yet vital service to billions of mobile users. It has been a killer application in mobile network since its origin. For sake of guaranteed quality of service (QoS), voice calls have been traditionally supported through circuit-switched (CS) technology, where a dedicated channel (or circuit) is established for the transmission of voice traffic. However, this scheme becomes invalid any longer, as mobile network is rapidly advancing to Long Term Evolution (LTE), the 4th-generation (4G) standard, which supports packet-switched (PS) technology only. As a result, voice service has to migrate from CS to PS, due to this fundamental, irreversible change in LTE network architecture.

VoLTE (Voice over LTE) is thus proposed to fulfill this evolution [1, 2]. Its design seems quite straightforward. It carries voice traffic in packets over the IP-based LTE network, no longer through an dedicated circuit. To facilitate voice communication, each VoLTE call also maintains a separate signaling session. This is akin to Voice-over-IP (VoIP) over the Internet. To ensure carrier-grade call quality comparable to CS calls, it leverages high-priority delivery offered by the LTE network for both signaling and voice sessions.

---

*The first two authors contribute equally to this work.

HotMobile'16, February 26–27, 2016, St. Augustine, FL, USA.

© 2016 Copyright held by the owner/author(s). Publication rights licensed to ACM.
ISBN 978-1-4503-4145-5/16/02...$15.00

DOI: http://dx.doi.org/10.1145/2873587.2873604

While promising, VoLTE has been going through a bumpy ride in its deployment. After its first commercial launch in 2012 [3], only 20 carriers out of 480 LTE networks have deployed VoLTE by October 2015 [4]. Among them, most carriers do not offer massive deployment. For example, the first rollout in major US carriers (Verizon, AT&T, and T-Mobile) was in late 2014, but until now, its nationwide deployment has not been achieved yet [5,6]. In fact, most carriers kept on promising but deferring its public launch again and again [7].

Inspired by such strenuous deployment, we seek to explore why. Our goal is two-fold. First, we conduct an assessment on VoLTE and investigate whether it is worth the effort to deploy VoLTE based on its performance, deployment cost and operation complexity, as well as benefits offered to different parties; second, we explore whether there exists an alternative lightweight voice solution, achieving comparable voice performance but at lower cost. Intuitively, our study is motivated by one common wisdom. We believe that strenuous deployment is often associated with inherent technical hurdles beyond operations.

To this end, we first investigate the current VoLTE solution from its deployment cost and operational complexity. It does require sophisticated support at the infrastructure. Specifically, IMS (IP Multimedia Subsystem), as well as complex functions, are needed inside the LTE network, leading to heavy investment cost and operational complexity. We further compare performance of VoLTE and popular VoIP applications (*e.g.*, Skype, Hangouts) when running in the LTE network. To our surprise, we discover that VoLTE offers no categorically better quality than VoIP in most cases. Moreover, we identify that the key quality guarantee comes from its cellular-specific QoS management, irrelevant to complex IMS. This implies that it is possible to enable PS-based voice solution in a simpler form.

Consequently, we propose VoLTE*, a lightweight voice solution to 4G LTE networks. Its core idea is to largely retain the Internet VoIP scheme at the device, while leveraging the priority service offered by the LTE core network. The LTE network only needs to offer *modest (and existing)* support for priority services, without implementing complex IMS and auxiliary functions. Instead, we largely leverage the existing VoIP service over the top.

The rest of the paper is organized as follows. §2 describes basic background on VoLTE. §3 investigates the cost and performance of VoLTE. §4 and §5 present the design and discussion of VoLTE*, respectively. §6 compares with related work. §7 presents the future work and §8 concludes the paper.

2. VOLTE PRIMER

VoLTE (Voice over LTE) [1,2] is designated as the ultimate voice solution to the 4G LTE mobile users. It seeks to migrate the tradi-

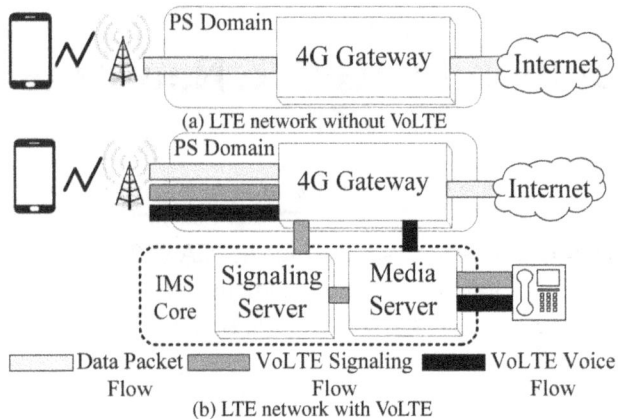

Figure 1: LTE network architecture with(out) VoLTE.

tional circuit-switched (CS) voice service to the packet-switched (PS) one. As illustrated in Figure 1, each VoLTE call maintains two communication sessions, one on the data plane and the other on the control plane. The control-plane session is to exchange the call signaling messages through the popular Session Initiation Protocol (SIP) [8]. The data-plane session handles the voice packet delivery via the Internet Real-time Transport Protocol (RTP) [9]; it is established on demand by the control-plane session. To ensure call quality comparable to typical CS calls, it leverages the multiple service classes (*e.g.*, the guaranteed bit rate and different priorities) offered by LTE. Both of VoLTE signaling and voice are delivered through the LTE's data channel that serves normal data services, but are offered higher priority than the data services.

Two subsystems in LTE networks are involved in the VoLTE operation. The first one is the IP Multimedia Subsystem (IMS) core, which is developed to support all-IP telephony and multimedia services [2]. It consists of the media gateway and the VoLTE server. The media gateway is to deliver real-time multimedia (*e.g.*, voice) traffic to VoLTE users, or to traditional telephony users. The VoLTE server provides call session control functions among the device, the media gateway and the 4G gateway. Note that the IMS core is not limited to the VoLTE support. It can be further upgraded to support other multimedia services, such as video conference call.

The second one is the existing packets-switched delivery subsystem. Its major component is the 4G gateway, akin to edge routers in the Internet. Its main role is to offer PS connectivity to and from the mobile device. To support VoLTE, the 4G gateway relays packets on both control and data planes between the device and the IMS core. In addition, the 4G gateway is also responsible for other control functions, *e.g.*, IP address allocation, packet filtering, policy enforcement and charging support.

3. VOLTE OR NO VOLTE?

We now take a step back by looking at alternative solutions to voice service over mobile networks. Our first choice is the popular Internet VoIP applications, which can directly operate over the IP-based LTE network.

Conceptually, the Internet VoIP solution follows design tenets different from VoLTE. It uses the best-effort service offered by the Internet, but relies on the end-device intelligence to improve voice quality. This works well with the increasing capabilities at the smartphone device. In contrast, VoLTE still mainly relies on the network infrastructure and phone hardware chip for call quality assurance, though it does migrate some functions to the phone software.

We next examine two other aspects of VoLTE operations: deployment overhead and call quality. We defer the discussion of the billing cost for users to Section 4. Our key finding is that VoLTE does not offer clearly better call performance than VoIP over LTE networks; in most of our tested cases, they are comparable. However, VoLTE incurs much higher deployment cost for operations.

3.1 Deployment and Operation Cost

The deployment is driven by two goals: voice call service among VoLTE users, and phone calls between VoLTE users and traditional phone users. Therefore, the deployment cost comes from two sources. The operator has to newly deploy the IMS core, and has to make changes on existing subsystems. In this case, two existing subsystems (PS domain, OAM (Operation, Administration and Maintenance) [10]) in the current 4G network infrastructure need to be updated. In addition, the CS domain components in 2G/3G infrastructure also need to be upgraded to support SRVCC (Single Radio Voice Call Continuity) [11], which migrates an ongoing 4G VoLTE call to the 2G/3G CS call once the user leaves the 4G coverage.

Specifically, the IMS core needs to be deployed. During VoLTE operations, it interacts with the mobile device, and potentially the legacy phone systems to translate the VoLTE signals and voice packets to the CS-based format. The PS subsystem in the LTE network needs to upgrade all four components: the user device, the 4G gateway, the base station and the mobility management entity. Its OAM needs to be updated to support new functions for VoLTE users: call charging and device authentication. In the legacy 2G/3G networks, the mobility component MSC (Mobile Switch Center) needs to be upgraded to interact with 4G VoLTE users.

In contrast, existing VoIP services (*e.g.*, Skype, Hangouts) do not require new deployment or infrastructure upgrade on the LTE network. We also note that translation servers are already deployed for years. They enable calls to traditional phone users from the VoIP user. However, we do identify a subtle issue for roaming users. Consider the scenario when the 4G network does not have full geographic coverage. When the user leaves the 4G coverage, the standard 4G→2G/3G handoff procedure is triggered. The ongoing VoIP call is then migrated from the 4G to the 2G/3G network. This process does not require infrastructure upgrade. Carriers leverage the existing servers from the VoIP service providers, and rely on the conventional handoffs to handle the insufficient 4G coverage. However, the charging function needs collaboration between the 4G carrier and the VoIP providers. In the current practice, Internet VoIP users are not billed by the service providers unless the calls are with traditional phone users.

3.2 Comparable Call Performance

We compare VoLTE and VoIP service (Google Hangouts is used) in terms of call setup time, voice performance and call drop rate. We conduct a medium-scale experiment: 10 static locations, 20 routes for mobility, and 50 people who are involved in the subjective test of voice performance. We show that they have comparable performance in all three aspects. However, VoLTE performs better in some congested scenarios . Note that we consider the locations with different signal strength based on user perception: strong (> -90 dBm), medium ($\in (-115, -90]$ dBm), and weak (≤ -115 dBm), which indicates the weakest level of the phone's signal strength icon.

Note that VoLTE is still at its early stage, so its performance may be further improved after more feedbacks are collected.

Call Setup Time. We examine the call setup time in four call scenarios: (1) VoLTE-to-VoLTE; (2) Hangouts-to-Hangouts; (3)

VoLTE-to-CS; (4) Hangouts-to-CS, where A-to-B represents that the caller with technology A makes a call to the callee with technology B. We thus assess both calls using the same technology and calls requiring PS/CS translation. The call setup time is the duration from the time the caller dials to that the callee's phone rings.

Figure 2 plots the call setup time for the tested four cases in two areas with weak and strong signal strength, where both the caller and the callee stay. The result of the medium signal strength is similar and omitted. We make two observations. First, the call setup time performed by Hangouts is comparable to that of VoLTE when both users use the same technology (*i.e.*, Scenarios (1) and (2)). They have median values around 5.0 seconds with smaller than 10% difference in three kinds of signal strength. Neither is better in all cases. Second, when the PS and CS translation is needed (*i.e.*, Scenarios (3) and (4)), Hangout requires 3.7–4.8 more seconds in the median values than VoLTE.

As a result, the control-plane performance by the signaling servers of VoLTE and Hangouts is comparable. However, when both PS and CS domains are involved, the translating gateway in the LTE network yields better performance than the Hangouts service provider.

Voice Quality. We compare voice quality of VoLTE and Hangouts. Since we are unable to capture VoLTE voice packets, which are handled within the hardware, we cannot apply traditional evaluation techniques of VoIP to conduct the comparison. We thus compare the recorded audio of the VoLTE and Hangouts calls. For the tested audio samples, we use four reference speech materials from ITU (International Telecommunication Union) recommendations. They include two male and two female American English speakers. Each consists of four simple, meaningful, and short sentences.

We do comparison study based on the subjective measurement method stipulated by ITU [12]. The subjective approach is used because the perception and evaluation of the voice performance is ultimately subject to users. The tests include both ACR (Absolute Category Rating) and CCR (Comparison Category Rating). ACR requires testers to give opinion scales from 1 to 5 on the quality of the audio they heard. In CCR tests, testers are presented with a pair of VoLTE and Hangouts audio files on each trial, and then give a score from -3 (much worse) to 3 (much better). The score, 0, denotes about the same. Note that the order of the pair audio files is randomly chosen for each trial.

The audio is transmitted through the call from the sender phone, and recorded at the receiver phone. We prevent background noise from our recordings. The tested audio sample is played by a computer to the sender phone through a connected audio line. The audio received by the receiver phone is forwarded to a computer through another connected audio line, and then recorded by a software, called Audacity [13], in 16-bit, 44.1kHz format. We also keep the volume settings of all computers and phones identical for all the experiments.

We do three recordings for each of four tested samples in each scenario. We consider five scenarios: (1) both phones are in the strong-signal area, (2) both are in the weak-signal, (3) the receiver is in a crowded but strong-signal area, (4) the receiver is in mobility (crossing cells), and (5) the receiver is in the strong-signal area and the sender is a CS-based phone. Note that in latter three scenarios, the sender has strong signals. We recruit 50 university students to do subject measurement, and the experiment settings required by ITU [12] are as follows. The tests are conducted in a quiet room with around 90 m^3 by eligible listeners (*e.g.*, they have not participated in any subjective test during the recent six months). Each test takes around 35 minutes, so the listener's fatigue is considered negligible.

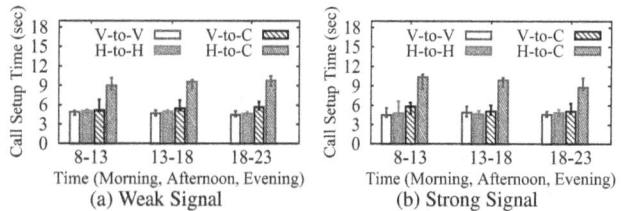

Figure 2: Call setup time (maximum, median, minimum) in weak-signal(a) and strong-signal(b) scenarios.

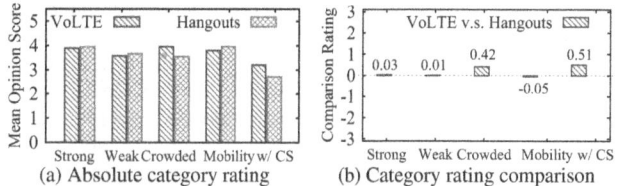

Figure 3: Voice quality comparison between VoLTE and Hangouts (VoIP).

Figure 3(left) shows the average ACR scores of VoLTE and Hangouts audio in the five scenarios. In Cases (1), (2) and (4), the differences between VoLTE and Hangouts in all the cases are below 0.2. They can be considered to be comparable. In both Cases (3) and (5), VoLTE performs better than Hangouts by about 0.4. It shows that the former's high-priority bearers are effective in the crowded area and its translating gateway for CS performs better. Figure 3(right) shows the average CCR scores by comparing VoLTE with Handouts. The results are similar to the ACR scores. Except Cases (3) and (5), they are comparable. Note that ITU recommends that both ACR and CCR should be considered for their average values. Note that our finding that VoLTE and VoIP are comparable, is consistent with other studies. For example, NSN (Nokia Siemens Network) Smart Labs claimed that from their experimental results [14], VoLTE and VoIP applications achieved a pretty similar mean opinion score (MOS), which is a numerical indication of the users' perceived quality of received media after compression and/or transmission.

Call Drop Rate. We consider the call drop rate mainly in three cases. We first test the static case for 10 locations with strong/medium/weak signal strength. We test two mobility cases without and with inter-system switch (*e.g.*, 4G→2G/3G). Each mobility case has 10 different routes. Each location or route is tested with 20 2-minute calls. It is observed that the call drop rates of VoLTE and VoIP are comparable. Both of them do not have any call drop in the static case. In the mobility case without inter-system switch, VoLTE does not drop any calls, whereas VoIP has small ratio of 0.5%. When an inter-system switch occurs, their call drop rates increase to 8% and 4%, respectively. VoLTE has a higher drop rate, rooted in its SRVCC. It proceeds an intricate cross-system/domain handoff. Specifically, a VoLTE call has to be migrated from a 4G packet-switched voice service to a 3G circuit-switched service (i.e., cross-system/domain handoff). However, the VoIP calls do not require to cross domains, but switch only between different PS systems, 4G PS and 3G PS. Its procedure is much less complex than that of crossing both systems and domains. The complex procedure results in higher failure rates of VoLTE.

4. VOLTE* DESIGN

We now describe a new proposal, called VoLTE* (shown in Figure 4), which seeks to achieve the best of both worlds. VoLTE*

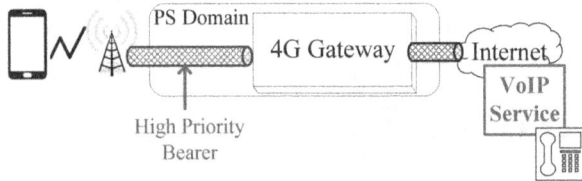

Figure 4: VoLTE* overview.

Service Class	Description
First	Akin to VoLTE
Business	Always better than best-effort
Deluxe Economy	Better than best-effort when needed
Economy	Best Effort

Table 1: Four service classes of VoLTE*.

uses the Internet VoIP scheme, but leverages the priority service offered by the LTE network infrastructure. We show that both LTE carriers and mobile users can benefit from this solution alternative. On one hand, it will serve the general public well for its lower cost and comparable quality to VoLTE, as well as more choices. On the other hand, operators also gain from the prioritized delivery in LTE networks.

Note that we are not championing to abandon VoLTE. VoLTE remains appealing to certain niche user groups who demand high-quality, guaranteed voice calls all the time (*e.g.*, police officers, company executives, medical emergency workers). The carriers with the VoLTE deployment can serve these kinds of demands. However, VoLTE* is proposed for the carriers which do not afford or are reluctant to spend the cost of the VoLTE deployment and maintenance.

4.1 VoLTE*: **How it Works**

VoLTE* supports four service classes of call services, as shown in Table 1. This is to exploit the diverse priority bearers offered by the LTE infrastructure. We retain two classes for VoLTE (*i.e.*, First class) and best-effort VoIP (*i.e.*, Economy class). Note that the first class offers the VoLTE-like call quality, but does not rely on the VoLTE deployment. The Business class always offers better service than Economy. Carriers may provide it using the bearer with the priority-level 7 [15], which is also assigned for voice. Both control and data planes can be carried at this priority level. Note that, this bearer has higher priority than that used for the Economy class (*i.e.*, 9), but has lower priority than those used for VoLTE control (*i.e.*, 1) and data (*i.e.*, 2) planes. Users of the Economy class thus pay less than that of the First class. The Deluxe Economy class provides users with adaptive VoIP service. A user is typically served as the Economy class, but will be adaptively upgraded to the Business class whenever needed (*e.g.*, too much resource is consumed by Economy users). This enables the user to receive call service better than Economy but worse than Business.

VoLTE* aims to put more functions into the user device and seeks for the network to provide only compact support for voice.

4.1.1 *Functions at User Device*

The VoLTE* application is given privilege to manage the bearers by sending AT commands [16] to the hardware of user device. The AT commands are defined for the software to control network service access. They are commonly used in practice. For example, Android OS uses them to dial call and establish data connections through Radio Interface Layer (RIL). By AT commands, VoLTE* is capable of activating, modifying and deactivating its serving bearers.

4.1.2 *Essential Support at Network*

In the network, four major supports are required. First, the network provides only differential pipe service, but does not manage them. It initially creates two VoIP bearers for signaling and voice. Afterwards, the differential priority services are configured upon the VoLTE* application's request. Second, the network leverages

the existing VoIP services, so that it does not need to deploy the IMS core. To guarantee the performance of VoIP signaling/voice outside its network, carriers can rely on the IPX (Internetwork Packet Exchange).

Third, the detection of congestion occurrence needs to be supported for the Deluxe Economy class. It can be done by the existing LTE mechanism of packet delay budget (PDB) for the VoIP bearers. PDB defines an upper bound for the packet delay between the phone and the 4G gateway. When PDB is not met due to non-radio-quality issues (learned from the base station), the LTE network upgrades the VoIP bearer to Business class. Once the PDB of all Economy users in a cell is satisfied, the users will be downgraded back to the Economy class. Fourth, most VoIP service providers rely on peer-to-peer voice communication. Carriers can enable Mobile-to-Mobile communication for the voice session. If both VoLTE* ends belong to the same carrier network, they can exchange voice packets directly through the LTE network without reaching the Internet.

We want to note two things. First, the VoLTE* service can support the handover from 4G to 2G/3G systems without additional requirements on the network. The reason is that VoLTE* is a packet-switched service, which is supported by all of 2G/3G/4G systems. Therefore, the handover involves only an inter-system switch, which has been supported by most of mobile networks [17].However, the data rate of 2G/3G might not always satisfy the demand of VoLTE*; it varies with carriers or locations [18]. For example, the average upload/download rate in Sprint 3G is merely 0.6 Mbps / 1.2 Mbps, whereas the average upload/download rate in T-Mobile is 7.4 Mbps / 31 Mbps [18]. Second, VoLTE* can meet the common lawful requirements of mobile carriers, such as emergency calls, interception of suspicious calls, tracking of users' locations, etc. For the dialing of emergency calls, VoLTE* can leverage the Emergency Bearer Service procedure [17], which is stipulated by the standard, to establish a bearer for the emergent services. However, the other two requirements can also be supported by VoIP service providers or/and carriers. For example, Microsoft allows FBI to access its Skype system to intercept calls [19]and carriers can help VoIP service providers to track the VoLTE* users' locations by their IP addresses. Since VoLTE* users' IP addresses are assigned by carriers (4G:P-GW [20], 2G/3G:GGSN [20], or carriers' NAT servers), carriers can obtain the IMSIs (International Mobile Subscriber Identity) [21] of VoLTE* users by their IP addresses and discover their locations through the paging procedure using IMSIs [20, 22].

4.2 VoLTE* **Benefits All Parties**

We believe that mobile users, carriers, and VoIP service providers can all benefit from VoLTE*.

Mobile Users: Better Services at Cheaper Fare. Users benefit from VoLTE* in both lower charge and richer services (*e.g.*, video calls). First, the charge for call service can be cheaper. A survey [23] shows that an American user spends averagely around 450 minutes per month when talking over the phone. We compare the current 1-minute-call charge between typical cellular call service and VoIP service (Hangouts is used) in four major US carriers based on the average usage (*i.e.*, 450 mins) and heavy usage (*i.e.*,

Charge (cent/min)		T-Mobile	AT&T	Verizon	Sprint
Cellular Call	450 mins	6.7	8.9	7.8	6.7
	900 mins	3.3	4.4	3.9	3.3
Hangouts	450/900 mins	1.2	1.2	0.6	0.9

Table 2: The charge comparison of cellular call and Hangouts call service from four major US carriers.

900 mins). For all the carriers, most plans have either unlimited call with an amount of data service or data service only. We thus consider the charge of call service based on the former plans with the smallest amount of data service, and then subtract the charge of the data service from their total price. The charge of the data services is based on the data plane with the most expensive data unit, *i.e.*, 1 GB data service only. We can then obtain the monthly price, from $30 to $40, and, from $10 to $20, for the unlimited call service only and 1 GB data service only, respectively.

The comparison results are given in Table 2. In Hangouts, the total volume of signaling and voice packets is around 0.6 MB (signaling takes 9.3% of traffic) per 1-minute call. Note that we consider the volume of signaling messages based on the average call duration of an American, 1.8 minutes [24]. For example, there are 250 calls with 450 minutes. We observe that the 1-minute-call charge for Hangout and cellular voice for normal users is ¢0.6-¢1.2 and ¢3.3-¢8.9 per minute, respectively. The 1-minute call charge for cellular voice service is 2.8−13.0 times than that of Hangouts. It shows that users still benefit from VoLTE* of better voice quality even when carriers double the charge for the Business and Deluxe Economy service classes.

Second, multimedia call services are already provided by current VoIP service providers, whereas VoLTE mostly supports voice calls only to date. For example, Hangouts supports video call and multimedia content sharing (*e.g.*, slides) during a call, and such multimedia services are quite mature and stable already. In contrast, VoLTE is still at its early deployment stage with basic voice call service.

Note that not all consumers are willing to pay for the prioritized VoIP traffic. This is why we propose four different service classes of VoLTE*. If some consumers do not want to pay for it or are reluctant to pay too much, they can still have voice service with lower classes. Moreover, we believe that the service classes with traffic prioritization can still be cheaper than VoLTE, since VoLTE* does not require the high cost of IMS deployment.

Carriers: Get More Revenue from Priority Delivery. According to [23], mobile users spend less time on talking, while taking more time on text messaging and Internet access. Call services via VoLTE thus generate less revenue for operators over time. With VoLTE*, operators avoid deployment cost and maintenance of VoLTE, yet still providing their 4G users with comparable voice service. New revenue streams also come from the prioritized delivery service by the carrier network. Moreover, the offered services can be easily extended to other multimedia ones, such as video conference calls, with the help of current VoIP services.

VoIP Service Providers: More Active Users. For VoIP service providers, although they provide carriers with free voice service, they benefit from more *active* users who remain online more often when accessing VoIP services.

5. DISCUSSION

We here discuss both technical and non-technical drawbacks of VoLTE*. They may be the reasons why carriers will still keep VoLTE but not switch to VoLTE*, even if the high cost of IMS deployment is required.

Technical Drawbacks. VoLTE* does not support two major network features which are leveraged by VoLTE. First, VoLTE* does not support the VoLTE-like energy saving mechanism. VoLTE uses a fixed packetization interval, 20 ms, so that base stations can schedule voice packets delivery for better energy saving. However, the sizes of VoIP packets usually vary. Second, VoLTE* does not support the VoLTE-like coverage enhancement, where the Transmission Time Interval (TTI) bundling [25] is employed. It transmits duplicate VoLTE voice packets in consecutive time slots (up to 4) while users are at the cell edges. Based on the estimation of a report [26], it can improve uplink coverage by 2−4 dB.

Moreover, VoLTE* requires carriers to spend efforts on developing a set of new interfaces, which are used by VoIP service providers to employ the mobile networks' high-priority bearers. It is because they have not been proposed in the literature or defined in the standard. Without prudent designs, they may make a security breach toward the core network, because they allow the network outsiders to manipulate the core network operations.

Non-technical Drawbacks. VoLTE* requires carriers to collaborate with VoIP service providers, but the sharing of both customers and the revenue may bring carriers some business concerns. We here present two examples, but the concerns are not limited to them. First, carriers may have risks of hurting their business by sharing customers. For example, the VoIP providers may do other commercial behaviors, which cannot be controlled by the carriers, to the customers, and they may cause customers' complaints. Moreover, it is difficult to resolve the sharing issues, if the collaboration of VoIP providers and carriers is terminated.

Second, it may be more difficult than usual for carriers to push new services. Once they rely on the VoIP providers to offer multimedia services, their plans would be impeded by the providers. In addition, they require to share the revenue of new services with the VoIP providers, and determine a new business model for each new service.

6. RELATED WORK

VoLTE has been actively investigated in industry (*e.g.*, [26–28]) and recently started to attract research attention [29–33]. Most efforts focus on its performance measurement [26, 27, 30] or deployment planning to improve performance [29]; Several recent efforts investigate VoLTE security [28, 31–33]. In particular, Jia *et al.* reveals that the early deployment of VoLTE in US suffers various performance problems [30] while mobile network industry advocates VoLTE with better or comparable voice quality [26, 27]. Our recent work and Kim *et al.* uncover that the VoLTE deployment is vulnerable to many attacks, including free data access, over-billing, denial of data service, voice mute and energy drain [31–33]. This is partly due to imprudent implementation at the early phase, partly due to complexity and substantial changes to the existing LTE architecture caused by VoLTE support. This also motivates us to revisit the current VoLTE solution and devise an alternative solution.

Recent years witness other LTE voice solutions: circuit-switched fallback (CSFB), single radio voice call continuity (SRVCC), simultaneous voice and LTE (SVLTE). CSFB migrates 4G LTE users to 3G/2G networks and leverages their legacy CS domain to support voices call [34]; Our previous studies reveal its performance issues and security implication (potential harm to normal data services) [32, 35]. SRVCC complements VoLTE and hands over VoLTE voice calls to 2G/3G networks in case of no LTE coverage [11]; SVLTE supports data in 4G LTE and voice in 3G/2G CS at the same time but it requires dual radio interfaces [36]. All are interim solutions since they require non-LTE networks (3G/2G). In this work, we focus on the voice solution that uses LTE only.

7. FUTURE WORK

In order to promote VoLTE*, we plan to pursue the following two items in our future work.

An Automated Tool for Large-scale Experiments. For the large-scale experiments of the comparison between VoLTE and VoIP applications, we seek to develop an automated tool of trace collection and release it to normal users. It will collect the traces which are required for three performance metrics of call performance: call setup time, call drop rate and voice quality. To measure the former two metrics, the tool will record the signaling messages of call setup, call accept, and call failure. To gauge the voice quality, it will log the voice packets of both VoLTE and VoIP applications, and apply the evaluation techniques of VoIP performance.

Promoting VoLTE* to the Industry. We plan to promote VoLTE* to not only the carriers which have not deployed VoLTE, but also the 5G standardization groups. First, we will seek the opportunities to collaborate with any carriers to deploy VoLTE*. We can learn whether there are any more practical issues, and then address them. We can further gain the lessons of how the Internet service providers and carriers collaborate to offer services, which can be applied to the future mobile Internet services. Second, we will actively participate in the standardization process of 5G to promote VoLTE*.

8. CONCLUSION

Bearing the telecom-based design mindset, VoLTE calls for substantial upgrades on the infrastructure side (complex functions in the core), and device updates as well. In this work, we offer an assessment on whether it warrants the effort to deploy VoLTE or not. Our criteria are based on its deployment cost and operation complexity, as well as the benefits offered to different parties. It is unfortunate, that our answer seems to be negative. Though VoLTE remains appealing to those niche groups of users who demand high-quality, high-reliability, guaranteed calls all the time, it is not necessary to be so complex.

The lesson we learned is that VoLTE leverages the higher priority services (compared with the low-priority, best-effort delivery) in mobile networks to ensure quality calls. The priority services are provided by the LTE network, but not from the IMS subsystem. The VoLTE implementation thus does not require the deployment of IMS, a main roadblock for its fast rollout. As the device becomes more powerful over time, it is prudent to place more intelligence at the device rather than the network. It soulds obvious to the Internet community, but not to the mobile networking camp in practice.

Acknowledgements

We would like to thank Dr. Kurtis Heimerl and the anonymous reviewers for their valuable comments. This work is supported in part by the National Science Foundation under Grants No. CNS-1421933, CNS-1422835, CNS-1528122 and CNS-1527613. Any opinions, findings, and conclusions or recommendations expressed in this material are those of the authors and do not necessarily reflect the views of the National Science Foundation.

9. REFERENCES

[1] Voice over LTE. http://www.gsma.com/technicalprojects/volte.
[2] 3GPP. TS23.228: IP Multimedia Subsystem (IMS);Stage 2, 2014.
[3] MetroPCS, SK Telecom, LG Uplus Claim VoLTE First, 2012. http://www.telecomengine.com/article/metropcs-sk-telecom-lg-uplus-claim-volte-firsts.
[4] Volte market revenue share of 12% to be held by video calling and supplementary services in 2020, Oct 2015. http://www.prnewswire.com/news-releases/volte-market-revenue-share-of-12-to-be-held-by-video-calling-and-supplementary-services-in-2020-530219051.html.
[5] AT&T: 2015 will be the year of mass market VoLTE. http://www.fiercewireless.com.
[6] VoLTE gears up for mass market. http://www.telecomasia.net.
[7] Ericsson: Volte deployment delays not surprising due to network complications, 2014. http://www.fiercewireless.com.
[8] RFC3261: SIP: Session Initiation Protocol, June 2002.
[9] RFC 3550: RTP: A Transport Protocol for Real-Time Applications, Jul 2003.
[10] 3GPP. Operation, Adminstration, Maintenance (OAM).
[11] 3GPP. TS 23.216: Single Radio Voice Call Continuity (SRVCC), March 2011.
[12] P.800: Methods for subjective determination of transmission quality.
[13] Audacity. http://audacity.sourceforge.net/.
[14] Is volte better than ott voip for carriers and customers. http://pressanykey.co.nz/wordpress/volte-better-ott-voip-carriers-customers/.
[15] 3GPP. TS23.203: Policy and Charging Control Architecture, 2013.
[16] 3GPP. TS27.007: AT command set for User Equipment (UE), 2011.
[17] 3GPP. TS23.401: GPRS Enhancements for E-UTRAN Access, 2011.
[18] P. Magazine. http://www.pcmag.com/article2/0,2817,2485838,00.asp, 2015.
[19] Microsoft allows nsa/fbi to access outlook, skype, other communication software. http://www.webpronews.com/microsoft-allows-nsafbi-to-access-outlook-skype-other-communication-software-2013-07/.
[20] 3GPP. TS23.060: GPRS; Service description; Stage 2, 2006.
[21] H. Holma and A. Toskala. *WCDMA for UMTS: HSPA Evolution and LTE*. John Wiley & Sons, Inc., New York, NY, USA, 2007.
[22] 3GPP. TS24.301: Non-Access-Stratum (NAS) protocol for Evolved Packet System (EPS); Stage 3, Jun. 2013.
[23] Experian: Americans spend 58 minutes a day on their smartphones. http://www.experian.com.
[24] Average Local Mobile Wireless Call Length in the United States from 1987 to 2012. http://www.statista.com.
[25] 3GPP. TR36.824: LTE coverage enhancements, 2012.
[26] N. Networks. From Voice over IP to Voice over LTE, 2013. http://tinyurl.com/q79vyu6.
[27] Qualcomm. The Voice Evolution, 2012. http://tinyurl.com/q5pe99h.
[28] VoLTE: Progress and Problems, April 2014. http://www.rcrwireless.com/article/20140416/networks/volte-progress-problems/.
[29] A. P. S. Louvros and A. Gkioni. Voice Over LTE (VoLTE): Service Implementation and Cell Planning Perspective. In *System-Level Design Methodologies for Telecommunication*, pages 43–62. Springer, 2014.
[30] Y. J. Jia, Q. A. Chen, Z. M. Mao, J. Hui, K. Sontinei, A. Yoon, S. Kwong, and K. Lau. Performance characterization and call reliability diagnosis support for voice over lte. In *MobiCom*, 2015.
[31] C.-Y. Li, G.-H. Tu, C. Peng, Z. Yuan, Y. Li, S. Lu, and X. Wang. Insecurity of voice solution volte in lte mobile networks. In *CCS*, 2015.
[32] G.-H. Tu, C.-Y. Li, C. Peng, and S. Lu. How Voice Call Technology Poses Security Threats in 4G LTE Networks. In *IEEE Conference on Communications and Network Security (CNS)*, September 2015.
[33] H. Kim, D. Kim, M. Kwon, H. Han, Y. Jang, D. Han, T. Kim, and Y. Kim. Breaking and fixing volte: Exploiting hidden data channels and mis-implementations. In *CCS*, 2015.
[34] 3GPP. TS23.272: Circuit Switched (CS) fallback in Evolved Packet System (EPS).
[35] G. Tu, C. Peng, H. Wang, C. Li, and S. Lu. How Voice Calls Affect Data in Operational LTE Networks. In *MobiCom*, Oct. 2013.
[36] Sonlte. Notes on Simultaneous Voice and LTE (SVLTE).

When IPs Fly: A Case for Redefining Airline Communication

John P. Rula* Fabián E. Bustamante* David R. Choffnes‡
*Northwestern University   ‡Northeastern University

ABSTRACT

The global airline industry conducted over 33 million flights in 2014 alone, carrying over 3.3 billion passengers. Surprisingly, the traffic management system handling this flight volume communicates over either VHF audio transmissions or plane transponders, exhibiting several seconds of latency and single bits per second of throughput. There is a general consensus that for the airline industry to serve the growing demand will require of significant improvements to the air traffic management system; we believe that many of these improvements can leverage the past two decades of mobile networking research.

In this paper, we make the case that moving to a common IP-based data channel to support flight communication can radically change the airline industry. While there remain many challenges to achieve this vision, we believe that such a shift can greatly improve the rate of innovation, overall efficiency of global air traffic management, enhance aircraft safety and create new applications that leverage the capability of an advanced data channel. Through preliminary measurements on existing in-flight Internet communication systems, we show that existing in-flight connectivity achieves order of magnitude higher throughput and lower latency than current systems, and operates as a highly reliable and available data link. This position paper takes a first look at the opportunity for IP-based flight communication, and identifies several promising research areas in this space.

1. INTRODUCTION

The global airline industry is experiencing exceptional growth. In 2014 alone, it supported 33 million flights carrying over 3.3 billion passengers [10], and these numbers are expected to grow steadily over the next 20 years at a 2.5% annual rate [8]. At the same time, the system is already exhibiting a high degree of fragility [1] with over 22% of all flights delayed and 2.6% of flights cancelled during the same period [21].

A key component of airline operations is the global air traffic management system (ATM), coordinating the activities of aircrafts and air traffic controllers. This system schedules flight plans, reports aircrafts locations, and coordinates take-offs and landings for the tens of millions of flights carried out annually.

Despite the massive scale and complexity of this operation, the communication system powering it has evolved little since its inception. In the past sixty years, airline communication has seen only 3 major improvements from the initial Mode A transponder system from the 1950s, to the Mode S of the late 1980s to the upcoming ADS-B (expected by 2018). As an example, all position and navigation data today is communicated over either VHF audio transmissions or plane transponders – measuring several seconds of latency and single bits per second of throughput. Similar to the state of computer networking four decades ago, each component in the existing flight communication system builds on custom hardware and several proprietary protocols.

In contrast, over nearly the same period, IP networks have evolved to link every conceivable device from personal computers and handhelds to home appliances and data centers, and touch nearly all aspects of our lives, including our in-flight experience.

While the evolution of airline and IP communication systems could not be more different, the applications and environments they support are converging. IP communication is increasingly reliable, supports higher data rates and has scaled from hundreds to billions of connected devices. *We argue that shifting the airline communication system from a confederation of proprietary protocols to a common IP-based data channel can radically change the airline industry.*

Existing aircraft Internet connectivity for *consumer* use shows the maturity of this technology and helps make the case that IP is a promising avenue for future aircraft communication systems. There are, however, a number of technical challenges for realizing this vision, not the least of which is a provably safe, secure, and reliable deployment over IP. We outline open research questions involving novel mechanisms for network addressing and mobility management, as well as entirely new transport protocols which are unique to the high speed, high latency environments of aircraft data communication. While there are many non-technical challenges to the realization of our proposed idea, we argue that the unavoidable roadblock facing industry progress would be a sufficiently strong motivator for change.

2. AIRCRAFT COMMUNICATION TODAY

In the following paragraphs, we provide an overview of aircraft communication for both traffic management and in-flight communication services. We then put the performance of different technologies discussed in context comparing them in terms of generic network properties such latency and throughput.

2.1 Air Traffic Management

The global ATM system is one of the most highly utilized and complex distributed systems in existence. Its duties include real-time tracking of tens of thousands of aircraft at any point in time, scheduling these planes through take-offs, landings and transit corridors, as well as communicating related information to and from the planes themselves.

Existing ATM communication systems involve several independent communication loops including (*i*) the Air Traffic Control Radar Beacon System (ATCRBS) including radar surveillance stations and plane transponders (*ii*) communication between aircraft and air traffic control personnel and (*iii*) inter-plane communication. The system's objectives are locating aircraft position, velocity and altitude, coordinating and scheduling aircrafts through shared airspace, and communicating navigation instructions to aircraft.

Radar Surveillance Systems. Ground radar stations make up the largest component of global ATM. These consist of both primary and secondary surveillance radar stations, PSR and SSR respectively. PSR are powerful transmitters typically located at airports. PSR systems track aircraft by measuring the reflections from radar emissions. Secondary radar utilizes transponders within aircraft – communicating by broadcasting interrogative signals and measuring the responses from aircraft transponders to locate individual aircraft. SSR systems are less powerful systems, which are geographically distributed throughout airspace not covered by primary systems. The time between updates can vary from 5 seconds at primary radar sites to 12 seconds at secondary surveillance stations [17].

Airborne Transponder Equipment. Aircraft transponders – both Mode A/C and the newer Mode S – are devices, which when pinged by a ground radar station, respond with a high-power encoded pulse with plane identification and navigation information [16]. Transponders are used to supplement secondary surveillance radar systems (SSR), which unlike primary radar systems, cannot accurately determine aircraft altitude except at close range. Once polled, each transponder replies with a response consisting of that aircraft's altitude and identification code.

Automatic Dependent Surveillance – Broadcast (ADS-B). ADS-B is a cooperative surveillance technology where aircraft broadcast their location determined from satellite navigation systems (e.g. GPS) [20]. ADS-B is part of the NextGen program and is meant as a solution to the coverage problem of ground stations. This system replaces radar interrogators with inexpensive listen-only ground stations, and to improves latency between location updates to one second. ADS-B is currently deployed on several commercial airlines and is a requirement of the FAA by 2018.

Airborne Data Communication. Data communication to aircraft is encoded and transmitted over the existing VHF radio infrastructure used for voice communication, called the VHF Data Link (VDL) [7]. A common use of VDL are the Aircraft Communications Addressing and Reporting System (ACARS), which communicates small messages to and from aircraft such as flight status reports and air traffic control messages such as clearances. An enhanced VDL Mode 2 is required on all commercial aircraft by 2016 as part of the NextGen program.

Plane-2-Plane Communication. The air collision avoidance system (ACAS) – part of the Mode S transponder system – allows planes to interrogate other proximal planes [13]. Using the radio signal properties of each response along with the provided altitude information, the ACAS alerts pilots to impending airborne collisions.

2.2 In-Flight Communication

Recently, a number of commercial airline services have begun to offer Internet access as an amenity on flights. These In-Flight Communication (IFC) systems can be divided into two groups based on their underlying technologies: Direct Air-To-Ground Communication and Mobile Satellite Service.

Direct Air-to-Ground Communication. Direct Air-To-Ground Communication (DA2GC) utilizes cellular technology to communicate between the aircraft and the ground. These systems are implemented using three key infrastructure pieces: the Aircraft Station (AS), the Ground Station (GS) and the DA2GC network core. The aircraft station consists of the radio receiver and transmitter, as well as network appliances for handling in-flight entertainment systems common on many aircraft. Ground Stations are towers that communicate with passing flights. These stations are similar to cellular towers, with the exception that their radio transmitters are directed upward, and that they are placed at much a greater distances from each other (e.g. 50 to 150 km radius). DA2GC systems also operate their own core networks analogous to cellular core networks, which handle user mobility and tower hand offs. Existing DA2GC systems operate on 2-3G cellular technologies for the air-to-ground link. Although systems using newer LTE technology have been proposed [2, 5], none have been deployed as of December 2015. Traffic from flights is received by each GS, and tunneled through to the DA2GC's core network before egressing into to the public Internet.

Mobile Satellite Service. Mobile Satellite Service (MSS) relies on geostationary satellite relays to establish connectivity, and its connectivity is therefore not confined to only areas with ground towers. Each satellite system leases a fraction of the transponders available on geostationary satellites. Due to the large distances traversed by wireless signals in satellite communication, and the large path-fading effects of transmission, satellite transmissions are divided into several beams of a few degrees of latitude and longitude, which are leased individually by companies. This means that satellite providers are also subject to geographic coverage constraints based on the availability of satellites and the relationship each provider has with satellite owners.

2.3 Putting Performance in Context

Given that many of these technologies transmit specialized information over proprietary protocols, we choose to compare them in terms of their generic network properties (e.g. latency, throughput, etc). Framing the problem of ATM in this light helps reveal many shortcomings in existing

Technology	Year	Goal	Eff. Latency (sec.)	Eff. Throughput (bits/s)
Mode A/C	1956	Aircraft identification (A) and altitude (C)	5-12	1-2.4
Mode S	1988	Multiple response modes; other navigation data in response	5-12	4.6-11.2
ADS-B	Exp. 2018	Broadcast position and navigation data automatically	1	120
VDL	Exp. 2016	Digital communication of ATC information	6.05	31,500
MSS	2001	Consumer Internet connectivity	0.5	200,000,000
DA2GC	2009	Consumer Internet connectivity	0.05	400,000,000

Table 1: Current (and proposed) aircraft communication technology. The table also includes a short description of the particular technology as well as the year of adoption, or expected adoption. IFC technologies provide up to between 2 and 6 orders of magnitude greater throughput, and 1 to 2 orders of magnitude lower latency than existing aircraft communication systems.

communication systems. Table 1 lists different aircraft communication systems, both for ATM and IFC, including their years of adoption, general goals and their effective communication latency and throughput.

Radar interrogation frequency can range between 5 to 12 seconds depending on the type of radar station used (near airports this frequency is close to 5 seconds, and elsewhere it drops to a 12 second interval). Each message only transmits 56 or 112 bits per reply, translating to a data link rate of between 1 bit per second using Mode A and a 12 second sweep, to 11.2 bits per second using Mode S near an airport. Even the next-generation ADS-B only improves latency to 1 second with an effective throughput of 120 bits/sec. As the table shows, existing IP-based IFC systems provide between *two to six order of magnitude greater throughput*, and *one to two orders of magnitude lower latency*. This is unsurprising when one considers that aircraft position reporting is dependent on the surveillance radar it is paired with.

In the following sections, we highlight the opportunities that potential IFC technology provides, and demonstrate that IFC technologies are already sufficiently fast and reliable to support and enhance a wide range of air traffic management applications.

3. THE CASE FOR IMPROVED AIRCRAFT COMMUNICATION

The continued expansion of the global air traffic network is pushing the current system near its maximum capacity [1]. This is demonstrated by the increasing numbers of delayed and cancelled flights – 22.3% and 2.6% respectively in 2014 [21]. In this section we make the case for a common IP-based communication channel could greatly improve the efficiency and effectiveness of global air traffic management.

Limited System Innovation.

A key problem with the existing ATM system is its reliance on specialized hardware and protocols. This reliance increases the cost and deploying time for system upgrade or expansion as any proposed upgrade requires a complete retrofit of the global airline fleet. The system of custom hardware also requires all new technology to be backwards compatible. In the case of SSR systems, all messages must be compatible with the original transponder system (Mode A) deployed in the 1950s.

By comparison, IP networks have shown to be easily adaptable to a range of applications and environments [4]. We believe the airline industry could benefit from a similar

surge of innovation after adopting a single, open architecture supported by commodity hardware and software.

Improved Spatial Efficiency.

The required separation distance between aircraft depends, in part, on the availability of aircraft location information, and its update rate. Radar separation standards require three-mile distances between aircrafts as long as both aircrafts are within forty miles of the same radar station, or 5 miles otherwise [19]. Much of this large safety factor is due to the latency of existing SSR systems, that can ranging between 5 and 12 seconds under good conditions and can be many times higher in cases of radio interference or component failure.

In addition to transponder transmission delays, these clearances must also account for other delays caused by this manual access control for radio resources. The command and control loop between the controllers and the aircraft also affects separation specifications. Air traffic controllers provide the required separation by issuing clearances, including routings, vectors (headings), and altitude assignments through a common VHF voice channel assigned to a given airspace.

Recent advances on next-generation plane transponders, ADS-B, illustrate some of the benefits of improved communication. Planes equipped with ADS-B broadcast their GPS locations every second. This has been leveraged in recently tested updated landing protocols showing savings of 40 to 70 gallons of fuel *per landing* and an increase in runway capacity of 15% [3]. It should be clear that while ADS-B represents a substantial improvement in aircraft positioning communication, it only one component of the ATM command and control loop.

Real-time plane data communication.

We believe that (near) real-time communication of flight location and diagnostic information can address several existing issues. For instance, such a service could stream portions of the near 500 GB of flight and instrument data generated per flight [15] to ground teams, leveraging the additional bandwidth offer by an IP-based communication service.. This information could then be used for more sophisticated, real-time diagnostics which may help detect technical issues before they become a hazard.

Real-time aircraft communication can also help diagnose and prevent several types of aircraft disasters, and may be able to mitigate these situations before they occur. Possessing up-to-date locations of aircraft could help to

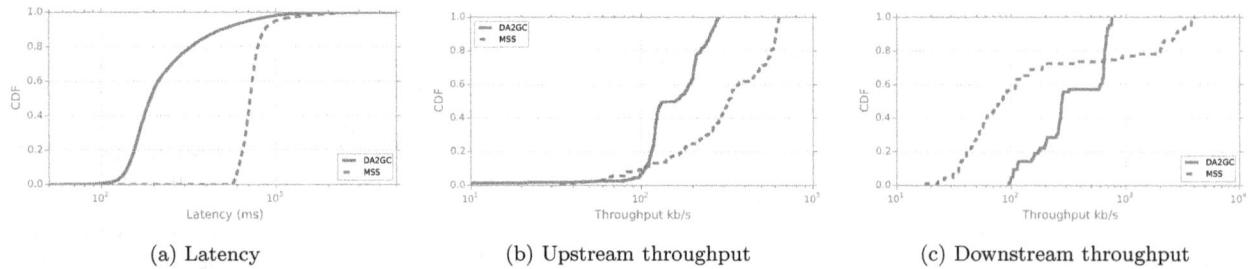

| (a) Latency | (b) Upstream throughput | (c) Downstream throughput |

Figure 1: Measured performance of existing IFC technology for both MSS and DA2GC. Even measurements taken during contentious periods on a shared link show orders of magnitude improvements over existing aircraft communication technology.

solve cases of missing transcontinental flights, and more accurately diagnose their causes to prevent future incidents. Analysis of real-time flight information could also alert of anomalous flight behavior (e.g., in cases of hijacking).

Increased Aircraft Awareness.

Increased communication bandwidth would allow aircraft to receive vastly more information about their surroundings – including detailed weather reports, air traffic control information and the locations of nearby aircrafts.

For instance, the current state of traffic collision and avoidance systems (TCAS) passively listen to plane transponder messages to detect and alert pilots to impending collisions. These systems, which rely on radio transmission between aircrafts, have a existing range of 3.3 (nautical) miles, leaving only 40 seconds in many instances (at 300 mph) to respond to a detected collision [13]. The information passed through a higher capacity data channel could include the locations and navigation data of aircraft within hundreds of miles, giving much earlier warnings for potential midair collisions.

Airborne Distributed Systems.

The switch to a standard IP interface could usher in the deployment of Airborne Distributed Systems through a peer-to-peer (plane-to-plane) topology [11]. These ad-hoc airborne networks could enable planes to share additional information for enhanced collision avoidance applications, by providing accurate position and altitude information along with current heading and flight plans. Aircraft could extend their proximity awareness beyond their current radio reach by sharing their view points with neighboring aircraft through the use of a distributed data store such as a distributed hash table (DHT).

Additionally, these peer-to-peer networks could be used as a backup air traffic control service in the case of air traffic control failures. [1] In this scenario, aircraft would coordinate approach vectors landing schedules in an ad-hoc manner, thus adding further levels of resiliency and safety to the system.

3.1 Industry Approaches

The need for enhanced communication and information propagation is a known issue in the airline and air traffic management industry. Indeed, the speed of information

---

[1]http://www.wired.com/2014/09/faa-chicago-fire-air-traffic-control/

Carrier	Date	Time (hrs)	Tech.
United Airlines	Feb-22-2015	1.34	DA2GC
US Airways	Mar-04-2015	4.92	DA2GC
Delta Airlines	Mar-12-2015	3.92	DA2GC
United Airlines	Mar-08-2015	4.03	MSS
United Airlines	Feb-24-2015	1.97	MSS
Southwest Airlines	Mar-10-2015	1.92	MSS
United Airlines	Mar-16-2015	3.66	MSS
United Airlines	Aug-30-2015	1.94	DA2GC
United Airlines	Sep-29-2015	3.87	MSS

Table 2: Flights used in our experimental results.

communication has been recognized as one of the key bottlenecks in the global airline industry [9].

Many of the enhancements proposed in the Next-Gen program involve reducing the latency inherent in several ATC feedback loops [18]. For example, in addition to improving location accuracy, the enhancements with ADS-B cuts down the time between location updates from 12 seconds to 1 second, reducing flight times and increasing runway capacity.

In addition, third party companies sell and operate data-link services between aircraft and airline operation systems. For instance, the Aircraft Communications Addressing and Reporting System (ACARS) allows digital messages to be transmitted over VHF radio to and from aircraft. ACARS has seen a wide variety of uses from aircraft status transmission, to graphical weather reports, to crew messages, to ground clearances. Introduced in 1978, ACARS messages have become an integral part of air traffic management due to the significant improvements in system coordination they provide [9].

While it is clear the airline industry understands the importance of information communication, we believe that their solutions fall into the same patterns of dedicated hardware and independent communication channels which left then with their existing ossified system. The majority of the NextGen enhancements upgrade *existing* interfaces, require new and incompatible hardware, and do little to unify the multiple communication channels. *We know of no other attempts in industry to unify aircraft communications across a common channel, IP or otherwise, as we propose.*

4. PRELIMINARY ANALYSIS

To gain an understanding of the potential of an IP-based communication systems for providing enhanced service for ATM, we look at the latency and throughput capacity of existing IFC services sold on many commercial flights across the continental United States and elsewhere (Table 2).

We conducted a series of experiments during each flight, continually measuring the latency and loss to www.google.com from our instrumented laptop. Concurrently, we ran Network Diagnostic Tests (NDT) [14] repeatedly to characterize the upstream and downstream throughput available to in-flight users.

We find existing IFC to provide far superior performance than existing ATM communication systems. Figure 1 shows performance metrics for each IFC technology across all flights in our dataset. We observe at least an order of magnitude greater performance across all metrics. The largest gains come in the ability to transmit 100s of kb/s in contrast to the 10s of bits per second currently available to transmit aircraft position. IFC is also capable of reducing the latency of these updates to a median value of 200 ms on DA2GC systems.

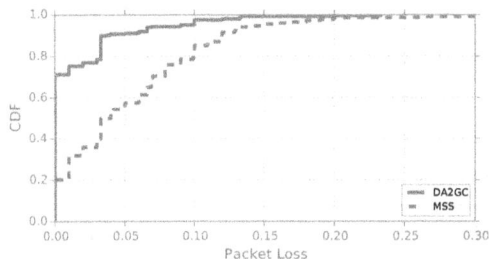

Figure 2: Aggregate packet loss measured for IFC technologies. Both technologies provide highly available data links. In the case of DA2GC, nearly 75% of measurements experience no packet loss.

In the case of aircraft communication, reliability and availability are in many cases greater in importance than system performance. Through active measurements of deployed IFC links, we find that even single systems provide adequate reliability and availability. We measured reliability through ping packet loss rate, aggregated every minute, and latency consistency. Packet loss rates for each technology are shown in Figure 2. We see that DA2GC has a median loss rate of 0% and a 95th percentile of 8% packet loss. Satellite service approaches loss rates of 4% at median and 14% at the 95th percentile.

Our results reveal a highly available Internet service during each flight. In our entire dataset, we found only one instance of 100% packet loss in the case of DA2GC, and only 13 instances in MSS. These periods of unavailability would be unacceptable for critical flight operations. However, consider that the IFC systems measured are designed for consumer use as a luxury service, and operate with a small fraction of the spectrum allocated to aviation operations. We believe that existing IFC could easily be enhanced to provide high levels of reliability and uptime.

A hybrid solution could address many of these reliability issues with satellite communication serving as a backup link to DA2GC. Indeed, such ideas for IFC are being currently explored [6]. Reliability can be further improved by adding redundant links to aircraft to supplement each technology or to be used as a backup in case of single link failure. Equipping aircraft with multiple links (multihoming them), would ensure the link reliability necessary for such a system.

If we assume packet loss events are independent between the two technologies, utilizing multihoming between these two technologies could result in a combined 0.08% chance of packet loss rate from our dataset.

5. FUTURE RESEARCH DIRECTIONS

There are numerous technical challenges which must be address before the promise of IP-based aeronautical networking can be realized. In addition, the unique domain of airborne networking opens up several new research areas. We describe several of these challenges and promising research areas below.

Best effort issues.

As a best effort service, IP does not offer any guarantees of protection against failure. One of the largest challenges for aeronautical networking is ensuring the reliability this IP channel matches, and even exceeds the current standard. Reliability over the radio link can be accomplished by multi-homing planes through the use of multiple redundant radios. These can include multiple IFC technologies such as DA2GC and MSS, or even sending high priority packets over existing VHF data links in certain cases.

Transit links between radio stations and air traffic control would also need to be configured to minimize dropped packets, especially those containing critical status messages from aircraft. Proactive congestion control on this internal network will be required to ensure near lossless operation.

Media Access Control.

Airline communication over a shared radio link faces new and interesting challenges. Due to the distances between broadcasting planes, there is a high likelihood of hidden terminal interference at receiving towers. The high latencies of each radio transmission mean that existing schemes like CSMA would need large back-off values, incurring inefficiencies in the wireless channel. It may be necessary for a more centralized method for channel assignment and broadcast slots for nearby aircraft. The extensive work on coordinated channel access in cellular networks involving dynamic channel allocation (DCA) [12] can be adopted.

New Transport Protocols.

The higher latency and loss rates of in-flight communication pose problems for existing transport protocols like TCP. In addition, the needs of air traffic communication are different than general packet delivery, where messages must support multiple and simultaneous levels of delivery effort and prioritization. For instance, certain messages such as navigation changes would require the highest priority and effort for delivery, whereas a periodic status report from a plane's existing beverage levels could be lost or delayed without consequence.

New transport protocols could potentially utilize encoding techniques such as forward error correction (FEC) for high priority traffic as well as principles from delay tolerant networking for lower priority traffic.

Mobility Management.

The constant high speed of travel and prerecorded flight plans enable new ways of routing packets to these mobile hosts. The large distances travelled during many commercial flights, especially International flights, require new systems for IP mobility management for a global scale. The existing methods of routing all packets through a single home-agent would incur excessive delays on flights over large distances.

Future aircraft mobility management systems can leverage the fact that commercial airlines follow pre-approved flight plans, and therefore have predictable mobility patterns. Such a system could potentially incorporate these flight plans into routing protocols for efficient routing of aircraft messages. Research on predictive mobility patterns for routing in mobile sensor networks directly applies to this.

Security.

Any new technology brings to bear new, poorly understood attack surfaces. By using well understood and tested Internet-connected software and services, we can reuse decades of security research products to improve defenses against attack. For example, we envision using standard PKI-based cryptographic techniques to authenticate and secure communication. Additionally, we can use multiple communication channels (IP and non-IP systems) to provide fault tolerance.

6. CONCLUSION

In this paper we advocated for a shift of air traffic management to a common IP-based data channel to support flight communication. We identified several opportunities where this improvement in networking capability could greatly increase the scalability of the global airline system. Our preliminary analysis of in-flight communication systems showed these existing systems provide a promising avenue for future communication systems, and a fruitful new area of mobile networking research.

7. ACKNOLEDGEMENTS

We would like to thank our shepherd Ben Greenstein, our anonymous reviewers, and Aaron Schulman for their feedback. This work was supported in part by the National Science Foundation through grant CNS 1218287.

8. REFERENCES

[1] P. Bonnefoy and R. Hansman. Scalability and evolutionary dynamics of air transportation networks in the united states. In *7th AIAA ATIO Conf.* American Institute of Aeronautics and Astronautics, 2007.

[2] S.-P. Chen. Perfomance analysis and optimization of da2gc using lte advanced technology. In *Proc. Int'l Conf. on Communications, Vehicular Technology, Information Theory and Aerospace & Electronic Systems (VITAE)*, 2014.

[3] Cheryl Harris Sharman. Feds Push Satellite Technology to Make Skies (and Runways) Friendlier. http://www.scientificamerican.com/article/feds-push-satellite-tech/, November 2008.

[4] D. Clark. The design philosophy of the darpa internet protocols. *ACM Sigcomm CCR*, 18(4):106–114, 1988.

[5] Electronics Communications Committee. Broadband direct-air-to-ground communications (da2gc). Technical Report ECC-214, CEPT, May 2014.

[6] Electronics Communications Committee. Adjacent band compatibility studies for aeronatucal cgc systems operating the the bands 1980-2010 mhz and 2170-2200 mhz. Technical Report ECC-233, CEPT, 2015.

[7] European Telecommunications Standards Institute. VHF air-ground Digital Link (VDL) Mode 2. Technical Report ETSI EN 301 841-1, ETSI, January 2010.

[8] Federal Aviation Administration. Faa aerospace forecast: Fiscal years 2015-2035. Technical Report OK 15-0814, Federal Aviation Administration, 2015.

[9] R. J. Hansman. The impact of information technologies on air transportation. In *AIAA Aerospace Sciences Conference, AIAA*, volume 1, 2005.

[10] IATA. Fact Sheet: Industry Statistics. https://www.iata.org/pressroom/facts_figures/fact_sheets/Documents/fact-sheet-industry-facts.pdf, June 2015.

[11] K. Karras, T. Kyritsis, M. Amirfeiz, and S. Baiotti. Aeronautical mobile ad hoc networks. In *Proc. European Wireless Conference*, 2008.

[12] I. Katzela and M. Naghshineh. Channel assignment schemes for cellular mobile telecommunication systems: A comprehensive survey. *Personal Communications, IEEE*, 3(3):10–31, 1996.

[13] J. Kuchar and A. C. Drumm. The traffic alert and collision avoidance system. *Lincoln Laboratory Journal*, 16(2):277, 2007.

[14] M-Lab. NDT (Network Diagnostic Test). http://www.measurementlab.net/tools/ndt.

[15] Matthew Finnegan. Boeing 787s to create half a terabyte of data per flight. http://tinyurl.com/h5d2zfv, July 2015.

[16] V. A. Orlando. The mode s beacon radar system. *The Lincoln Laboratory Journal*, 2(3):345–362, 1989.

[17] P. Park and C. Tomlin. Investigating communication infrastructure of next generation air traffic management. In *Proceedings of the 2012 IEEE/ACM Third International Conference on Cyber-Physical Systems*, pages 35–44. IEEE Computer Society, 2012.

[18] B. Rosenberg. Data comm. *Avionics Magazine*, July 2010:30–33, 2010.

[19] S. D. Thompson and J. M. Flavin. Surveillance accuracy requirements in support of separation services. *Lincoln Laboratory Journal*, 16(1):97, 2006.

[20] S. D. Thompson and K. A. Sinclair. Automatic dependent surveillance–broadcast in the gulf of mexico. *Lincoln Laboratory Journal*, 17(2):1–15, 2008.

[21] United States Department of Transportation. On-Time Performance - Flight Delays at a Glance. http://tinyurl.com/ov5xlyn.

A First Look at Unstable Mobility Management in Cellular Networks

Yuanjie Li
Dept. Computer Science
University of California, Los Angeles
Los Angeles, CA, USA
yuanjie.li@cs.ucla.edu

Jiaqi Xu
Dept. Computer Science Engineering
The Ohio State University
Columbus, OH 43210
xu.1629@osu.edu

Chunyi Peng
Dept. Computer Science Engineering
The Ohio State University
Columbus, OH 43210
chunyi@cse.ohio-state.edu

Songwu Lu
Dept. Computer Science
University of California, Los Angeles
Los Angeles, CA, USA
slu@cs.ucla.edu

ABSTRACT

Mobility management is a prominent feature in cellular networks. In this paper, we examine the (in)stability of mobility management. We disclose that handoff may never converge in some real-world cases. We focus on *persistent* handoff oscillations, rather than those *transient* ones caused by dynamic networking environment and user mobility (*e.g.*, moving back and force between two base stations). Our study reveals that *persistent* handoff loops indeed exist in operational cellular networks. They not only violate their design goals, but also incur excessive signaling overhead and data performance degradation. To detect and validate instability in mobility management, we devise MMDIAG, an *in-device* diagnosis tool for cellular network operations. The core of MMDIAG is to build a handoff decision automata based on 3GPP standards, and detect possible loops by checking the structural property of stability. We first leverage device-network signaling exchanges to retrieve mobility management policies and configurations, and then feed them into MMDIAG, along with runtime measurements. MMDIAG further emulates various handoff scenarios and identifies possible violations (*i.e.*, loops) caused by the used policies and configurations. Finally, we validate the identified problems through real measurements over operational networks. Our preliminary results with a top-tier US carrier demonstrate that, unstable mobility management indeed occurs in reality and hurts both carriers and users. The proposed methodology is effective to identify persistent instabilities and pinpoint their root causes in problematic configurations and policy conflicts.

1. INTRODUCTION

Mobility management (MM) is widely regarded as a fundamental service to the evolving Internet. To support billions of mobile devices (including smartphones, tablets, wearables, IoT, *etc.*),
the 4G/3G/2G cellular network plays a pivotal role. To date, it is the only deployed large-scale system that successfully offers wide-area, ubiquitous Internet access and mobility support.

A key MM function to 4G/3G/2G network is *handoff*, which migrates the device from one serving cell (also known as base station) to another new one *when necessary*. The necessity is defined to satisfy versatile (sometimes conflicting) demands such as sustaining pervasive network availability, offering seamless voice/data support, providing high-speed data service, balancing the traffic load between cells, to name few.

Stability is a desirable property in MM. It states that MM should converge to certain choice given an invariant setting. It is desirable because each handoff comes at a cost. Each handoff incurs multi-round signaling exchanges and causes data/voice suspension or degradation. The more frequent handoffs, the higher cost to carriers and users.

In this paper, we take the first effort to examine the structural property of stability in MM. We are particularly interested in whether MM in reality suffers from persistent loops and whether such loops are caused by fundamental conflicts (*e.g.*, inconsistent policies, uncoordinated configurations), rather than by transient factors such as radio dynamics and user behaviors [1,2]. Our work is inspired by the observation that, while each individual handoff policy or procedure may be well justified, the interplay among multiple handoffs can be problematic. Note that, each individual cell or the mobile device may customize its local policy in determining the target cell. The handoff decision is thus affected by each other, and prudent coordination is required. Otherwise, policy conflicts or misconfigurations lead to unstable handoffs.

We start with a real-world persistent-loop example to motivate our study (§3). We disclose its causes and the potential damages. It turns out that, a user-deployed femtocell introduces *conflicting* preference settings with two existing 3G and 4G cells, thus causing persistent loops among these three cells. It incurs 3–8x signaling overhead and 10-fold or more slowdown in file downloading. We then formulate the (in)stability problem and derive the necessary and sufficient conditions for stability (§4). Based on these rules, we further devise MMDIAG, an in-device approach to detect and validate possible instability in MM (§5). We leverage signaling exchanges between the device and the serving cell in the standard specifications to tackle the challenge without requiring access to network-side information. We build an automatic detector which enumerates each possible scenario and examines its likelihood of

HotMobile '16, February 26-27, 2016, St. Augustine, FL, USA

© 2016 ACM. ISBN 978-1-4503-4145-5/16/02. . . $15.00

DOI: http://dx.doi.org/10.1145/2873587.2873599

violating the stability. Finally, we validate our identified findings through real experiments. Our preliminary study via a top-tier US carrier shows that instability indeed exists and our proposed approach is effective (§6).

The paper makes three contributions.

- We present the first work to uncover persistent instability caused by misconfigurations and policy conflicts in mobility management, to the best of our knowledge.

- We devise MMDIAG, a device-based solution to identifying mobility instability in cellular networks.

- We conduct real experiments and validate the identified problems in an operational carrier network. We find that inconsistent mobility management between (macro)cells and femotcells are the main source of many handoff loops.

2. UNDERSTANDING MOBILITY MANAGEMENT IN CELLULAR NETWORKS

We first introduce necessary concepts on mobility management.

Handoff procedure flow.   To depict the handoff procedure flow, we use a typical scenario: the user is about to move out of the coverage of the current serving cell. Figure 1 gives an illustrative example. Initially, the phone is served by Cell 1. As it moves toward Cell 2 (away from Cell 1), the serving cell switches from Cell 1 to Cell 2 via handoff (③).

The handoff procedure can be divided into three phases: *pre-handoff*, *handoff* and *post-handoff*. The *pre-handoff* phase decides whether to trigger a handoff, depending on user mobility, radio quality variation, load balancing, *etc.*. In the above example, the serving cell asks the phone to measure radio quality (defining measurement parameters and criteria that trigger reports) and invokes a handoff decision upon receiving the radio quality report from the phone. Afterwards, the serving cell requests a handoff to the target cell and performs admission control. Once accepted, the handoff request is acknowledged by the target cell. The serving cell executes the handoff by sending a handoff command to the phone. The phone changes its radio configuration (matching with the target cell) accordingly and responds with a handoff confirmation message to the target cell. In this process, the user traffic is still delivered via the original cell (likely with poor performance) until the handoff completes. In the final *post-handoff* phase, it performs *location update* and reconfigures the data/voice forwarding path if the new cell belongs to a different location area. This is to let the cellular network learn the current location of the phone. During this phase, it may also release resources at the source cell, update QoS profiles and the IP address, perform authentication *etc.*, depending on the handoff type. Finally, the phone continues its traffic delivery through the new cell. In reality, various handoffs take place (see Table 1) and their detailed procedures might vary. However, they all require the trigger-and-decision process to prepare for a handoff and perform multiple-round signaling message exchanges to execute the handoff.

MM-related procedures.   There are several procedures related to MM. Table 1 lists the main procedures and their standard specifications, covering *initial attach, cell (re)selection, active handoff, voice support via CSFB and SRVCC, offloading, load balancing* (*e.g.*, via self-organizing networks). Each works with certain radio access technology (RAT, say, 4G/3G/2G), and/or various service types (say, active data/voice/both or idle).

Specifically, the *initial attach* and *cell-(re)selection* procedures are used to look for a serving cell or another better cell when the

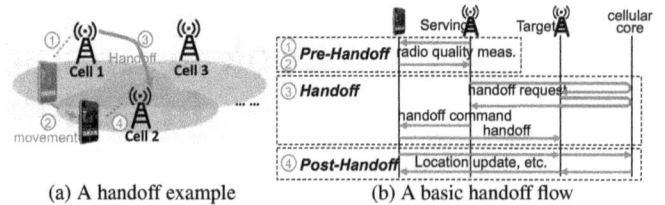

(a) A handoff example   (b) A basic handoff flow

Figure 1: Illustration of a handoff and its procedure flow.

Procedure	Standard	RAT	Service
Initial attach	23.401 [3]	all	idle
Cell (re)selection	25.304 [4],36.304 [5]	all	idle
Active handoff	23.009 [6]	all	active
CSFB and SRVCC	23.272 [7],23.216 [8]	4G	active(voice)
Femtocell offloading	25.367 [9]	3G,4G	active & idle
WLAN offloading	23.261 [10]	3G,4G	active & idle
Load balancing	32.500 [11]	all	active

Table 1: Main procedures (related to MM) in 3GPP standards.

device has no active association with the serving one (idle). They are performed regardless of whether mobility is involved or not. The *initial attach* procedure is used to establish an association with a serving cell when the device just powers on or recovers from the out-of-service state (*e.g.*, the airplane mode). The *cell reselection* is used to switch its association when the device camps on a serving cell but has no active connectivity. In both idle cases, the handoff decision and execution are made by the user device. The decision is mainly based on the measured radio quality from different cells, the cell preference and radio evaluation criteria preconfigured by the device or reconfigured by the associating cell (*cell-reselection* only). The device receives configurations and commands over the broadcast channel in the current cell.

The *active handoff* procedure[1] regulates the cell switching for ongoing services, and its primary goal is to ensure seamless services. It exhibits many forms, including inter-RAT handoff (*e.g.*, 4G↔3G) and intra-RAT handoff (*e.g.*, within 4G), soft handoff (with simultaneous connectivities to multiple cells) and hard handoff (disconnect-and-connect). Moreover, cellular networks also support handoff for different purposes. For instance, 4G LTE leverages 3G/2G systems to carry voice through CSFB (Circuit Switched Fallback) and SRVCC (Single Radio Voice Call Continuity), thus invoking 4G↔3G/2G handoffs.

To enable opportunistic wireless access, the cellular network may offload traffic to small cells or user-deployed femtocells. It also allows for traffic redirection to different cells for load balancing or other carrier-specific optimizations. In these cases, both the user and the network are involved. They use different decision criteria based on many factors, such as radio quality evaluation threshold and cell preference, runtime traffic load, service type, and so on. These criteria and factors are not necessarily regulated by standards, but can be customized by carriers. However, the active handoff decision is fully controlled by the network, particularly via the serving cell.

3. A MOTIVATING EXAMPLE

We motivate our work with a real-world example. The discovered persistent loop differs from the transient ping-pong effect, which oscillates between cells due to frequent movement and wireless channel dynamics. As a matter of fact, the instability prob-

---

[1]We use "*active handoff*" to differentiate it from the case of switching the serving cell without active services.

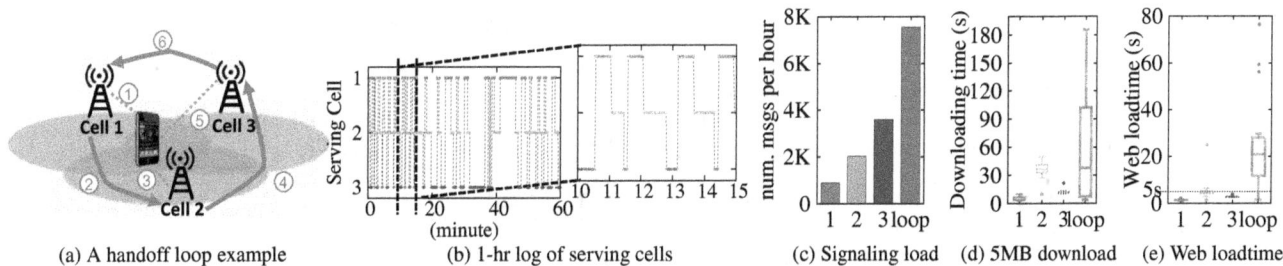

Figure 2: A persistent handoff loop among three cells and the consequent overhead and performance degradation.

lem is caused by policy and configuration conflicts rooted in MM. That is, even given an invariant setting, the handoff process still never converges. Instead, inconsistent handoff decisions are made in turn, and the serving cell consequently oscillates among multiple cells under the invariant setting.

Figure 2a illustrates the example. The phone is placed at a spot covered by three cells, but repetitive handoffs (Steps 2, 4 and 6) are triggered in turn once the phone switches the serving cell. As a result, the phone oscillates among three cells. In our experiment, we place the phone in the idle mode (no voice/data) for 40 hours at this location. We record the network status (serving cell ID and RAT) per second. The loop repeats every several minutes (see 1-hour trace in Figure 2b), and it does not converge during the 40-hour test. We further test different phone models (Samsung S4/S5 and LG Optimus G), and verify that the finding is independent of phone models. Note that such oscillations are not caused by radio signal variations. The loop still exists even in an ideal scenario without any channel or traffic dynamics.

It turns out that, this persistent loop is caused by conflicting handoff configurations among different cells. In this example, Cells 1, 2, 3 are a 4G cell, a 3G femtocell and a 3G cell, respectively. Cell 2 is deployed by users while the other two cells are deployed by carriers. The carrier aims to offer high-speed access *and* balance the traffic load. This can be realized through configuring the MM preferences at different cells. In the example, Cell 1 believes that Cell 2 has a higher preference to itself for the offloading purpose. Cell 2 configures equal preference to all its neighboring cells and selects the one with strongest radio coverage. Cell 3 (3G) always prefers Cell 1 (4G) for its high-speed data service, as long as the Cell 1's radio signal is not weak. Unfortunately, these *independent* preference settings at different cells lead to inconsistent results. When Cell 3 has stronger coverage than Cell 2, it results in the persistent loop $c_1 \rightarrow c_2 \rightarrow c_3 \rightarrow c_1 \rightarrow \cdots$.

Such a loop is undesirable, and it does hurt both the carrier and the user. Without converging to any cell, the mobile carrier fails to achieve the expected goals. Our 40-hour test further shows that more than 90% of loops can be formed within 200 seconds. That is, three handoffs approximately take place every three minutes. With such high-frequent switches, it fails to offer high-speed 4G access or achieve cost-effective offloading to the Femtocell. Even worse, it incurs a large amount of signaling overhead between the device and the network. Figure 2c compares the incurred signaling messages per hour with the case using each cell only. On average, this loop incurs 7555 signaling messages per hour, 8.5, 3.5, 2.2 times over those only using Cells 1, 2, 3 respectively. Finally, this results in data performance degradation. Data transfer speed decreases and the response is delayed. In addition to the experiment in the idle mode, we load a small webpage (www.cnn.com, interactive) and download a 5MB file to assess the negative impacts. We choose

these two representative apps, since they take both the access speed and the response time into account. The results are similar to those running other apps and speedTest. Figures 2d and 2e show the boxplots of their (down)loading times. In the worst case, it takes at most 12 seconds to download a 5MB file and about 3 seconds to load the web page using 4G; However, the current practice takes 180 seconds and 76 seconds. It suffers the 10-fold slowdown (15 fold in the worst case) in file downloading, and large performance slump in web browsing (11x on average, 33x in the worst case).

We further examine why handoff instability incurs these negative effects. As described in §2, each handoff execution requires signaling message exchanges and it takes time to get ready to serve the mobile device using the new cell. Even worse, *location update* is mandatory in most cases. It has to add multi-round message exchanges related to radio resource allocation, data forwarding-path reconfiguration and authentication (see the standard TS24.008) We find that a *location update* typically takes 3–6 seconds in the absence of failures. This matches previous studies (*e.g.*, [12, 13]). Frequent location updates intermittently suspend traffic delivery, thus incurring significant delay, loss and throughput slump.

4. THE INSTABILITY PROBLEM IN MM

We now formulate the instability problem of mobility management in cellular networks. We look into under what conditions unstable handoffs occur in reality, particularly those caused by uncoordinated policy conflicts. We focus on the persistent loops rather than those transient ones (*e.g.*, ping-pong effects), because they have lasting negative impacts and can be prevented with appropriate mobility management. We examine the trigger-and-decision phase, while assuming that the handoff execution exactly follows its decision.

We model a handoff procedure as a transition from the serving cell s to the target cell t out of the available candidate set C: $s \rightarrow t, t \in C$. We define the decision function as $t = F_s(s, C)$. The handoff decision depends on the criteria used by the serving cell or the mobile device, as well as the neighboring cell measurement performed at the mobile device (but configured by the serving cell). For simplicity, we assume the environment is invariant. Consider the same device is used in all the decision functions, we simplify it as $t = F_s(s)$. Once the serving cell switches, the decision criteria and measurement will change accordingly. Finally, it can be expressed as a deterministic process

$$s \rightarrow F_s(s) \rightarrow \cdots c_i \rightarrow [c_{i+1} = F_{c_i}(c_i)] \rightarrow \cdots, c_i \in C.$$

We claim that, stability is guaranteed if the handoff process always converges to the target t, regardless of its initial value s. If this property is violated, a *persistent loop* happens within a subset of candidate cells. Note that, our work focuses on whether it converges, and does not discuss how long it takes to converge. We now give necessary and sufficient conditions for stability.

17

THEOREM 1. [**Necessary condition**] *There exists at least one cell who allows a handoff decision to itself, namely, $\exists t \in C, t = F_t(t)$.*

PROOF. This is proved by contradiction. Assume that it converges to t when no cells satisfy $c = F_c(c), c \in C$. Given the serving cell t, its next cell is not t. It leads to contradiction. □

THEOREM 2. [**Necessary and sufficient condition**] *It converges, if and only if (1) there exists at least one cell specified in Theorem 1: $\exists t \in C, t = F_t(t)$; (2) there exists a handoff path from the initial cell s to the desirable cell t.*

PROOF. We only need to prove that they are sufficient. Assume there exists a handoff path from $s \to \cdots \to t$. Follow this path, it converges to t since $t = F_t(t)$. So the handoff process converges. □

Bearing these stability conditions in mind, we next devise an automatic detector to infer possible instability.

5. MMDIAG DESIGN

We design MMDIAG, an in-device diagnosis tool to detect and validate instability in MM. We take the device-based approach, since the carriers are reluctant to provide public access to their mobility management configurations and runtime information for handoff decisions. Our approach is deemed a viable solution, because we can leverage the signaling exchanges to bypass this major constraint. The underlying premise is that, the serving cell has to send their main parameters and decision logics to the device.

Inspired by this, we design MMDIAG as follows. Figure 3 plots its architecture, which is divided into two phases: detection and validation. In the detection phase (left), the core is an MM automata, which explores possible instability cases through an instability analyzer and reports counterexamples if found. It models the MM decision logic based on the 3GPP standards and feeds this model with real configurations collected directly from the device and indirectly from the serving cell, as well as dynamic environment settings created for various scenarios. The instability is inferred through examining two instability conditions given in Theorems 1 and 2. Once they are found, we move to the device-based validation phase (right). For each counterexample, we set up the corresponding experimental scenario and conduct measurements in operational networks for validation. We next elaborate on each component.

Instability analyzer. The key is to model the decision process in MM. This model determines the target cell using three factors: the *decision logic*, the *configurable parameters* and the *runtime observations*.

The decision logic is the algorithm to select the target cell, represented by F_s. We support the standard procedures specified in Table 1 and extract their logic engines from their specifications. For instance, *cell reselection* selects the one with the strongest radio coverage among those most preferable cells. That is,

$$F_s(s, C) = \arg \max_{c \in C'} radio(c),$$

$$C' = \{c | prefer(c) = \max_{i \in C} perfer(i), c \in C\}.$$

The configurable parameters are used to feed the logic. They are defined in the standards but can be customized by carriers and vendors. Table 2 summarizes related configurations specified in the standards. In the above example, cell preference $prefer(c)$ maps

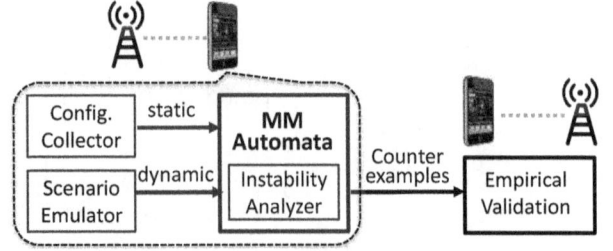

Figure 3: The MMDIAG architecture.

	Category	Parameter	State	Description
Net-work	Candidate cells	*MeasObj*	Active	Cells to be monitored
		carrierFreqList	Idle	Frequencies to be monitored
	Access control	*Handover restriction list*	Active	List of forbidden target cells
		Closed Subscriber Group	Idle	List of users with the cell access
	Radio evaluation	*eventA1 ~ eventA5* *eventB1 ~ eventB2*	Active	Thresholds and report event criteria
		Thresh1 ~ Thresh3	Idle	Thresholds for cell re-selection
		TimeToTrigger	Active	Measurement duration for each cell in the active mode
		$T_{reselection}$	Idle	Measurement duration for each cell in the idle mode
	Traffic eval.	*event4A* and *event4B*	Active	threshold for users' traffic volume report
	Cell preference	*cellReselPriority*	Idle	Cell reselection priority
		SPID	Active	Subscriber ID for RAT/Freq. priority
	Mobility method	*InactivityTimer*	Active	Timer for active→idle state transition
Device	Radio	Network mode	both	Frequency bands to be enabled
	Operation mode	Usage setting	both	Voice-centric or data-centric
		Voice preference	both	indicate if preferring PS or CS voice

Table 2: Summary of standardized configurations related to mobility management.

to a priority value, CELLRESELPRIORITY, which can be directly obtained from the handoff request message.

The runtime observations serve as the input to the handoff decision. The idle-state handoff adopts the cell-radio-quality assessments as the input. The active-state handoff uses both the radio quality and customizable observations (*e.g.* cell loads), which are fed through the *configuration collector* and the *scenario emulator*.

To infer whether the handoff converges, the Instability Analyzer first checks the necessary condition (Theorem 1). If no cell satisfies Theorem 1, it directly reports an instability counterexample with all the configurations and runtime measurements. Otherwise, we proceed to check the sufficient condition (Theorem 2). For each cell, we enumerate the possible paths. Note that this simple scheme may not be scalable; it can be improved as part of our future work.

Configuration collector. We collect surrounding cells' handoff policies and configurations from the signaling messages sent by the serving cell. We retrieve configuration parameters through the mapping defined by the standards. To collect signaling messages, we enable the diagnostic mode (*e.g.* dialing secret code *#0808# for Sumsang Galaxy S5) at the mobile device. We log signaling messages through MobileInsight [14], an in-device cellular signaling collector developed by us. This acts like QXDM [15] and XCAL [16], proprietary software used by professionals to record message exchanges over the air. To collect a complete set from all cells, the device proactively switches to every 3G/4G cell at each location. Given each cell, we collect handoff parameters (see Table 2) from the radio resource control (RRC [5, 17]) layer and mobility management layer (MM [18, 19]).

Scenario emulator. Based on the handoff decision logic, we create runtime scenario parameters (*e.g.*, radio signal strength and traffic loads) and feed them into the MM automata. This is not easy because these parameters are not formally defined by the 3GPP standards, but largely dependent on carrier requirements and user demands. Testing all combinations is neither feasible nor necessary. For scenarios with an unlimited number of options (*e.g.*, user mobility at various speeds, traffic arrival patterns), we take the random sampling approach. We first retrieve the configuration values and then divide the runtime value range into several ranges. We assign each usage scenario with certain probability, and randomly sample values within these ranges. For the scenarios with a limited number of options (e.g., device switch on/off, data/voice service), we enumerate all possible combinations. This approach is similar to our prior studies [12, 20]. However, it differs from the previous work in that we examine configurations and policies on the management plane, whereas the prior work examines protocol interactions on the control plane.

Empirical validation.   Using counterexamples as the input, the validation phase needs to construct test scenarios, run experiments, collect real traces, and confirm whether a loop appears. The real challenge is to *precisely* re-create the counterexample scenario. For example, MMDIAG infers that one persistent loop would incur as long as Cell 1 is stronger than -108 dbm and 3 dbm stronger than Cell 2 (see the example later). However, in reality, it is not easy for us to find such a location. To this end, we pre-collect a radio map through extensive measurements in indoor and outdoor testbeds. We further use them as hints to approximately locate the spots of our interests.

6. PRELIMINARY RESULTS

We conduct experiments in two metropolitan areas in Los Angeles and Columbus using a top-tier US carrier. We run both outdoor and indoor experiments. The outdoor experiments cover 63 different locations over 240 km^2 in LA and 260 km^2 in Columbus. Each location is separated by at least two kilometers apart, to obtain diverse cell coverage. We also collect information on indoor experiments at 50 spots in an 8-floor office buildings and an apartment, respectively. In this indoor setting, we mainly collect the radio quality observations at various spots, since most cells, as well as their configurations, are similar across locations. We also deploy four 3G Femtocells in the office and at home for indoor tests. We use four Android phone models: Samsung Galaxy S4, S5 and Note 3, and LG Optimus G. The results are similar for all phone models. Our dataset confirms that today's cell deployment is dense and hybrid. At most locations, there are about 8–16 cells available (11 cells on average).

MMDIAG reports 17 types of conflicts that might cause loops at the idle state and one type of loop at the active state. They are all validated in real experiments. Figure 4 summarizes the loops at the idle state. The smallest loop involves 3 cells, while the largest one has 7 cells. These happen when they use various RATs (4G, 3G, 2G) or different frequency bands[2]. Furthermore, they can be classified into three categories: 4G-Femtocell-3G loops (8 types), 4G-Femtocell-3G-2G loops (8 types), and 4G-only loop (1 type). Note that the the specific deployment location of the femtocell does not affect the discovery of loops involving the femtocells. Our outdoor tests confirm that, all 2G/3G/4G Macrocells have the problematic configurations, and a potential loop might exist as long as a Femtocell was deployed at the spots. We further test with femtocell deployment in campus buildings, and conduct indoor experiments at all viable locations. Among the tests, 25% of locations incur loops. Based on the root causes, these loops can be further classified in three categories:

[2]https://en.wikipedia.org/wiki/List_of_LTE_networks

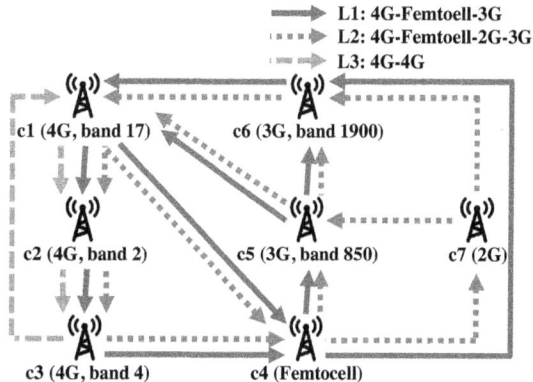

Figure 4: Idle-state persistent loops detected in US-I.

C1: Uncoordinated handoff goals.   In this category, 8 variants of loops are reported, and all happen between 4G Macrocell, Femtocell and 3G Macrocells. The example in §3 illustrates the smallest loop, with c_1 = 4G, c_2 = Femtocell and c_3 = 3G. These loops are caused by conflicting preference settings for conflicting goals: the 4G Macrocells intend to offload user to the private Femtocells, but 3G Macrocells prefer to move the user to the high-speed 4G cell.

C2: Device-side preference misconfiguration.   MMDIAG further reports 8 variants of loops between 4G Macrocells, Femtocell, 2G and 3G Macrocells. Compared with C1, when leaving the Femtocell, the mobile device hands off to 2G first, then switches to 3G Macrocells. This happens when the Femtocell's signal strength is weak (<-115dBm) but still higher than 4G's high-preference handoff threshold (-116dBm in this scenario). It turns out that, this additional handoff is caused by improper preference configurations at the mobile device. With weak signal strength, the device may temporarily lose association to the Femtocell. According to the standards [5], the device resumes the service by scanning all cells and associating to the first available one. The order of the scanning cells is based on a pre-configured preference list stored at the phone's SIM card. For certain phones, 2G is listed as the highest preference, so the phone moves to 2G instead of 3G. Once associated with 2G, the device would immediately switch to 3G, 4G and 3G Femtocells. This way, the persistent loop continues.

C3: Imprudent 4G infrastructure upgrade.   The last instance is a 4G-only loop. We observe that, US-I is upgrading its 4G infrastructure and deploying cells over a new frequency band (c_2 in Figure 4). Before the upgrade, existing 4G cells (c_1 and c_3) assign equal preferences to each other. US-I intends to migrate users to the new cells, which offer higher speed. To this end, some old cells (c_1) configure the new cells with higher preference. However, not all cells' preferences are updated in a timely fashion: preference ties still happen on some cells (c_2). Such partial upgrade fails to migrate the user to the new cells. This loop has no direct impact on users, because all cells belong to the same location area. However, it incurs larger 4G-Femtocell-3G and 4G-Femtocell-2G-3G loops, and indirectly amplifies their negative impacts.

C4: Uncoordinated load balancing.   MMDIAG reports one loop between two 4G cells at one location. Both cells try to offload the user to each other when both signal strengths are higher than a threshold (here, -106 dBm). However, such load-balancing policies are not coordinated, so the user oscillates between cells when both cells' signal strengths are higher than -106 dBm. Fortunately, this loop is not commonly observed. Among all 4G cells we have collected, 67% of them use the same policy for the active-state handoff, but its neighboring cells are not observed to use the same rule except at one location. At this location, we conduct 6-hour ping tests and observe 8 loops (every 45 minutes on average) and the minimum one lasts only 43 seconds.

7. RELATED WORK

In recent years, mobility management has been well examined in the context of cellular networks. These studies focus on handoff optimization [1, 2, 21], offloading [22, 23], TCP/app performance [24] and cross-layer optimization [25, 26]. In contrast, we demonstrate that improper interplay between handoff policies and misconfigurations can lead to instability. Our work is inspired by our prior efforts on the control-plane protocol verification [12, 20], but focuses on the management plane rather than the control plane.

Instability and policy misconfigurations have been studied in other problem contexts, including BGP routing divergence [27], DNS [28], home networks [29], and data center networks [30], *etc.*. Our work complements these efforts, but applies domain-specific analysis to study (in)stability in mobility management.

8. DISCUSSION AND CONCLUSION

Mobility support offers an indispensable utility function in 2G/3G/4G cellular networks. However, its management is more complex than expected. In practice, it allows for customizable policies and configurations at each cell and each device, to accommodate diverse demands from carriers and users. In this work, we conduct the first study to look into its persistent instability problem. We propose a device-based methodology to detect possible loops and validate them through real experiments. We show that, persistent loops may occur without proper parameter configurations or/and coordinated decision logics. They can result in heavy signaling overhead and significant performance degradation.

This work is still at its early stage. Several issues remain to be explored. First, we focus on the stability property only. It can not cover all desirable features; Other structural properties can be violated along with policy conflicts and misconfigurations. For example, the handoff converges to an undesirable choice (*e.g.*, 3G/2G even when 4G is available [13]). Second, we look into deterministic factors and do not take transient factors (*e.g.*, channel or traffic dynamics) into consideration. In reality, Non-deterministic factors need to be accounted. It is thus more challenging for stability analysis. Third, our approach may fail to identify all the unstable cases without all essential information on the network side. It thus calls for a holistic approach with cooperations from both parties. Fourth, the current work focuses on instability *only within* cellular technologies. Loops between different radio technologies (say, between WiFi and cellular networks) may exist, due to the offloading criteria between WiFi and cellular, similar to mobility management policies and configurations. Last but not the least, we focus on detecting the loops, but not fixing them. The future work is to sketch a solution that facilitates to both detect and fix the problems in MM. To this end, MMDIAG can be used to report identified problems to carriers. It can also assist end devices to break loops when they occur. Given hints of possible loops, we need to further check runtime measurements and detect whether a loop occurs. As long as the device confirms that the loop is caused by policy conflicts and/or misconfigurations, it take actions to intervene the loop; For instance, in the motivating example (§3), it can move to 4G and disable the path to the 3G Femtocell (thus hiding the existence of 3G femtocells). This prevents the further occurrence of loops.

Acknowledgments

We greatly appreciate the insightful and constructive comments from our shepherd, Dr. Aaron Schulman, and the anonymous reviewers. This work is supported in part by the National Science Foundation under Grants No. CNS-1423576, CNS-1421440, CNS-1526456 and CNS-1526985.

9. REFERENCES

[1] C. Brunner, A. Garavaglia, M. Mittal, M. Narang, and J. V. Bautista. Inter-system Handover Parameter Optimization. In *VTC Fall*, 2006.

[2] A. Lobinger, S. Stefanski, T. Jansen, and I. Balan. Coordinating Handover Parameter Optimization and Load Balancing in LTE Self-Optimizing Networks. In *VTC Spring*. IEEE, 2011.

[3] 3GPP. TS23.401: GPRS Enhancements for E-UTRAN Access, 2011.

[4] 3GPP. TS25.304: User Equipment (UE) Procedures in Idle Mode and Procedures for Cell Reselection in Connected Mode, 2012.

[5] 3GPP. TS36.304: E-UTRA; User Equipment Procedures in Idle Mode, 2015.

[6] 3GPP. TS23.009: Handover Procedures, 2011.

[7] 3GPP. TS23.272: Circuit Switched (CS) fallback in Evolved Packet System (EPS), 2012.

[8] 3GPP. TS 23.216: Single Radio Voice Call Continuity (SRVCC), 2011.

[9] 3GPP. TS25.367: Mobility procedures for Home Node B, 2014.

[10] 3GPP. TS23.261: IP flow mobility and seamless Wireless Local Area Network (WLAN) offload; Stage 2, 2014.

[11] 3GPP. TS32.500: Self-Organizing Networks (SON); Concepts and requirements, 2014.

[12] G.-H. Tu, Y. Li, C. Peng, C.-Y. Li, H. Wang, and S. Lu. Control-Plane Protocol Interactions in Cellular Networks. In *SIGCOMM*, 2014.

[13] G. Tu, C. Peng, H. Wang, C. Li, and S. Lu. How Voice Calls Affect Data in Operational LTE Networks. In *MobiCom*, Oct. 2013.

[14] Mobileinsight project. http://metro.cs.ucla.edu/mobile_insight.

[15] QUALCOMM eXtensible Diagnostic Monitor. http://www.qualcomm.com/media/documents/tags/qxdm.

[16] Mediatek. Xcal-mobile. http://www.accuver.com.

[17] 3GPP. TS36.331: E-UTRA; Radio Resource Control (RRC), 2012.

[18] 3GPP. TS24.008: Mobile Radio Interface Layer 3, 2012.

[19] 3GPP. TS24.301: Non-Access-Stratum (NAS) for EPS; , Jun. 2013.

[20] G.-H. Tu, Y. Li, C. Peng, C.-Y. Li, and S. Lu. Detecting problematic control-plane protocol interactions in mobile networks. *IEEE Transactions on Networking (TON)*, pages 1–14, March 2015.

[21] M. Liu, Z. Li, X. Guo, and E. Dutkiewicz. Performance Analysis and Optimization of Handoff Algorithms in Heterogeneous Wireless Networks. *IEEE Transactions on Mobile Computing*, 7(7):846–857, July 2008.

[22] A. Balasubramanian, R. Mahajan, and A. Venkataramani. Augmenting mobile 3g using wifi. In *ACM MobiSys*, June 2010.

[23] W. Dong, S. Rallapalli, R. Jana, L. Qiu, K. Ramakrishnan, L. Razoumov, Y. Zhang, and T. W. Cho. ideal: Incentivized dynamic cellular offloading via auctions. *TON*, 22(4):1271–1284, 2014.

[24] F. P. Tso, J. Teng, W. Jia, and D. Xuan. Mobility: A Double-Edged Sword for HSPA Networks: A Large-Scale Test on Hong Kong Mobile HSPA Networks. *IEEE Transactions on Parallel and Distributed Systems*, 23(10):1895–1907, 2012.

[25] N. Balasubramanian, A. Balasubramanian, and A. Venkataramani. Energy consumption in mobile phones: A measurement study and implications for network applications. In *IMC*, 2009.

[26] U. Javed, D. Han, R. Caceres, J. Pang, S. Seshan, and A. Varshavsky. Predicting handoffs in 3g networks. In *MobiHeld*, 2011.

[27] T. G. Griffin and G. Wilfong. An Analysis of BGP Convergence Properties. In *ACM SIGCOMM*, 1999.

[28] V. Pappas, Z. Xu, S. Lu, D. Massey, A. Terzis, and L. Zhang. Impact of Configuration Errors on DNS Robustness. In *SIGCOMM*, 2004.

[29] B. Aggarwal, R. Bhagwan, T. Das, S. Eswaran, V. N. Padmanabhan, and G. M. Voelker. NetPrints: Diagnosing Home Network Misconfigurations Using Shared Knowledge. In *NSDI*, 2009.

[30] P. Sun, R. Mahajan, J. Rexford, L. Yuan, M. Zhang, and A. Arefin. A Network-State Management Service. In *ACM SIGCOMM*, 2014.

Towards Mobile Handheld Imaging Devices

S. M. Iftekharul Alam
Purdue University
alams@purdue.edu

Jack Brassil
Princeton University
jbrassil@cs.princeton.edu

ABSTRACT

A new generation of smartphone accessories are emerging to support 2-d and 3-d printing and model creation. These mobile, handheld devices require continuous self-location with position accuracy approaching 0.001 inch, well beyond the capabilities of commercial, consumer-grade wireless positioning technologies. We consider the problem of accurately tracking the motion of a handheld device that provides free-hand, high-resolution image 'drawing' while being swiped across a fixed planar surface. We review the capabilities and limitations of existing short-range localization technologies, including optical navigation sensors, ultrasonic positioning devices, and Inertial Measurement Units (IMU). We describe the testing apparati we constructed to establish the ground truth position of a device. We show how combining the complementary capabilities of these sensors can accurately locate a handheld device, potentially enabling a new class of smartphone imaging peripherals and applications.

1. INTRODUCTION

Mobile handheld imaging devices promise users the freedom of untethered portability and ease-of-use. Unlike conventional labeling or portable printing products, we envision a device that a user continuously swipes back-and-forth across a media surface to collect or deposit an image, entirely under user control. Despite early interest in prototypes from consumers worldwide, developing such a device while maintaining the high-resolution, artifact-free image quality that printer users expect has proved stubbornly difficult [1]. Innovations are required in diverse disciplines ranging from inkjet pen design, ink chemistry, nonlinear motion estimation, nozzle firing control systems, energy efficiency and low latency communications.

We do not strive to tackle all these challenges here. Instead we observe that many of the large physical components of a conventional printer are directed at precisely aligning a printhead with media; this includes mechanical paper feeders, alignment rails and belts, stepper motors, etc. We seek

to replace these bulky mechanical components with sensors to localize the handheld (with respect to media) at absolute positioning accuracy approaching 0.001 inch (1 mil). Achieving sub-millimeter translation accuracy, fine angular rotation accuracy, and reliable motion estimation requires a sophisticated positioning subsystem, possibly including multiple ultrasound transmit-receive pairs, optical navigation devices (i.e., mouse sensors), accelerometers, and gyroscopes. Each sensor type has unique limitations, but somewhat complementary capabilities; a diverse set of sensors can provide high accuracy, reliability, and availability.

Note that such a device must self-locate, or acquire its own position. If localization is performed off-device (e.g., in an ultrasound receiver or a smartphone app), that information must be transmitted to the device at a high update rate with low latency. Even at modest hand speeds of 1-2 in./sec., imaging at 300 dpi demands device localization at 1 mil accuracy, position update rates exceeding 1000 Hz, and low jitter sub-millisecond wireless communication latencies; several of these parameters exceed commercial product capabilities by an order of magnitude or more. Consumer ultrasound based positioning systems [9] lack sufficiently high position update rates for mobile imaging. Optoelectronic navigation systems [6] used in prototype free-hand printers [1] suffer from growing error with distance traveled, and complete position loss due to surface "liftoff" of even a few millimeters. In this paper, we devise a positioning subsystem that combines sensing capabilities of ultrasound and optical sensors and leverages compute and communications capabilities of modern smartphones to achieve sub-millisecond accuracy and communication latency.

Figure 1: An illustrative example of drawing an image by manually swiping a mock handheld printer (red/black) with associated external ultrasound receiver (white) and smartphone.

The key contributions of our research are

- a system architecture comprising a set of complementary sensors and associated fusion algorithms that can

HotMobile '16, February 26-27, 2016, St. Augustine, FL, USA

© 2016 ACM. ISBN 978-1-4503-4145-5/16/02. . . $15.00

DOI: http://dx.doi.org/10.1145/2873587.2873590

localize a translating, rotating device at sub-millimeter accuracy, and

- a set of novel test tools to establish position ground truth for short-range applications, and

- positioning tools and methods that are extensible to emerging applications including 3d model development.

The remainder of this paper is organized as follows. Sensor capabilities and limitations are discussed in the next section. The proposed device architecture is described in Section 3. Our experiments with integrating diverse sensor technologies are discussed in Section 4, which we divide into subsections focusing on measuring 1-d translation, rotation, and arbitrary 2-d movement. Each subsection also describes the specialized test rigs we developed to establish ground location truth. Finally, related work is reviewed in 5, and we state our conclusions.

2. SENSOR BACKGROUNDER

Accurate *absolute* localization within $1\ m^2$ is often best performed with ultrasound positioning. Inexpensive ultrasound stylus technology exploits the relatively low speed of sound (330 m/s) while sampling at low single-digit MHz rates [9]. In a typical pen application, dual transducers in a fixed location "receiver" bilaterate an ultrasound transmission (Figure 2) by measuring transmission delay differences from a stylus-tip based transmitter; synchronization of each receiver's clock is established by the transmission of a periodic, faster propagating infrared signal from the pen tip.

The position update rates supported by commercial products is very modest (e.g., 50-150 updates/sec.) but adequate for display-oriented cursor or pointer control applications such as electronic whiteboarding. Technical challenges affecting positioning accuracy include surface/air turbulence, thermal variations, multipath reception, and imprecise methods for coverage area landmark position calibration. Ease-of-use challenges include finger/hand obstruction, variable transmitter orientation (i.e., pen angle), clumsy manual calibration steps, and human ultrasound hearing exposure safety concerns [4]. While commercial systems advertise positioning accuracies of approximately ± 1 mm. [2], our experiments demonstrated 0.3 mm is typically achieved with fixed pen angle.

Optoelectronic navigation (i.e., mouse) sensors analyze sequential surface images to measure *relative* movement [12]. An onboard digital signal processor correlates consecutive images, using surface features to determine changes in orthogonal direction and magnitude of displacement (δ_x, δ_y). Typical low-end sensors for computer mouse application register only 400 counts/inch or CPI, and are polled at rates as low as 100-125 Hz). But recent advances is optical sensors include larger pixel arrays (e.g., 30-40 pixels/dimension), higher polling rates (e.g., 500-2000 Hz), high count densities (e.g., 8000-12000 CPI), and accurate tracking at high speeds and accelerations (e.g., 50-200 in/sec, 50G).

Optical sensors suffer from the fact that measured displacement errors accumulate with distance traversed. A key requirement of our application – the ability to traverse a circuit of tens of inches and accurately return to a starting point – can be very inaccurate. Since optical sensors measure displacement relative to the instantaneous device orientation, continuous rotation tracking and compensation

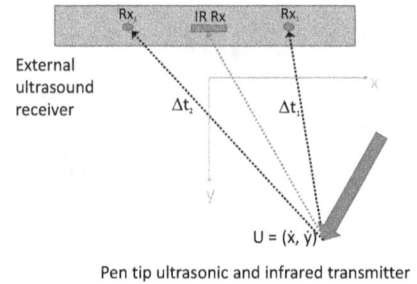

Pen tip ultrasonic and infrared transmitter

Figure 2: Differential time-of-flight bilateration with an ultrasonic 'pen' transmitter and an outboard receiver with 2 transducers. Periodic infrared pulses establish receiver time synchronization.

is required when measuring distance traveled. Hence these sensors have found limited use in demanding position tracking applications [6]. Technical issues with navigation sensors include media type (e.g., paper) and sensor height sensitivity requiring CPI calibration, and potential instabilities at high polling rates (e.g., exceeding 1000 Hz). Ease-of-use issues include tracking loss due to surface liftoffs as low as a few millimeters.

Like optical sensors, IMUs (i.e., gyroscope, accelerometer) measure relative motion and suffer accumulated errors. A key benefit is their ability to measure orientation in 3 orthogonal dimensions. While measuring absolute displacement is generally difficult relative to other sensors, these devices excel at rapid detection of undesired device motions (e.g. surface liftoff, direction reversal, etc).

3. SYSTEM ARCHITECTURE

We next explore the design and operation a mobile printing device, focusing on the demanding requirements on its positioning subsystem. To minimize size, complexity and cost, we envision a battery operated device serving as a peripheral to a smartphone or tablet computer. The smartphone provides functions including a user interface, position engine, pen/scanner firing controller, communications system, and image pre-processing unit. Upon pressing an on/off firing button, the device deposits ink when passing over the target print area only when position and trajectory estimates are within a desired tolerance (determined by target image quality); experiments suggest that speeds of 1-2 in./sec acceptably balance ease-of-use and image quality [8]. Motion-aware on-off nozzle firing produces a 'scratch off lottery ticket' reveal, where parts of the image are drawn with initial user swipes and backfilled on subsequent passes over unfinished image areas. If the device location (or predicted near-future location) is determined off-device (e.g., in a smartphone app), that information must be transmitted to the device at a high update rate with low latency.

A key design concern is the division of labor between device and smartphone to process sensors, and calculate and communicate device position. Rather than exhaustively identify alternative system designs, we present one *illustrative* approach where the handheld device comprises the following positioning components:

1. an ultrasound transmitter with line-of-sight commu-

nication to a physically separate, media-affixed, dual transducer receiver to provide absolute position,

2. two optical navigation sensors to measure instantaneous device orientation and minute displacements,

3. a low power communications system (e.g., BLE), and

4. an IMU to detect device motion deemed outside a desired range for accurate position prediction.

The system operates as follows. A smartphone app preprocesses a conventional image format and downloads a device-specific representation to an image buffer via the communication channel. The handheld device continuously transmits ultrasound signals to the ultrasound receiving unit, and periodically transmits IR synchronization signals at rate R_{IR}. Upon receipt of a synchronization signal, the ultrasound receiver bilaterates the ultrasound signal, and forwards current period absolute position data to the smartphone at rate R_B over a second (logical) communication channel. The smartphone app further processes the incoming raw position updates, performs local functions (e.g., UI updates), and communicates position and firing control information to the handheld over the communication channel at rate R_U.

Handheld motion triggers relative displacement updates from its optical sensors at relatively high polling rate R_M, $R_M \gg R_U$, to be processed locally. The translation data from these separate, imperfect, noisy sensors is fused (e.g., using linear state estimators such as Kalman filters) to improve position accuracy. Figure 3 shows how relatively frequent optical sensor updates $\mathbf{M}$ can be used to refine position between less frequent ultrasound updates $\mathbf{U}$, improving location accuracy over a predicted piecewise linear path.

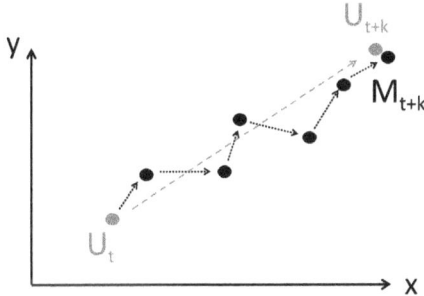

Figure 3: High-rate optical navigation sensors' relative position updates $\mathbf{M}$ refine intermediate positions between slower ultrasound updates $\mathbf{U}$.

In addition, the dual opposing optical sensors separated by a known distance D are processed locally to measure rotation from the initial orientation as user arm swipes move the device roughly along a fixed radius arc during each polling period. The time between a pen fire request and actual ink drop on the media is a small but significant lag requiring dead reckoning. We estimate position and speed at time t_n based on kinematic equations, and drops are fired only when the previous n sensor samples and instantaneous IMU measurements indicate the device is moving at near constant velocity. Typical hand swiping motion [10] has been well-researched, and our conjecture is that users can be guided toward maintaining roughly constant velocity by observing the positive feedback of fewer print artifacts and faster print

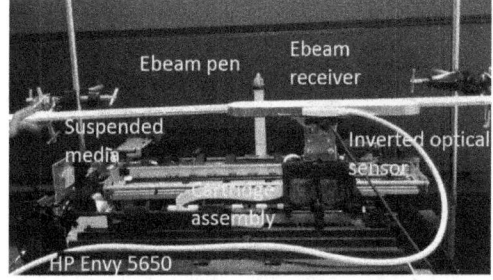

Figure 4: Test harness based on an HP Envy 5650 establishes ground truth for 1-d motion.

completion. A distance between the optical sensors and the surface of roughly 1-5 mm. must be preserved to maintain continuous sensor output.

4. EXPERIMENTATION

Establishing ground truth device location and measuring minute movements are major technical challenges that require developing special purpose localization test equipment. In this section we describe how we tackled this in steps. First we explore the problem of tracking a handheld device moving at constant speed and fixed orientation along a straight line. We then consider measuring the device's angle of rotation, as the device orientation will change continuously during arm swiping motion. Finally, we examine the problem of tracking 2-dimensional motion with arbitrary acceleration and rotation.

4.1 Measuring translation

To track the handheld device moving at constant velocity we developed a testbed based on a modified HP *Envy 5650* inkjet printer with customized position control firmware. This allowed us to repeatedly move the cartridge assembly at speeds up to 10 in/sec over a 10 in. span while collecting time-stamped position data at accuracies of 1/600 in. Figure 4 shows how we emulated the positioning subsystem. A Luidia eBeam *Edge* [2] ultrasonic receiver and an inverted Razer Orochi gaming mouse (i.e., Avago ADNS 3988 sensor) were affixed to the moving cartridge assembly platform. These devices were chosen in part for their wired USB interfaces, permitting us to initially bypass varying wireless communication latencies. In various experiments the devices were connected to measurement applications we wrote on either a Ubuntu Linux 3.1.1 desktop, or a Nexus 5 smartphone running various Android OS versions; some older version required modifications of the stock OS to support functions such as multiple mice. The optical sensor lightly grazed a suspended surface as the assembly moved. The ultrasonic transmitter (i.e., pen) was inverted and positioned at moving platform height.

We performed a large number of experiments while changing operational parameters (e.g., speed, optical sensor CPI from 400-3200 CPI, etc.). In some experiments we used alternate ultrasound pen technologies, including the wireless *equil*© SmartPen, with software tools for position capture based on the Equil SDK [11]. In each experiment the cartridge assembly stopped briefly at each end of the assembly rail and reversed direction; after a brief acceleration period the device maintained a fixed, controllable speed.

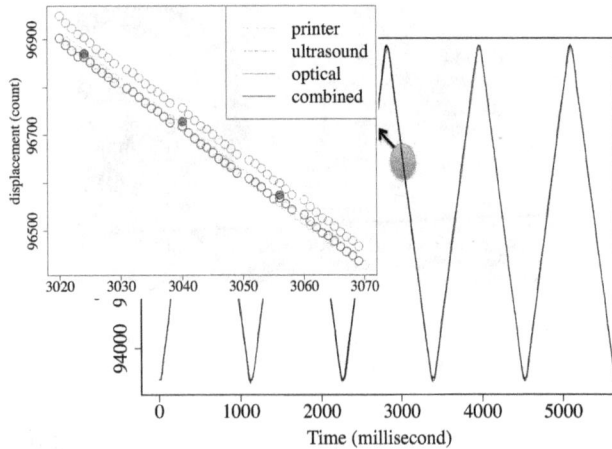

Figure 5: The amount of printhead displacement measured by different methods (ground truth, ultrasound, optical, and fusion) during the repeated 1-dimensional, back-and-forth motion of the testbed printhead. A closer look is overlaid to show sensor tracking during constant velocity operation.

We were pleased that optical device tracking was excellent over the entire regime of parameters, including motion at speeds of 10 in./sec, far exceeding our application requirements. In analyzing our results we separately considered the constant speed regime (middle of span) and the acceleration/deceleration regimes (end of span). But the low position update rates of low-cost commercial ultrasound technology are far too low to independently track acceleration regions accurately; note that a device moving at 1 in/sec moves 10 mils between 10 ms updates.

In order to achieve an improved trajectory estimate of printer head movement, we fuse data collected from both ultrasound and optical sensors mounted on the head. Suppose that at time t_0 the printer head is at some known position $x(t_0), y(t_0)$, the ultrasound subsystem absolute position estimates arrive at times t_j, $j = 1, 2, ...$, and the system's overall best estimate of device position is $\hat{x}(t_j), \hat{y}(t_j)$. Then at intermediate times $t \in (t_j, t_{j+1})$ we refine the head position estimate by accumulating the optical sensor's counts δ_x, δ_y, such that

$$\hat{x}(t) = \hat{x}(t_j) + \sum_{t_j}^{t} \delta_x; \quad \hat{y}(t) = \hat{y}(t_j) + \sum_{t_j}^{t} \delta_y. \quad (1)$$

Figs. 5 & 6 show an example of successfully fusing sensor data to improve positioning accuracy. Frequent optical sensor updates (shown in blue) are used to refine position between less frequent ultrasound updates (shown in red). Combining those updates produce an improved trajectory estimate (shown in black) that is closer to the actual device position (shown in green).

Note that optical sensor position measurement errors are tiny but accumulate with distance traveled, while ultrasound measurement errors are relatively large with a roughly fixed bias, that is somewhat independent of motion (and position). Hence, the question arises of the minimum distance traveled over which the optical sensor likely accumulates more error than found in a biased ultrasound position update.

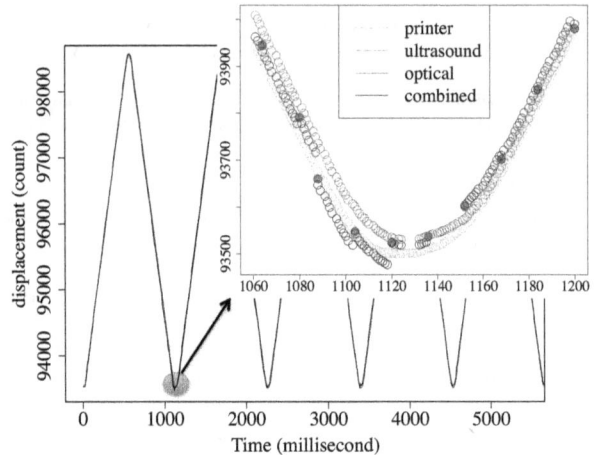

Figure 6: The overlaid graph shows a closer look at sensor tracking and reports the amount of printhead displacement measured by different methods during the direction reversal.

Suppose that we model the optical sensor position errors in each dimension and in each polling period as a gaussian random variable with distribution $N_m(0, \sigma_m{}^2)$, and that of the ultrasound sensor as $N_u(\mu, \sigma_u{}^2)$. To simplify further we assume that each sensor's noise is independent from measurement to measurement, across dimensions, and across sensors. Then if there are N optical sensor polling periods between ultrasound updates, the cumulative optical sensor noise is $N_m(0, \sum_N \sigma_m{}^2)$. The magnitude of the error (i.e., $z = \sqrt{x^2 + y^2}$) for each sensor in each polling period is given by a Rayleigh distribution. If we assume that noise is symmetric across the x and y coordinates, then we can show that the accumulated optical sensor error is less than the ultrasound error for N consecutive polling periods such that

$$1 - \frac{1}{2}\left[erf\left(\frac{x + \frac{\mu}{\sqrt{2}}}{\sqrt{2}\sigma_t}\right) + erf\left(\frac{x - \frac{\mu}{\sqrt{2}}}{\sqrt{2}\sigma_t}\right)\right] > 0, \quad (2)$$

where $\sigma_t^2 = \frac{1}{2}\left(\sigma_u^2 + N\sigma_m^2\right)$. Hence, we can use Eq. 2 to limit the number of previous mouse polling periods used for current position estimation, after which we "reset" mouse displacement counters to flush accumulated errors.

4.2 Measuring Angular Rotation

Continuously tracking the orientation of the handheld device is critical for 2 reasons. First, optical sensors measure displacements relative to their local axes, which is familiar to all computer mouse users. Second, inkjet printhead nozzles are typically organized in a rectangular array. Hence printhead orientation is required to determine the position of individual nozzles to fire. To measure device orientation we adopted the well-established approach of mounting two, identical surface-tracking optical navigation sensors separated by distance D on the device base. This approach has seen common use in multiple applications [7], including for relatively coarse position tracking in robotic vehicles. Here, however, we seek to overclock state-of-the-art sensors to track displacements on the order of *tick lengths* of $1/CPI$ inches. To emulate this system we initially constructed a test harness joining two Logitech G502 gaming mice (i.e., Pixart ADNS 3366 sensor) on a rotating platform as depicted in Fig. 7. Our initial metrics of interest were the devices' 1)

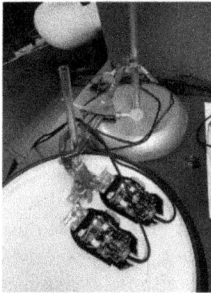

Figure 7: A test rig to measure rotation tracking of dual optical sensors suspended above a rotating turntable.

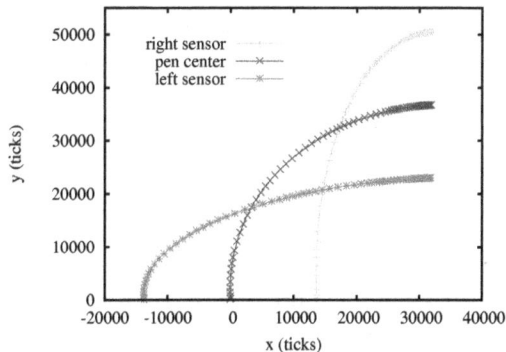

Figure 8: Dual optical navigation sensors track a device moving clockwise along a quarter circle while rotating 90° counterclockwise.

ability to track angular rotations accurately while traversing circles of varying radii, and 2) ability to traverse relatively long circuits and accurate return to a starting point.

The vast majority of the software needed to read and process mouse device events is widely available in the public domain. To determine device orientation we relied on the idealized optical mouse based odometry developed in [3]. Overall, we found optical sensor tracking to be excellent, given the caveats we discuss in Section 4.4. The devices were tested at 10,000 CPI and a 1 kHz polling rate, well below their maximum manufacturer specifications. That said, instabilities can be observed in some settings at polling rates exceeding 1500 Hz. Further, the devices are sufficiently sensitive at CPI settings exceeding 10,000 that they measure the "noise" of ambient room vibrations when the device is not actually moving.

Figure 7 depicts one experiment where our emulated device was rotated 90° counterclockwise *while* clockwise traversing a curve that is roughly a 3.375 in. radius $\frac{1}{4}$-circle. Note that at the end of this experiment the sensors are vertically aligned and should have identical measured x-coordinates; indeed the calculated positions were $31,617$ and $31,611$ ticks for the right and left sensors, representing a measurement error of only 0.6 mil after traversing 3.14 and 7.46 in., respectively. Angular error was approximately 0.1% through the $\frac{1}{4}$-circle.

4.3 Measuring Arbitrary 2-D Motion

Determining ground truth is a fundamental issue addressed in localization problems at all scales. But at sub-millimeter scales determining positioning system accuracy is partic-

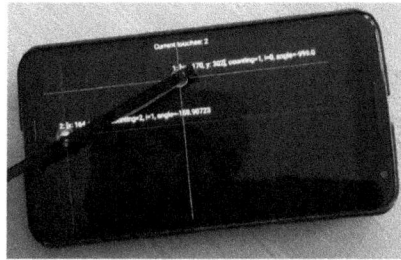

Figure 9: A *soft* pantograph tracks device translation and rotation using the high-resolution Nexus 6 multi-touch screen.

ularly challenging. We observe, however, that the multi-touch display of a mobile computing device *itself* represents a highly accurate, readily available positioning system.

To exploit the presence of this display, we have constructed a modern analogue to the classical mechanical pantograph – a *soft pantograph*. Reconstruction of line drawings at variable scale via mechanical linkages or extension arms was invented in the 17th century. Many object/drawing duplication methods (e.g., engraving, sculpting) continue to create copies pantographically. Fig. 9 shows a rigid mechanical arm extending from a handheld device (not shown) to be positioned. Two capacitive probe tips extend down from the far end of the arm, separated by a known fixed distance S. The tips rest on the multi-touch screen of a Nexus 6, which features a 560 dpi screen resolution.

We modified an open source Android app to detect and process the probe tip locations. The probe tip information is collected, time stamped and processed by the smartphone. The processing includes calculating probe tip position and motion, and the exact position and orientation of the handheld. These results are transferred to the handheld device over a short-range wireless channel (e.g., BlueTooth or WiFi). Hence, by exploiting the multi-touch display we have created a test apparatus that provides absolute motion and orientation ground truth for a peripheral device traversing a planar surface.

4.4 Sensor Calibration

Extremely careful device calibration is required to address systematic motion estimation errors [5]. Several system parameters must be precisely known including 1) the separation distance D between optical sensors, and 2) the *actual* CPI of left and right optical sensors on the target media. Other parameters such as the relative angular skew of the left and right optical sensor coordinate systems also should be measured and corrected. Many parameters can be determined and adjusted at time of manufacture. As an example of how we calibrated optical devices in a lab setting, we rotated the turntable of Fig. 7 through $N * 360°$, while the sensors recorded displacements. The left and right sensors were located at known radii r_l and r_r from the turntable center, permitting calculation of actual CPI for each sensor.

A particularly challenging area for further study is *field* calibration, particularly if performed by non-technical device owners. As one example, spinning a device about itself could serve as a simple calibration step. Interestingly, this appears to be one area where multiple sensors help – one sensor can facilitate the calibration of another sensor type.

5. RELATED WORK

The HP Capshare 910 consumer image scanner/portable copier product [7] used a pair of optical sensors to track device orientation. The devices were separated by 3 in., aligned with but straddling a scanning window set perpendicular to the direction of device motion. The scanner arguably validated a market for portable imaging products [13]. But the technical challenge associated with developing handheld printers capable of freehand drawing on media free of registration marks has appeared insurmountable. While a variety of handheld labeling devices such as the HP *SP400* and Xyron *Design Runner* continue to focus on mobile text printing opportunities, existing commercial products have yet to achieve goal of drawing high resolution color images.

More recently a surge of related product concepts is gaining support through crowd sourcing. *InkShield* is a KickStarter-funded project that tethers an unenclosed print cartridge to an Arduino computing platform [14]. Ink is deposited by manually sliding the cartridge itself across a page; no positioning is supported. A second related KickStarter-funded project is the ZUtA Labs *Robotic Printer*, an automated compact vehicle equipped with a print cartridge that drives over media to deposit ink [15]. This solution requires a smooth horizontal surface for media and prints cannot be interrupted. The handheld device we envision is most similar to PrintDream's proposed *PrintBrush* standalone printer [1], though only prototype devices have been demonstrated years after the project was announced. Moreover, the maximum inter-swath gap error reported on its specification sheet indicates 0.4mm which is one order of magnitude less than the accuracy (0.001 inch required to print a full-color 300-dpi image) our system strives to achieve.

Finally, we note that there is a vast scholarly literature of closely related technical developments in ultrasonics, indoor positioning, robotics, and pen computing.

6. CONCLUSION

Advances in smartphone and sensor technologies have led us to investigate the feasibility of handheld imaging devices. We have been motivated by the possibilities presented by handheld printing devices, though highly accurate positioning systems might see more extensive application in 3-d printing and model creation. We have showed that handheld positioning can be refined by fusing information from state-of-the-art sensors. We caution, however, that this is a work-in-progress, and a considerable amount of empirical evaluation and algorithm design must be performed to validate these proposed approaches, in particular confronting positioning lag and measuring rapidly changing device velocity. An equally interesting and challenging set of problems lies in developing the handheld's inks and associated print subsystem.

In principle mobile handheld printers can deposit images on media affixed to non-planar and non-level surfaces (e.g., a poster on an easel, or wall). The freedom of these unconventional settings suggest that depositing images on unengineered media – possibly even materials ranging from paperboard to drywall to human skin – might have potentially disruptive applications.

We have dedicated considerable initial effort at developing the test tools necessary to investigate displacements on the order of fractions of mils. We are also optimistic that advances in 2-d short range positioning will lead to innovations in other domains. Possible applications might include novel input devices for 3-d CAD modelling, high accuracy localization for semi-autonomous micro-robots, and new Simultaneous Localization and Mapping (SLAM) algorithms.

Though introduced as a test tool, the soft pantograph achieves high positioning accuracy at low cost; modern multi-touch screens operate at 300-600 ppi and can be expected to improve with time. It is possible to envision embellishments that make the device suitable for non-test applications including software-based scaling, telescoping extension arms, variable probe tip technologies (e.g., resistive vs. capacitive), ternary probe configurations, and active probe tips for pixel-level accuracy.

Acknowledgment: The authors would like to acknowledge contributions from Andy Liao and Vijay Nayak of HP Inc.

7. REFERENCES

[1] "PrintDreams", http://www.printdreams.com/
[2] Luidia, Inc., "eBeam Edge Technical Specification", http://www.e-beam.com/business/ebeam-edge/tech-specs.html
[3] A. Bonarini, et al, "Dead Reckoning for Mobile Robots Using Two Optical Mice," *ICTA*, 2004.
[4] M. L. Lenhardt, "Airborne ultrasonic standards for Hearing Protection", *9th Intl. Conf. on Noise a Public Health Problem (ICBED)*", 2008.
[5] J. Borenstein, L. Feng, "UMBMark - A Method for Measuring, Comparing, and Correcting Dead Reckoning Errors in Mobile Robots," *University of Michigan Technical Report UM-MEAM-94-22*, 1994.
[6] Michal Bachraty, Milan Zalman, "2D Position Measurement with Optical Laser Mouse," *Proc. of NSSS Slovakia*, 2010.
[7] "HP Capshare Data Sheet", http://www.shopping.hp.com/shopping/pdf/c6301c.pdf, 1999.
[8] Andy Liao, Vijay Nayak, "Mobile Printer Positioning Requirements", *private communication*, 2014.
[9] C. Medina, J.C. Segura, A. De la Torre, "Ultrasound Indoor Positioning System Based on a Low-Power Wireless Sensor Network Providing Sub-Centimeter Accuracy", *Proc. of Sensors 2013*, vol. 13, 2013.
[10] J. Gordon, M.F. Ghilard, S.E. Cooper, C Ghez, "Accuracy of Planar Reaching Movements", *Experimental Brain Research*, vol. 99, 1994.
[11] "Equil SDK for Git", http://support.myequil.com/customer/en/portal/articles/1995007-equil-sdk-for-git
[12] D. Sekimori, F. Miyazaki, "Precise Dead Reckoning for Mobile Robots Using Multiple Optical Mouse Sensors", *Informatics in Control, Automation and Robotics II*, J.Filipe et al Eds, Springer, 2007.
[13] "Hewlett Packard CapShare 910 Scanner Review", http://www.xbitlabs.com/articles/other/display/capshare-910.html, 1999.
[14] N. Lewis, "InkShield", https://www.kickstarter.com/projects/nicholasclewis/inkshield-an-open-source-inkjet-shield-for-arduino
[15] ZUtA Labs Ltd., "The Mini Mobile Robotic Printer", https://www.kickstarter.com/projects/1686304142/the-mini-mobile-robotic-printer
[16] "PixArt Imaging Inc.", www.pixart.com

Scale-based Exploded Views: A Selection Method for Mobile Devices

Zezi Ai
Dalhousie University
Halifax, Nova Scotia
(902) 494-2093
azizabdurexit@gmail.com

Kirstie Hawkey
Dalhousie University
Halifax, Nova Scotia
(902) 494-2093
hawkey@cs.dal.ca

Stephen Brooks
Dalhousie University
Halifax, Nova Scotia
(902) 494-2512
sbrooks@cs.dal.ca

ABSTRACT

Utilizing 3D models for repair operations is crucial to mechanical engineers and exploded view diagrams are an effective way to explore the inner structure of models. We evaluate a low-complexity scale-based exploded view method designed to help find and select small and occluded objects within 3D models on mobile devices. We separate models by categorizing each object into different layers based on size. Then, at a particular layer, the explosion is under the direction of a user-controlled probe that sprawls exploded components to facilitate object selection. In a comparative evaluation with an alternative low cost explosion technique, our method significantly reduced the number of wrong targets selected when performing several selection tasks. This is important given that our application is targeted for use in mobile-assisted manufacturing and repair environments, which have a low tolerance for user error.

Keywords

3D selection; exploded view; mobile interaction.

1. INTRODUCTION

3D models have been extensively used in manufacturing for several decades. Mechanics and engineers design, examine, repair, and maintain complex machinery with the help of 3D digital models. Digital assistance becomes more important as the models become ever more complex, far beyond what a human can memorize. Thus, improvements to the process of understanding the internal structure of 3D models are needed.

However, many approaches are only applicable to desktop computers and workstations with powerful GPUs and CPUs. Increasingly, mobile devices are being used in industry to improve workflow efficiency on the factory floor. For example, aircraft mechanics deal with complex 3D models during their construction and maintenance tasks. Even a small delay on the repair assemblies of a plane has a high cost. The physical distances involved in such an environment are also considerable. Our site visits to the Boeing manufacturing plants proved a humbling

HotMobile '16, February 26-27, 2016, St. Augustine, FL, USA.
© 2016 ACM. ISBN 978-1-4503-4145-5/16/02…$15.00.
DOI: http://dx.doi.org/10.1145/2873587.2873593

experience given that the size of the facilities are on a city block scale and the planes are 250 feet long and 6 stories high.

Thus mobile devices have been proposed as a means of enabling just-in-time access to 3D virtual models. But 3D models can be difficult to render and interact with on such devices. In this paper, we introduce a scale-based exploded view selection technique, which is as computationally simple as possible, that reveals exploded views of 3D virtual models incrementally based on the size of components. The system is evaluated with a comparative user study whose design was informed by on-going discussions and site visits with engineers at The Boeing Company.in this research, we are particularly interested in finding and selecting small and occluded components. The motivation behind this is the common and frequent scenario of an aircraft mechanic that wishes to repair or replace a broken part. Due to the sheer complexity of the aircraft, mechanics may attempt to look for the same part in 3D virtual model. However, given that a model for a Boeing 747, for example, may contain millions of individual parts, it may be impossible for the mechanic to recall the names of parts. Therefore, simple text searching would not be possible in many cases. One of the key pieces of information they have is the spatial location of each component within the 3D virtual model. This knowledge, combined with exploded view selection on mobile devices may help facilitate the selection of occluded parts.

2. PRIOR WORK

Perhaps the biggest challenge of depicting a solid 3D model is occlusion among structures. There are three main techniques that are used to interpret the inner structure of a technical model: ghosted views, cut-away views and exploded views.

Ghosting or x-ray visualizations render a transparent view from outside a surface to reveal internal structures. Ebert and Rheingans [8] introduced a physics-based rendering process that utilizes non-photorealistic rendering techniques. This is a volume illustration approach designed to improve the structural perception of models by the addition of illumination effects. However, this method is not suitable for real-time systems, especially for finding small and occluded objects within a 3D model because target objects could be changed constantly which requires real-time transparency allocation. Diepstraten et al. [6] presented an interactive real-time rendering of ghost view, which includes a hardware-accelerated depth-sorting algorithm to dynamically change the transparency. This method may solve real-time transparency for searching occluded parts but it doesn't support multi-transparency where target objects are blocked by more than one object. For example, finding the deepest objects in the center of a complex 3D model could be difficult for this method. Cut-away views are another method used extensively to handle occlusion within 3D models. Hodges [10] and Netter [15] introduced the concept that designing cuts on volumetric data should follow cognitive rules for reconstructing the missing geometry mentally. However, static cutaways can often only reveal little information and require a lot of manual operations. Bernhard et al. [2] described a low level automated cutaway technique. They used a deformable clipping plane for selective virtual resection. Viola et al. [19] introduced an importance-driven method to make parts with the highest priority clearly visible first. The high level automatic generation of cut-away and ghost views were introduced by Feiner and Seligmann [9]. They proposed algorithms for automatically displaying potentially obscured objects in a cut-away view. A more subtle interactive cutaway technique was proposed by Li et al. [12] to support the authored generation of cuts with editable auxiliary parameters. By increasing the transparency of the context, it gradually unveils internal objects. Although cut-away techniques are an effective way to remove occluding parts to unveil internal structures, it still does not resolve the problem of selecting small or occluded objects with 3D model because cut-away methods only show parts of target objects by removing occluding components. This makes target components hard to select when the target components are located deep inside of 3D model and it is even harder for users to select on touch screen devices since one's finger requires a bigger selecting area comparing to mouse selection on a desktop. Another key limiting factor of the above methods is the loss of surrounding contextual information. To overcome these challenges and help facilitate the procedure of selecting small and occluded components, exploded view techniques were proposed by McGuffin et al [13]. They let users cut into, open up, spread apart and peel away parts in real time, making the interior visible while still retaining context. However, the explosion is controlled manually. There are other systems that produce exploded views such as Driskill and Cohen [7] and Rist et al. [16], but the views are static. Bruckner et al. proposed a semi-automatic explosion technique to inspect the interior of a volumetric dataset in a feature-driven way [3]. But a limitation of most of these systems is that users have to decide the explosion directions and blocking relationships for all parts in the model, which is a tedious task when dealing with even moderately complex models. Agrawala et al. suggested an algorithm that can compute the order and direction in which parts can explode without breaking blocking constraints [1]. Later Li et al. went one step further and implemented an interactive exploded diagram generated automatically by the system. They used explosion graphs to encode how parts explode with respect to each other [11].

A lot of research has followed Li et al.'s work, one of which offers a solution to the visual clutter problem, which happens when many small pieces explode together. Tatzgern et al. [18] proposed compact explosion diagrams taking into account the similarity between objects. The system recognizes a representative among several identical group objects by evaluating the quality of their potential exploded view and only these representatives are exploded. Another force-based explosion technique presented by Sonnet et al. [17] interactively controls the local explosion in order to reduce the visual complexity of explosion diagrams. Sonnet et al.'s work was an extension of the visual access distortion technique by Carpendale et al. [4], which opens the line of sight by pushing away surrounding parts.

2.1 Limitations of Current Approaches
All of these prior approaches are designed for desktop computers with powerful hardware. For example, it was stated by Li et al. [11] that their system could only generate effective visualizations

of models with up to roughly 50 parts else it required too much computation to determine blocking and containing parts. The popularity and capabilities of mobile computing devices such as tablets and cellphones have been greatly increased the last several years and 3D games and maps have been developed for those devices, enabled by hardware acceleration. However, performance still does not approach that of desktop machines or dedicated game consoles. In addition, processors of mobile device such as Nvidia's Tegra series pale in comparison to the PC chips from Intel or AMD. Desktop computers also offer better performance in other aspects such as memory and hard drive capacity

We collected feedback from the engineers at the Boeing Company and they stated that exploded views are a very promising technology on the shop floor especially for maintenance. However, they also stated that these complex techniques from prior work, with blocking and collision detection, are not practical at the moment. And they do not use pre-structured exploded views for large-scale models because computational complexity becomes too large even for desktop computers, given their size and complexity of models (millions of parts). They indicated this is true even for just a section of a plane. Another issue they highlighted with the more structured and expensive exploded view approaches are that objects are not always placed in the right location for even simple linear explosions and that for radial explosions, things can get worse. This means there is a significant amount of tweaking needed in practice, even for relatively small models. Hand tweaking structured exploded views for models as large as a plane is impractical. They felt that a more automatic approach that can be cheaply computed on the fly for a local subset of the total model is therefore required.

To this end, we simplify the process of computing relationships between parts by allowing parts to pass through each other. As mobile devices have very limited CPU and GPU power, we were able to present exploded views of up to 450 parts. Furthermore, we do not need to perform a large-scale exploded view pre-computation on a massive model, which would be prohibitive for the application domain of interest. Given the necessity of simplifying the exploded view approach, it becomes critical to study how best to maintain usability and accuracy under such constraints. In this paper, we compare two exploded view techniques that are expressly designed enable selection of small and occluded objects.

Our method is also related to the approach described by Sonnet et al [17]. They use a 3D cube as an interaction tool to locally explore parts of a model by pushing each nearby component away. The 3D cube has a limited area of detection used to explore parts. We refined several aspects of this technique to make it more appropriate for finding and selecting small, occluded objects. First, we expand the scope of interaction area to encompass the whole model and, secondly, we permit exploration on a layer-by-

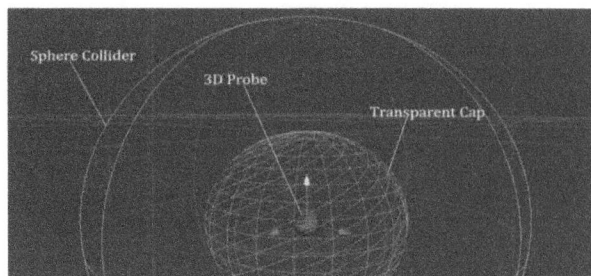

Figure 1. Structure of the 3D Interactive Probe

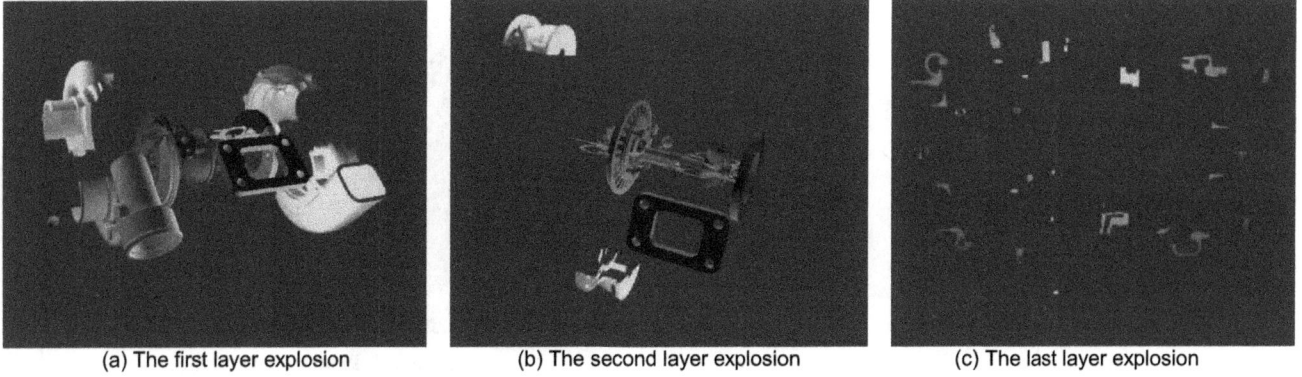

(a) The first layer explosion   (b) The second layer explosion   (c) The last layer explosion

Figure 2. Work flow of scale-based exploded view technique (SBET)

layer basis. Each component of the model can be categorized into one layer based on the bounding size of this object and only the objects in the current layer can be exploded.

3. SCALE-BASED EXPLODED VIEWS
We now describe our layer-based method for exploring 3D models on mobile devices to help find and locate small and occluded target components.

3.1 3D Interactive Probe
In our method, a 3D interactive probe (shown in Figure 1) is the main tool for exploring the model and finding occluded targets. The probe is comprised of 3 parts: the visible probe shown in red, a transparent cap and a sphere collider. The transparent cap is a transparent object, which is slightly larger than the 3D probe. The purpose of the transparent cap is to address the "fat finger" problem that users may encounter when they try to move 3D probe. However, we do not expand the visible area of the probe itself to avoid additional occlusion. The sphere collider is used to detect if any 3D objects are within the proximity of the probe.

3.2 Explosion Process
The effects of the probe can manipulate an entire layer of objects. A layer is defined as a subset of a model where each subset is defined by component size. For example, when the model is loaded, only parts that pass the size threshold will be exploded and all those exploding parts collectively define the first layer.

The process is shown in Figure 2 for layers of composed of component sets of decreasing size, from left to right. The largest components, which are located in the first layer, are exploded away as shown Figure 2(a). In the subsequent layer, as shown in Figure 2(b), the largest parts (that were previously exploded in 2(a)) disappear and the set of second largest components in the second layer are exploded at the users' direction. We can continue this process until the final layer that contains the smallest components, as shown in Figure 2(c). At any stage the user can select the target object of interest.

The set of thresholds T_i, are used to divide the model into different layers, and are set relative to the volume of the model. The initial value of the largest threshold T_0, is determined by the size of the largest objects of the 3D model. For each model, we calculate the size of largest components R and divide R by two and make it equal to T_0. Each sub-object's volume is calculated based on the bounding box, B. V_j represents the volume ($B_x \times B_y \times B_z$) of sub-object j. When V_j is larger than the current threshold, sub-object j will be assigned to the current layer, will be rendered in the same color (green color) and also will be exploded concurrently as we

can see in the Figure 2(a). The four green components belong to one layer and explode accordingly. The series of thresholds T_i, decrease by half in each subsequent layer, and the current effective threshold is incremented when the "+" and "-" buttons are pressed.

The number of sub-objects in each layer is determined by the comparison between threshold and each object's volume, meaning that the number of components in one layer is not fixed. For all objects with the 3D model, if any sub-object's volume value is larger than the current threshold, it will be categorize into one layer. The algorithm for pushing away each layer's objects is also computationally simple. Let P_{object} represent the position of a part in three dimensional space, P_{probe} is the position of probe, P_{ini} is the initial position of object when it is loaded to the scene, D_{ini} represents the initial distance between the probe and the object when the object first enters the sphere collider, D_{cur} is the distance between the probe and P_{ini}, and V_{ini} represents a vector with a length of D_{ini} and with a direction from the probe to the object. The simple pseudo code of the method is shown below:

> **if** $D_{cur} <= D_{ini}$ **then**
> $P_{object} = P_{probe} + V_{ini}$
> **else**
> $P_{object} = P_{ini}$

From the calculation above we can see that the 3D position of any object is determined by the position of the probe under the condition where $D_{cur} <= D_{ini}$. And when distance between probe and initial position D_{cur} is bigger than D_{ini}, the object returns to its initial position. The algorithm will apply to all objects within the current active layer in the model. This is concisely illustrated in Figure 3. The top row of the figure shows the probe outside the object's range, D_{ini}. The middle row shows the probe at the limit of the objects range with still no effect. The third row shows the push motion caused by the probe when within D_{ini}. The object is pushed away from the probe to maintain its distance

3.3 Prototype Interface
Figure 4 shows our prototype implemented for Android tablets. There are three main sections: the left side control area, the middle interaction view area and right side overview map area.

In the left area, there are several functional buttons, which control basic interactions with the model. Z axis movement of the probe (the small red ball), is controlled by the tablet's embedded accelerometer and it can be turn off or on by the buttons: "Start Tilt" and "Stop Tilt". The Up/Down/Left/Right direction panel near the top is used for adjusting the movement of the probe

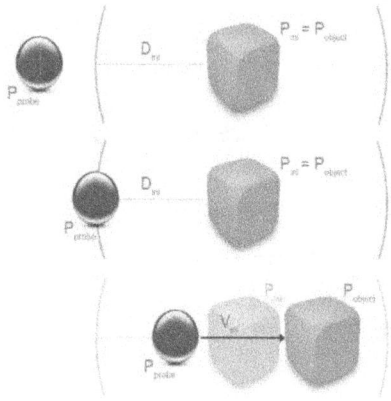

Figure 3. Illustration of the effect of the probe on an object's position that is within the current active layer.

by a small amount (in approximately 5mm steps) and the direction panel towards the bottom is used to move the camera in four directions. The "Reset Angles" buttons resets the rotation of the model back to initial state. "Pause the app" and "Move to next task" buttons are two high level functions used for running the user experiment that will be discussed in section 4. Lastly, the "+" and "-" buttons, along with the associated slider bar provide operations for the layer-based explosion process.

Touchscreen interactions mainly occur in the middle area. The system utilizes two finger pinching for zooming in and zooming out, where a pinch in moves the camera close to the model and pinch out moves the camera farther away. The minimum and maximum distances between the camera and model are pre-defined by the system so the view stays within a reasonable scope. The system also enables one finger for dragging the probe on the screen when the finger touches the selection area of the probe. One finger sliding performs rotation of the model when located within an empty area where no object is selected. The right area of the screen shows three views (left side, top-down and front side) of the 3D structure, which highlights the target object. These three pictures are pre-generated and statically placed at the right side. The purpose of these views is strictly for the user evaluation.

4. EVALUATION

The primary contribution of this paper is the evaluation of the performance of computationally simple approaches to exploded views designed for tablet interaction. Specifically, we conducted a controlled user study comparing our scale-based explosion technique (SBET) method with an alternate exploded view based selection approach. This alternate whole explosion (WE) technique simply explodes every component of the 3D model simultaneously (as shown in Figure 5), and does not constrain the dispersion of components based on layers of a particular size. WE technique is simplified method, which applied the idea from Li at al [11]. The explosion function uses the same algorithm as described in Section 3.2 for all parts of the model regardless of size.

4.1 Study Design

The goal of this study is to compare the effectiveness between two different low cost exploded view techniques for finding and selecting small and occluded objects in 3D virtual models on mobile devices. In addition to technique, we varied the complexity of the model and the target size as these could also have an impact on the performance of the selection techniques.

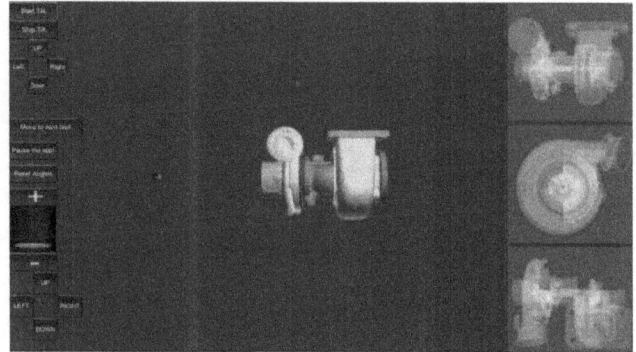

Figure 4. Prototype Interface

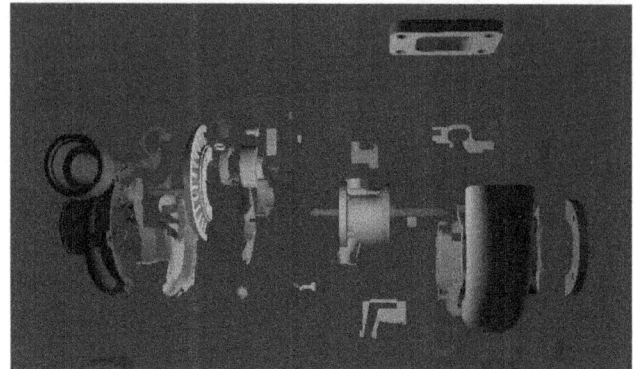

Figure 5. View of the alternative Whole Explosion (WE) technique.

We initially intended to use a within-subjects design; however, during pilot testing with 8 participants we observed a strong task learning effect that favoured the second technique used. We therefore used a 2x3x3 mixed design, with selection technique (SEBT, WE) as a between subjects variable and complexity (1: 150 parts, 2: 300 parts, 3: 450 parts) and target size (1: large, 2: medium, 3: small) as within subject variables. We recruited 36 participants (18 per technique) with each participant performing 9 selection tasks, which varied in complexity and size.

4.1.1 Study Protocol

In order to mimic a mechanic's procedure for finding and selecting parts in 3D models, we provided participants with three different pictures that showed the target objects from three different angles. A real mechanic would likewise have a good sense of where the object is within the overall structure from direct observation.

Before participants engaged in the study tasks, we had them practice with 4 training tasks to allow them to become familiar with the interface and techniques. The training process is identical to the actual study procedure except conducted with a simpler model and fewer tasks. After the training session, each participant was given 9 tasks (3 model complexity x 3 target object sizes) using only one of the two exploded view methods. The task sequence was counterbalanced. We recorded the length of time to finish each task and recorded the number of errors participants made during this process. Questionnaires and interviews were also collected after the tasks to obtain qualitative feedback.

4.2 Study Results

4.2.1 Study Protocol

Task finishing time is defined as the time from when the participant started touching the screen to the final selection of the

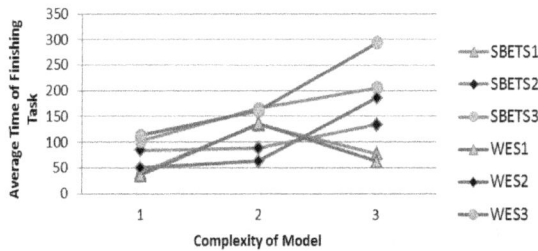

Figure 6. Task finishing time for each model complexity (1 = least complex, 3 = most complex) and technique/target size (SBETS1 = Scale-based Explosion Technique, Size 1 (large); WES3 = Whole Explosion Technique, Size 3 (small)).

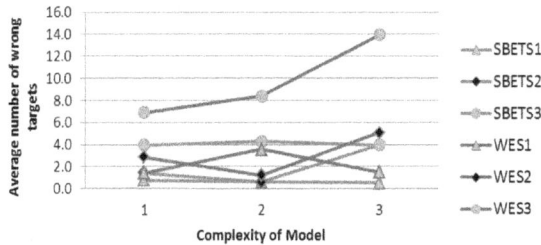

Figure 7. Number of incorrect targets for each model complexity and technique/target size.

correct target. Figure 6 illustrates the mean task finishing time of all participants combined with all three variables: complexity of model, size of searching target and method. As expected, as the complexity of the model increased and the target object size decreased, more time was taken to finish tasks. This applies to both techniques. However, there was one atypical case: complexity 2 and target size 1. Upon further investigation we found that this particular target was located in the center of model and the colour of the target object was similar to the surrounding components.

We analyzed the results with a split-plot ANOVA to see if any factor had significant effects on the average task finishing time. The results showed there was a statistically significant effect for complexity and target size (F1 = 18.30, P1 < .0005; F2 = 37.23, P2 <.0005). Also, the Partial Eta Squared value obtained for complexity and target size were .526 and .693 respectively, which suggested a very large effect size (.01= small effect, .06 = moderate effect, .14 = large effect [5]). The test of the between subjects variable's effect was not significant (F = .262, P = .612), meaning there was no significant difference in the average task finishing time between the two explosion techniques. The effect size was small (.008).

4.2.2 Number of Incorrect Targets Selected
Incorrect target selections occurred when participants mistakenly select objects other than the target object. Figure 7 shows the mean number of wrong targets selected in relation to target size, complexity, and technique. As the complexity of the model increased, the mean number of incorrectly selected targets increased for both techniques. As for task finishing time, the only atypical case was for target size 1 at complexity level 2. As with task finishing time, the similarity of the target object to the surround objects increased the error rate for the target size/model complexity combination. Figure 7 shows as the size of the target gets smaller, participants tend to select more wrong targets when they use the alternate WE technique. However, participants

selected approximately an equal amount of wrong targets across all the levels of complexities and sizes when they used SBET technique. As the complexity increases, the gap between the two different techniques at different target sizes increases in terms of wrong target selection. A mixed ANOVA revealed no significant difference for the effect of complexity (F = 2.727, P =0.08). However, there was a significant main effect of target size (F = 12.558, P <.0005); the effect size was large (0.432).There was also a statistically significant difference between the two techniques in the average number of wrong targets selected (F = 11.621, P = .002), with a large effect size.

4.2.3 Post Session Questionnaire
We administered a questionnaire after participants finished all 9 tasks. We asked participants to evaluate the technique they used in terms of the interface and system responsiveness, as well as other aspects on a scale from 1 to 5 (1 = strongly agree, 5 = strongly disagree). The results are shown in Figures 8-15.

More participants in the SBET condition agreed that the task was easy to perform (Figure 9), the target was easy to find (Figure 12), there was good system responsiveness (Figure 13), and the technique was helpful for finding small and large targets (Figure 15) than in the WE condition. Furthermore, fewer participants in the SBET condition (50%) thought that the technique was hard to use for finding small targets (Figure 14), than in the WE condition (94%). While a similar percentage of people agreed that both interfaces were easy to use (Figure 8), about 25% of participants disagreed on this matter.

Since the ease of finding and selecting small targets is a key goal for our method, these results are promising. However, it should be noted that the WE technique was rated better than the SBET technique when it comes to probe control (Figure 10) and micro-adjustment (Figure 11). We speculate that our SBET method required more complex interactions.

4.2.4 Interview
At the end of the session, we briefly interviewed each participant about their experience with the technique they used and asked them to speculate about the other techniques (i.e., the one that they did not experience), which was demonstrated to them.

Overall, 30 out of 36 participants reported that they thought the SBET technique would be more helpful when it comes to finding small targets that are not visually accessible at the beginning of the finding task. They believed that it reduced the level of difficulty and stress in the process when all the components are not scattered on the screen. In addition, they indicated that the level of difficulty did not vary much as the target's size became smaller and the model became more complex. They said it was very hard to focus on small targets in the WE technique when there were many components exploded simultaneously. However, some participants found that it was confusing when the targets disappeared in the previous layers in the SBET approach and there was a need to go back to the earlier layers to search for parts. Some other participants thought that WE would somehow be faster when locating large targets because its procedure is simple. However, some participants complained about the similarity of components that made finding parts hard in the WE method.

5. CONCLUSION
Overall, the average time of finishing the same tasks using two different methods did not vary significantly on the mobile device, but SBET performed significantly better with fewer incorrect targets selected. This result could be critical for our motivating

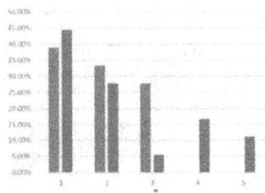

Figure 8: Ease of user interface

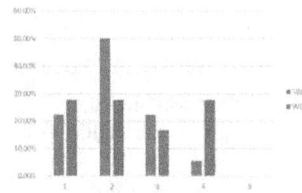

Figure 9: Ease of tasks

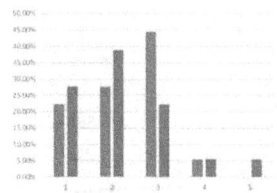

Figure 10: Ease of probe control

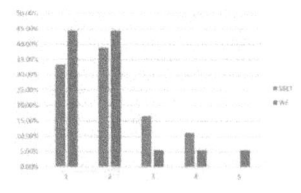

Figure 11: Micro Adjustment evaluation of probe

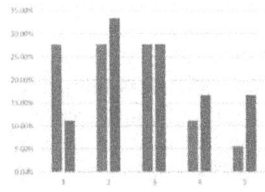

Figure 12: Ease of finding targets

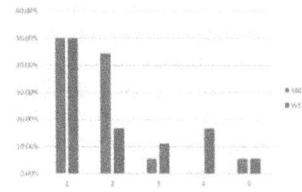

Figure 13: System responsiveness

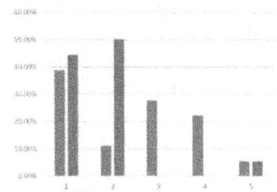

Figure 14: Hardness of finding small targets

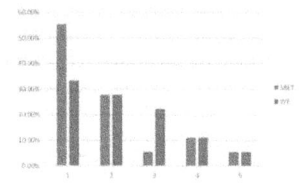

Figure 15: Helpfulness of selecting small and large targets

scenario if a mechanic tried to perform operations that depended on correct selection of a specific part. Although the timing for the selection of objects was not significantly different between two techniques, the higher number of errors in the WE method could substantially increase the average task completion time, depending on the ramifications on the additional errors. We can only speculate on the additional delays as it would be highly dependent on circumstances.

SBET has been shown to be good for finding small targets within a fairly complex model. The smaller the target becomes and the more complex the model is, the better the SBET tends to perform when compared to WE. Although our method showed stronger performance, we still need to address problems such as finding similar targets faster or better distinguishing target objects by colour from the surrounding parts. For future work, we are going to compare other possible exploded view approaches on low-end devices and evaluate how much of an impact the lack of blocking has on the final results.

6. REFERENCES

[1] Agrawala, M., Phan, D., Heiser, J., Haymaker, J.,Klingner, J., Hanrahan, P., and Tversky, B. Designing effective step-by-step assembly instructions. *ACM Trans. Graph*, 22(3) (July 2003), 828-833.

[2] Bernhard, O. K.-V., Preim, B., and Littmann, A. Virtual resection with a deformable cutting plane. In *Simulation and Visualization* (2004), 203–214.

[3] Bruckner, S., Grimm, S., Kanitsar, A., and Groller,M. E. Illustrative context-preserving exploration of volume data. *IEEE Transactions on Visualization and Computer Graphics*, 12(6) (Nov. 2006), 1559–1569.

[4] Carpendale, M. S. T., Cowperthwaite, D. J., and Fracchia, F. D. Extending distortion viewing from 2D to 3D. *IEEE Comput. Graph. Appl.* 17, 4, July 1997, 42–51.

[5] Cohen, J. Statistical Power Analysis for the Behavioral Sciences (2nd Edition), Routledge, July, 1988.

[6] Diepstraten, J., Weiskopf, D., and Ertl, T. Transparency in interactive technical illustrations. *Computer Graphics Forum*, 21, 2002.

[7] Driskill, E., and Cohen, E. Interactive design, analysis, and illustration of assemblies. *Symposium on Interactive 3D Graphics*, (New York, NY, 1995), 27–34.

[8] Ebert, D., and Rheingans, P. Volume illustration: Non-photorealistic rendering of volume models. In *Proceedings of the Conference on Visualization* (Los Alamitos, CA, 2000), 195–202.

[9] Feiner, S., and Seligmann, D. D. Cutaways and ghosting: satisfying visibility constraints in dynamic 3D illustrations. *The Visual Computer* 8, 5&6, 1992, 292 302.

[10] Hodges, E. R. S., and of Natural Science Illustrators (U.S.), G., Eds. The Guild handbook of scientific illustration. Hoboken, N.J. John Wiley, 2003.

[11] Li, W., Agrawala, M., Curless, B., and Salesin, D. Automated generation of interactive 3D exploded view diagrams. *ACM SIGGRAPH '08* (New York, NY, 2008), 101:1–101:7.

[12] Li, W., Ritter, L., Agrawala, M., Curless, B., and Salesin, D. Interactive cutaway illustrations of complex 3D models. *ACM Trans. Graph.* 26, 3 (July 2007).

[13] McGuffin, M., Tancau, L., and Balakrishnan, R. Using deformations for browsing volumetric data. In *Visualization* (2003), 401–408.

[14] Meybaum, H. Narusk, I. GrabCAD library. URL: http://www.grabcad.com/library/ [june 2013].

[15] Netter, F. H. Atlas of Human Anatomy, 2nd edition. Rittenhouse Book Distributors Inc., Jan. 1997.

[16] Rist, T., Krger, A., G. S., and Zimmermann, D. Awi: A workbench for semi-automated illustration design. *Advanced Visual Interfaces* (1994), 59–68.

[17] Sonnet, H., Carpendale, S., and Strothotte, T. Integrating expanding annotations with a 3d explosion probe. *Working Conference on Advanced Visual Interfaces*, AVI '04 (New York, NY, 2004), 63–70.

[18] Tatzgern, M., Kalkofen, D., and Schmalstieg, D. Compact explosion diagrams. *Symposium on Non-Photorealistic Animation and Rendering*, (New York, NY, 2010), 17–26.

[19] Viola, I., Kanitsar, A., and Groller, M. Importance-driven feature enhancement in volume visualization. *IEEE Transactions on Visualization and Computer Graphics*, 11, 4 (2005), 408–418.

Lighting Up the Internet of Things with DarkVLC

Zhao Tian, Kevin Wright[†], and Xia Zhou
Department of Computer Science, Department of Physics and Astronomy[†]
Dartmouth College, Hanover, NH
{tianzhao, xia}@cs.dartmouth.edu, kevin.wright@dartmouth.edu

ABSTRACT

Visible Light Communication (VLC) holds a great potential to solve the spectrum crunch problem and to provide scalable connectivity to zillions of mobile and IoT devices. However, VLC commonly requires LED lights to be on, which fundamentally limits the applicable scenarios of VLC and makes VLC less attractive to mobile and IoT devices with tight energy budget. We present *DarkVLC*, a new VLC primitive that allows the VLC link to be sustained even when the LED lights appear dark or off. The key idea is to encode data into ultra-short light pulses imperceptible to human eyes yet detectable by devices equipped with photodiodes. Realizing DarkVLC faces several challenges to generate and deal with the ultra-short light pulses reliably. We describe our preliminary efforts to tackle these challenges and build a DarkVLC prototype using off-the-shelf LEDs and low-cost photodiodes. DarkVLC fundamentally broadens the application scenarios of VLC and provides a new ultra-low power, always-on connectivity affordable for mobile and IoT devices.

CCS Concepts

•Networks → Wireless access networks;

Keywords

Visible light communication; Energy efficiency; Internet of Things

1. INTRODUCTION

Scaling out zillions of mobile devices and Internet of Things (IoT) encounters a critical roadblock: the radio spectrum crunch and the energy cost of communicating with a large number of embedded devices and sensors. Going beyond the radio spectrum frequency, Visible Light Communication (VLC) [7] holds a great potential to mitigate the radio spectrum crisis. It offers the following benefits: orders of magnitude (10^4) higher bandwidth than the radio spectrum, reusing existing lighting infrastructure, simple modulation and demodulation without complex signal processing (suitable for IoT devices with limited capability), being free of electromag-

HotMobile '16, February 26-27, 2016, St. Augustine, FL, USA
© 2016 ACM. ISBN 978-1-4503-4145-5/16/02. . . $15.00
DOI: http://dx.doi.org/10.1145/2873587.2873598

netic interference, and finally better security and privacy since light cannot penetrate walls.

When bringing VLC to the world of mobile and IoT devices, however, we face a fundamental constraint – VLC commonly requires the light to be on during communication. This constraint leads to two key problems. *First*, communication stops when lights are off (e.g., inside a dark car, during night when we are in sleep), which severely limits the applicable scenarios of VLC. Consider the use of VLC-enabled ceiling lights to provide network connectivity to the mobile devices or smart sensors in the environment (e.g., a home, office, car). The connectivity is lost once the ceiling lights are off, which can hinder a wide range of monitoring applications. *Second*, for mobile devices to transmit data using VLC, they have to emit visible light beams. Emitting visible light beams not only consumes a high power (∼900 mW [1]) quickly draining the device battery, but also creates unpleasant visual experiences to mobile users who are potentially carrying or wearing these devices. A recent design [15] encodes data into reflected light to eliminate the need of actively emitting light rays. However, it still requires ceiling lights to be on and the reflected light beams remain visually unpleasant for mobile users.

In this paper we propose *DarkVLC*, a new VLC primitive that allows a VLC link to be sustained even when the LED light appears dark or off. The key idea is to reduce the LED's duty cycle to an extremely-low level and encode data into ultra-short light pulses. The light pulses are imperceptible to human eyes, but light sensors (photodiodes) can detect these light pulses and decode data. By removing the constraint of requiring perceptible light beams, DarkVLC fundamentally broadens the applicable scenarios of VLC. It can be integrated with VLC in its normal mode (i.e., when lights are visually on), so that ceiling lights can transition from the normal mode with lights on to its dark mode when lights are off, allowing communication to be 24/7. DarkVLC also provides a new ultra-low power, always-on connectivity affordable for mobile and IoT devices to communicate with either the ceiling light in the uplink, or other mobile devices in a peer-to-peer manner.

The design and development of DarkVLC entail several challenges. *First*, it is non-trivial to emit and detect ultra-short light pulses using off-the-shelf LEDs and photodiode sensors. We need to switch the LEDs on and off at a ultra-high speed, requiring the LED/photodiode driver circuit, the wiring, and the micro-controllers attached to LEDs and photodiodes to react very fast with minimal delay (within tens of nanoseconds). *Second*, the ultra-low duty cycle imposes challenges on the design of modulation schemes. Common VLC modulation schemes either modify the LED duty cycle and thus cannot keep the light pulses imperceptible, or achieve very low data rates because of DarkVLC's ultra-low duty cycle, or require special hardware support. *Third*, the DarkVLC link can be fragile in practice, as ambient light, transmission distance and angle can all affect the detection of the ultra-short light pulses and lead to decoding errors.

This paper describes our preliminary efforts on tackling the above challenges. We judiciously design the driver circuit of both the transmitter and the receiver to generate and detect the ultra-short light pulses. To encode data, we explore the use of pulse position modulation (PPM), which can efficiently represent multiple bits as the occurrence of a single light pulse in the time domain. To diminish the interference of ambient light, we decode data by locating the rising edge of the encoded light pulse, which is more rapid than ambient light fluctuation. We have built a prototype of DarkVLC using a commercial LED and a low-cost photodiode. Our current prototype supports 1.77 Kbps data rate, generating 0.09 lx of luminance and consuming only 46.8 μW of transmit power. We conclude the paper by discussing remaining challenges and potential applications built atop DarkVLC.

2. DarkVLC DESIGN

We first describe the key concept of DarkVLC, i.e., adapting the LED's duty cycle to generate ultra-short, imperceptible light pulses. We then present our preliminary design to encode and decode data into patterns of light pulses. A prior study [3] has discussed the standard for lights to appear off and simulated resulting data rates. Our work goes beyond the analytical results and simulations. We tackle the practical challenges to realize DarkVLC.

Concept. In practice, an LED emits light rays by periodically transitioning between ON and OFF states. The resulting luminance is determined by both the peak light intensity and its duty cycle d (i.e., the percentage of the ON duration t_{ON} in a period t_{period}, $d = t_{ON}/t_{period}$). Thus, to reduce LED's luminance to an extremely-low level, we can reduce its peak light intensity and lower its duty cycle. Reducing the peak light intensity, however, results into lower light pulses and curtails the communication distance as light luminance degrades over the square of the distance [8]. To eliminate this undesired side effect, we keep the peak light intensity high and only reduce the duty cycle.

To reduce the duty cycle, we should narrow t_{ON} and widen t_{period}. The configuration of these two parameters is subject to the capacity of the electrical components and human eyes' perception (e.g., flickering effect). The minimal t_{ON} is determined by the response time of the LED, the rise- and fall-time of the switching circuitry [5], and the response time of the photodiode. Our experiments show that $t_{ON} = 100$ ns is feasible for off-the-shelf LED and low-cost photodiodes (§ 3). Configuring t_{period}, however, faces a tradeoff. On one hand, a larger t_{period} means a smaller duty cycle and thus lower luminance, better maintaining DarkVLC imperceptible. On the other hand, a larger t_{period} also lowers the switching frequency ($f = 1/t_{period}$) and possibly causes the flickering effect. Prior studies [16] show that human eyes can perceive light flashes if f is below 120 Hz or 160 Hz [16]. A lower switching frequency also constrains the link data rate. Therefore, we need to carefully configure t_{period} to achieve the best tradeoff between user perception and link data rate. In our current hardware setup (§ 3), we observe that $t_{period} = 5.2$ ms performs the best.

Modulation. Encoding data into the ultra-short light pulses is challenging because the light pulses have to be short (e.g, 100 ns) and sparsely spread in the time domain to keep the LED's duty cycle ultra-low (0.0019% in our experiment). Common VLC modulation schemes, however, either involve modifying the pulse duration (e.g., PWM [7]), or lead to much lower data rate. As examples, On-Off Keying (OOK) encodes only a single bit over a light pulse,

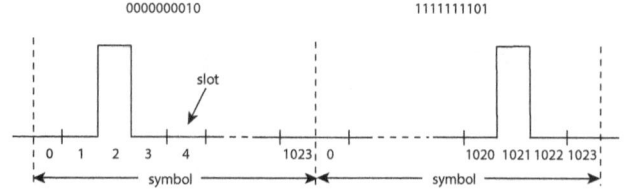

Figure 1: Pulse Position Modulation (PPM). A light pulse occurs only once per symbol. Each symbol is divided into 1024 time slots, thus the time slot where the light pulse resides represents 10-bit information.

while Frequency-Shift Keying (FSK) requires multiple light pulses to transmit a single bit. To achieve efficient encoding and boost the data rate, we choose Pulse Position Modulation (PPM) [7] to encode data. The key idea is to encode bits into the exact position of a light pulse in the time domain. More specifically, PPM divides time into symbols with equal length, where only a single light pulse occurs per symbol. Each symbol is further divided into 2^N time slots, and thus the exact time slot where the light pulse occurs represents N bits. Figure 1 shows an example where each symbol is divided into 1024 time slots and thus 10 bits are transmitted per symbol. While rich literature [19, 22, 23] has studied advanced forms of PPM to boost its data rate, these PPM variants are inherently unable to maintain a constant ultra-low duty cycle, a key requirement to realize DarkVLC. Thus, we use the basic PPM in our current design. We leave detailed discussions on these PPM variants to § 7.

Demodulation. The receiver decodes data by continuously sensing the incoming light intensity. To detect the occurrences of light pulses, a simple method is to collect the light intensity values within a symbol, average the observed light intensity values of each time slot, identify the time slot with the highest mean intensity value, and treat this slot as the light pulse position to decode bits. However, because of the ultra-short duration of the light pulse, ambient light fluctuation can mislead the receiver and cause errors in pulse detection. To diminish the interference of ambient light, we apply an edge-detection method to detect pulses. The key idea is to distinguish the ambient light fluctuation from the encoded light pulse based on the speed of the light intensity change. Our experiments show that the light intensity of an encoded light pulse rises much more rapidly than the ambient light fluctuation. Therefore, we first compute the first-order derivatives of the light intensity values. We then identify the local maximum to locate the edge of the encoded light pulse.

Accurate pulse detection also requires tight synchronization between the transmitter and the receiver. To help the receiver detect the beginning of a packet and align the slots, we design a preamble of pattern 11010101 using OOK and pulses are located at predefined slots. Since the receiver's ADC can occasionally lose sample points, we realign the slots once a rise edge is detected. The reason is as follows. When the ADC misses sample points, the rise edge is assumed to appear earlier than its actual occurrence. Given that we obtain only five samples for each pulse, losing even a single sample causes a significant misalignment of the slots. Losing the first sample does not immediately affect the decoding of the next pulse because we round it to the closest slot. However, errors can accumulate and lead to incorrect decoding in later slots. Therefore, to address the problem, each time we detect a rise edge, we determine the slot it belongs to, realign the slot to the rise edge, and shift the subsequent samples correspondingly.

| (a) Circuit design | (b) Hardware | (c) Testbed setting |

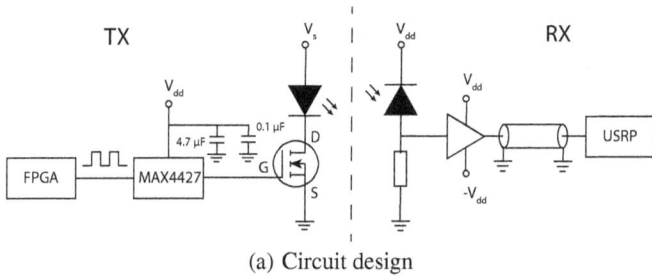

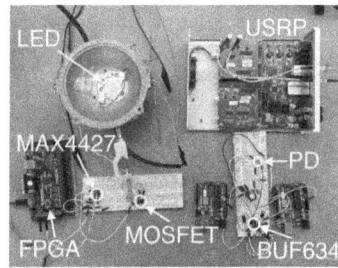

Figure 2: DarkVLC implementation. The LED is driven by a Xilinx Artix-7 FPGA through a MOSFET (STF5N52U) and a gate driver (MAX4427). The photocurrent generated by the photodiode is converted to the voltage signal by a resistor. The voltage signal is sampled by a USRP with an LFRX daughterboard. The voltage follower (BUF634) between the resistor and the USRP is for impedance matching.

3. DarkVLC PROTOTYPE

We build a proof-of-concept prototype for a DarkVLC link. The fast switching speed of the transmitter and receiver circuits is the key to realize DarkVLC. Next we briefly overview our implementation of the transmitter and the receiver. Figure 2 shows our circuit design and the prototype hardware.

Transmitter. We use CREE CXA2520 as the LED driven by an FPGA board. We choose an FPGA board as our micro-controller, because it offers the clock-level (10 ns) control granularity and can generate light pulses as short as 40 ns (limited by its I/O capacity 24 MHz [6]). In comparison, common micro-controllers (e.g., Arduino UNO) cannot provide clock-level control. To further boost the switching speed of the LED, we insert a dedicated gate driver between the micro-controller and the MOSFET. The gate driver can supply a burst current to switch the MOSFET. It also acts as a voltage amplifier if the output voltage of the micro-controller cannot reach the threshold voltage of the MOSFET.

We notice that wiring also affects the circuit switching speed. Long wires introduce the so-called transmission line [9], where signal reflection occurs, resulting into oscillating signals. This effect is non-negligible for our circuit with high frequency. We reduce the effect by minimizing the wire length. It will be less of an issue once we integrate these electrical components into a printed-circuit board (PCB) in the future.

Receiver. Our receiver photodiode is Honeywell SD5421 connected to a USRP radio. We choose USRP because it offers sufficiently high ADC sampling rate (100 MS/s). We equip the USRP with an LFRX daughter-board with a 50-Ω input impedance. We connect the photodiode to a 100-kΩ resistor. We use a unity gain voltage amplifier to transform the impedance so that the USRP does not load the signal source. Because of the bandwidth of our low-cost photodiode, our current prototype supports 100-ns light pulses. We plan to examine high-end photodiodes in our future work to further reduce the pulse duration.

Our current prototype uses customized hardware to demonstrate the concept and feasibility of DarkVLC. Moving forward, we plan to examine the prospect of implementing DarkVLC on existing mobile devices (e.g., smartphones). We will discuss associated challenges and research plan in § 5.

4. PRELIMINARY RESULTS

Using the DarkVLC prototype, we examine user's perception of DarkVLC and its practical performance under different link distance, viewing angle, ambient light condition.

Experimental Setup. We conduct experiments in a typical office environment, where sunlight and fluorescent light are present. We fix the LED on a stand with adjustable height. The LED is not covered by any lampshade (Figure 2(c)). By default, we place the photodiode right below the LED. We configure $t_{ON} = 100$ ns and $t_{period} = 5.24$ ms. All experiments are repeated 10 rounds.

4.1 User Perception

We start with examining the luminance level of DarkVLC, aiming to examine whether users can perceive DarkVLC's luminance under different ambient light conditions. We conduct the study with five participants (23 – 28 years old) in both day and night. We consider two viewing scenarios: (a) *Indirect viewing*, where we place a white paper below the LED, and ask the participant to look at the paper and report whether the LED is switched off. It tests whether the participant can perceive LED's luminance in the environment, which is also how we typically perceive light; and (b) *Direct viewing*, where the participant stares directly into the LED and reports if the LED is off. In each viewing scenario, we conduct 10 tests. In five of them we set the LED to the DarkVLC mode and in the other half we switch LED off. We mix them in a random order. The participant is unaware of the actual state of the LED.

Table 1 lists the percentage of times participants reporting lights to be off when the LED is actually off or in the DarkVLC mode, respectively. We observe that participants cannot differentiate DarkVLC and the light-off mode when they do not directly stare at the LED chip. This demonstrates that our LED duty cycle configuration is sufficient to keep light pulses imperceptible. Participants can identify the DarkVLC mode when they stare closely into the LED chip in a low ambient light condition (0.6 lx). This is only to test DarkVLC in an extreme case, since the LED chip is not covered by any lampshade and the participant is only 30 cm away from the LED chip.

We further systematically measure the luminance of DarkVLC with different duty cycles. We fix the light pulse duration to 100 ns and vary the period (t_{period}) from 0.04 ms to 5.24 ms. We place the light meter (Extech 401036) 15 cm away from the LED to measure the illuminance. We also plot the ambient light level I_0. We observe that the illuminance gradually drops to I_0 as t_{period} increases. In our default setting ($t_{period} = 5.24$ ms), the illuminance shift of the LED is only 0.09 lx. For reference, the full moon on a clear night produces about 3 lx of illuminance outside [3]. The same experiment conducted in the day shows that the variation of the ambient illuminance (60–110 lx) caused by cloud movements already exceeds the illuminance of the LED. Hence the luminance of DarkVLC is imperceptible in the day.

Table 1: User perception of DarkVLC, where the percentage measures the likelihood of users perceiving the light to be off.

Viewing	Ambient Light	Light-off	DarkVLC
Indirect	Day (385 lx)	92%	96%
	Night (0.6 lx)	100%	100%
Direct	Day (385 lx)	92%	88%
	Night (0.6 lx)	100%	12%

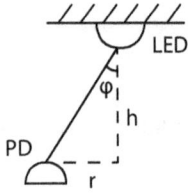

Figure 3: Experiment setup. By default $\varphi = 0$.

Figure 4: DarkVLC luminance w/ varying t_{period}.

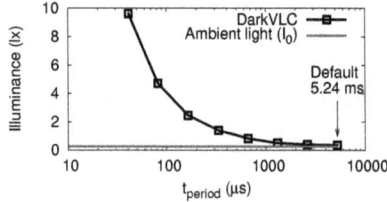

4.2 System Performance

We now measure the throughput and accuracy of DarkVLC, examining how the channel parameters and environment affect its performance (Figure 5(a)-(b)). In each experiment, the transmitter sends 2040 random bits of payload (one packet) in 1.152 s including overheads. The throughput is the number of bits (only payload) correctly received per second and the accuracy is the ratio of correctly received bits over all transmitted bits. We repeat each experiment 10 times and compute the average throughput and accuracy.

Overall, we observe that DarkVLC achieves 1.77 Kbps throughput with BER around 0.01%. The throughput is very stable with standard error below 1 bps. This aligns with the prior study [28] that verifies the stability and predictability of the optical channel.

Supporting Distance. To examine DarkVLC's supporting distance, we change the LED height while keeping the viewing angle φ as $0°$. Figure 5(a) shows the throughput and accuracy as the distance varies from 5 cm to 15 cm. We observe that our current prototype supports up to 10 cm distance. As long as the distance is within the communication range, the throughput is stable. Once the distance exceeds 10 cm, the throughput drops dramatically to 0. This is because the received pulse height is comparable to the noise (mainly circuit noise) and the receiver cannot decode any bits.

The limited supporting distance is due to the ultra-short pulse modulation, which prevents the light pulse from ascending to its normal peak intensity before it starts to fall. In our current prototype, the rise time of the LED is approximately 1 μs. Since we set the pulse width as 100 ns, the peak light intensity of the current DarkVLC is far below LED's peak intensity in its normal mode. Therefore, for a given noise level, the communication distance is largely affected. In comparison, using the same LED with pulse width longer than 5 μs, the supporting distance can be extended to 2 m. We will discuss our research plan to boost the transmission distance in § 5.

Viewing Angle. To examine the viewing angle of DarkVLC and the impact of the receiver misalignment, we horizontally move the photodiode away from the LED with the photodiode facing upright (Figure 3). We also vary the LED height h and repeat the experiments. Figure 5(b) plots the throughput and accuracy as the irradiance angle (φ) increases from $0°$ to $30°$. We observe that each height is associated with a corresponding maximum viewing angle. With the increase of distance, the support viewing angle decreases. At a height of 5 cm, the view angle is around $50°$ ($\pm 25°$).

Sensitivity to Ambient Light. We also evaluate DarkVLC under different ambient light conditions, including: (a) Daytime with other lights on; (b) Daytime with all lights off; (c) Night with other lights on; (d) Night with all lights off. Figure 5(a) indicates that ambient light does not influence the throughput and accuracy of DarkVLC. The reason is two-fold. *First*, the modulated light pulses change much more rapidly than the ambient light – let it be the natural (sunlight) or artificial (fluorescent or LED lamp) light. The sunlight is almost a DC signal, while the flashing frequency of a commercial LED lamp (Cree A19) is only 120 Hz (8 ms period). Our modulated light pulse rises and falls within μs. Thus our edge detection-based demodulation can effectively decode bits even with ambient light interference. The major noise that affects the SNR is from the circuit. *Second*, most photodiodes have a limited field of view (FoV), resembling a directional antenna. The receiver gain of signal with an incidence angle exceeding half of the FoV is very small. For SD5421, at $20°$ incidence angle, the received signal strength is only 10% of that at $0°$. Thus the possible ambient light perceived by the photodiode has been largely attenuated. In summary, our current design is robust against ambient light interference, demonstrating the efficacy of our pulse detection scheme.

4.3 Power Consumption

Finally, we measure the power consumption of DarkVLC and compare it to VLC in the normal mode with LED on. The experiment setting is the same as Figure 4. Figure 5(c) shows how the power of the LED changes with different duty cycle (fixed t_{ON}). We measure the average LED forward current with a multimeter and calculate the power by $P = V_s I$. The power of the LED used in common mode is 19.8 W, while the power of DarkVLC is as low as 46.8 μW. With fixed pulse width, the power of the LED is directly proportional to the duty cycle.

Our current demodulation requires the USRP radio as its ADC provides sufficiently high sampling rate (1 MS/s), which can be power-consuming for wireless devices. However, since IoT devices typically upload sensor data more frequently than receiving commands, the power consumed by receiving data can be insignificant. In addition, we plan to examine the following two methods to reduce the power consumption of data reception. First, we can add an analog circuit component that prolongs the pulses before the ADC such that the sampling rate can be reduced at the cost of lower data rate. Second, we can potentially replace USRP with low-power FPGAs (e.g., [25]). The embedded ADC of these FPGAs can support 1 MS/s sampling rate, yet consuming much lower power.

5. REMAINING CHALLENGES

Initial experimental results demonstrate the feasibility of DarkVLC. We also recognize the limitations of our current study and plan to address following remaining challenges.

DarkVLC Networking. We plan to study a network of DarkVLC links and seek efficient medium access control (MAC) protocols to maximize network throughput. Since light pulses are ultra-short and sparsely spread out (0.0019% of duty cycle), two uncoordinated DarkVLC links are very unlikely to collide. However, the resulting multiple light pulses in a symbol make the receiver unable to detect the source (i.e., transmitter) of each light pulse. Inspired by a recent study [10] on RF backscatter, we will examine physical-layer features of each transmitter to separate light pulses from different links. Another solution is for each DarkVLC transmitter to emit light pulses in a different color (i.e., frequency), which separates links in the frequency domain.

Boosting Link Distance. The supporting distance of our current

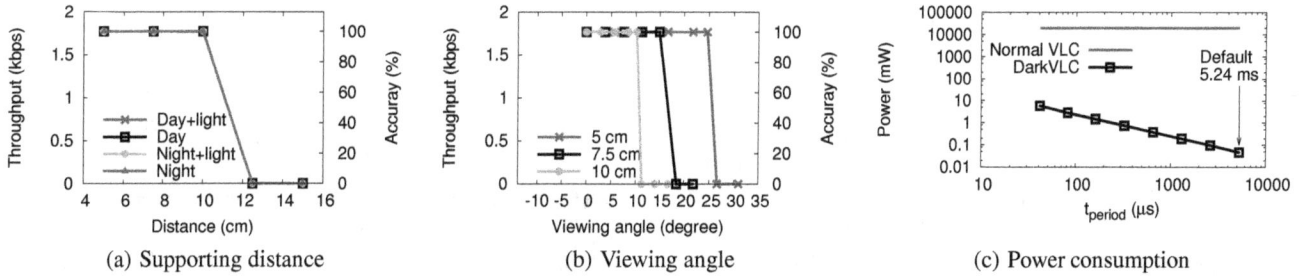

(a) Supporting distance

(b) Viewing angle

(c) Power consumption

Figure 5: DarkVLC's performance at different distances and viewing angles (a)(b). Its throughput is very stable with a standard error < 1 bps. (a) shows DarkVLC with varying distance in four ambient light settings: Day + light (385 lx), Day (149 lx), Night + light (105 lx), and Night (0.6 lx). (b) shows DarkVLC with varying viewing angle under three distances. (c) shows DarkVLC's power consumption with varying t_{period}. The transmit power of DarkVLC is 46.8 μW, multiple orders of magnitude lower than that of VLC in normal mode (19.8 W).

prototype is still very limited – only 10 cm. It is not a concern for short-range, device-to-device communication, yet is unable to support the communication between ceiling lights and IoT devices in the environment, which can be 1 – 3 m away. To significantly boost the transmission distance, we will examine LED chips with shorter rise time and optimize the LED driver so that the light intensity can rise to a higher peak within a short duration. We will refine the circuit design, especially the receiver circuit, to reduce the circuit noise and increase the photodiode's sensitivity. We will also consider signal processing techniques to minimize the impact of the hardware noise.

Adapting LED Duty Cycle. Our current design uses a fixed LED duty cycle to generate imperceptible light pulses. The ultra-low duty cycle limits the link distance and data rate. We plan to slightly relax the constraint and adapt the duty cycle based on the ambient light. As shown by our experiments and prior studies [20], our eyes are less sensitive to flashes in brighter environments. Thus when ambient light is brighter, we can slightly increase the LED's duty cycle by reducing the OFF duration (t_{OFF}) while still keeping light pulses imperceptible. A larger duty cycle leads to a shorter period (t_{period}) and thus higher link rate. As an example, doubling the duty cycle (0.0019%) used in the current DarkVLC prototype results into an illuminance level of only 0.09 lx, which is still imperceptible under a bright ambient light condition, yet the resulting data rate increases nearly twice using PPM. To enable such adaptation, we can consider LED itself as a sensor that senses the ambient light condition, which has been shown feasible in prior work [21], without embedding additional photodiodes.

DarkVLC on Mobile Devices. We will also explore the implementation of DarkVLC on off-the-shelf mobile devices such as smartphones, which are often equipped with LED and photodiode sensors. We face two key challenges. First, existing smartphones cannot support the LED switching speed required by DarkVLC to generate ultra-short flashes. Our initial experiments with Nexus 5 show that the the shortest flash the phone can generate is 32.86 ms on average, far too long for DarkVLC. Furthermore, the flash duration is unstable with a standard deviation of 2.36 ms. Second, restricted by the OS scheduling, current phones support only up to 100 S/s sampling rate [16] of the light sensor data. We will need solutions to gain finer-grained and more precise control of the flash duration, and speed up the sampling of the light sensor data.

6. DarkVLC APPLICATIONS

IoT Networking. DarkVLC can enable a new IoT network architecture built atop VLC. We can turn existing lighting infrastructure

into a backbone of the IoT network. The ceiling LED lights are connected to the Internet using power line communication (PLC) technology. The ceiling lights smoothly transition between the VLC's normal mode (when lights are on) to DarkVLC when lights are off (e.g., night). Shining a light onto IoT devices provides them with always-on connectivity and makes them searchable as part of the open web of things [2, 24]. IoT devices not only decode data from the ceiling light, but also emit or reflect [15] modulated lights using DarkVLC to sprinkle their collected data, or to send out periodic beacons (e.g., UriBeacons [24]) to facilitate device discovery and interaction.

Wireless Authentication. As mobile payment becomes increasingly popular, DarkVLC can serve as a new means for wireless authentication. DarkVLC reuses the LEDs and light sensors that existing mobile devices (e.g., smartphones, smart watches) are already equipped with. DarkVLC leverages imperceptible, directional light beams[1]. It is secure because light signal strength decreases dramatically with the increase in distance or viewing angle. Light can be easily blocked and its multi-path effect is minimal, preventing attackers from eavesdropping the authentication traffic.

Visible Light Sensing. DarkVLC also broadens the use case of visible light-based sensing. Recent works have proposed the use of visible light to track whole-body postures [17] or 2D finger movements [27]. These sensing systems do not require the VLC channel to deliver a high data rate, yet always-on connectivity is crucial to sustain light sensing. Therefore, DarkVLC is a very suitable candidate. By integrating DarkVLC into these sensing systems, we can achieve always-on behavioral monitoring even when lights are off (e.g., night), and realize unobtrusive near-field finger tracking without having LED lights visibly on.

7. RELATED WORK

VLC Modulation. We divide VLC modulation schemes into two categories: 1) Basic single-carrier pulse modulation schemes [7, 8] encode bits in the pulse presence, pulse width, pulse position, pulse amplitude, or the light polarization [26]. Specifically on pulse position-based modulation (PPM), rich literature have studied its variants to increase the data encoding efficiency and boost the data rate. As examples, MPPM (Multipulse PPM) [23] allows multiple pulses in a symbol and uses combinatorial pulse patterns to increase data rate greatly; DPPM (Differential PPM) [22] encodes bits in the number of empty slots between adjacent pulses, thus elimi-

---
[1]Infrared is also unobtrusive, but not all smart devices are equipped with infrared emitters.

nating the slots after each pulse in the basic PPM; EPPM (Expurgated PPM) [19] selects a subset of symbol patterns of MPPM and uses the bandwidth more efficiently than PPM; 2) Advanced multi-carrier modulation schemes (e.g., OFDM) provide higher data rates using more complicated hardware [7]. DarkVLC's modulation design is inspired by these prior schemes. It faces a new constraint of keeping light pulses imperceptible, which makes some prior design either not applicable or inefficient in data encoding. We focus on single-carrier pulse modulation schemes for hardware simplicity.

VLC Applications. Recent research has studied VLC applications that go beyond communication. Examples include indoor localization and sensing. VLC-based localization employs LEDs as anchors, which broadcast beacons containing light IDs and locations [13, 16]. A recent design [26] further allows any illumination light sources to be used for indoor localization. The idea of visible light sensing is to collect the light intensity values from photodiodes to track bodies [17] or finger movements [27]. All these current designs, however, require lights to be visibly on. They can leverage DarkVLC to broaden the sensing scenarios.

Infrared Communication. Another line of related research is on infrared communication, which is also imperceptible to human eyes and operates on optical wireless channels. Prior works [12, 4, 11] have extensively studied its modulation schemes and channel characteristics. However, since these modulation schemes are designed for infrared light that is intrinsically imperceptible to human eyes, when being applied in the DarkVLC link, most of them cannot keep the visible light pulses imperceptible. Compared to infrared communication, DarkVLC brings two unique benefits. First, DarkVLC reuses existing LED lights to enable imperceptible communication while infrared links require extra infrared emitters dedicated to communication. Second, operating on higher frequency, visible light is securer than infrared and is harder to be eavesdropped, since its reflectivity is lower than that of the infrared band [14].

Low-Power Communication for IoT devices. Active research focuses on low-power communication technologies for IoT devices. One representative example is RF backscatter, where the transmitter reflects incoming RF signals to encode data [18] and harvests energy from ambient RF signals. Backscatter often uses lightweight modulation (e.g. OOK) schemes and MAC protocols [10], as it demands simple circuit with low energy. DarkVLC is orthogonal to these designs and exhibits similar properties. It differs in that it operates on the visible light spectrum, offering one more option to achieve ultra-low power connectivity. A recent work [15] applies backscatter in VLC to design low-power uplink for IoT devices. DarkVLC can be integrated with this design to enable VLC backscatter when lights appear off.

8. CONCLUSION

We presented DarkVLC, a new communication primitive that encodes data into imperceptible, ultra-short light pulses, allowing a VLC link to be sustained even when the light appears dark or off. We demonstrated its feasibility by building a prototype using off-the-shelf LEDs and low-cost photodiodes. DarkVLC broadens the applicable scenario of VLC and significantly drives down the power consumption of a VLC transmitter. It provides a new ultra-low power, always-on connectivity affordable for mobile and IoT devices.

9. REFERENCES

[1] High Power Flash LED. http://www.samsung.com/global/business/business-images/led/file/product/it-c/201312/Data_Sheet_FH411B_SPFCW24301CL.pdf.

[2] The Physical Web. http://google.github.io/physical-web/.

[3] BOROGOVAC, T., ET AL. "Lights-off" visible light communications. In *Proc. of Globecom Workshop on Optical Wireless Communications* (2011).

[4] CARRUTHERS, J. B., AND KAHN, J. M. Multiple-subcarrier modulation for nondirected wireless infrared communication. *Selected Areas in Communications, IEEE Journal on 14*, 3 (1996), 538–546.

[5] CREE, INC. *Pulsed over-current driving of Cree XLamp LEDs: information and cautions.* REV 1B.

[6] DIGILENT, INC. *Digilent Pmod interface specification*, November 2011.

[7] DIMITROV, S., AND HAAS, H. *Principles of LED Light Communications: Towards Networked Li-Fi.* Cambridge University Press, 2015.

[8] GHASSEMLOOY, Z., POPOOLA, W., AND RAJBHANDARI, S. *Optical wireless communications: system and channel modelling with Matlab®.* CRC Press, 2012.

[9] GILMORE, R., AND BESSER, L. *Practical RF circuit design for modern wireless systems*, vol. 1. Artech House, 2003.

[10] HU, P., ZHANG, P., AND GANESAN, D. Laissez-faire: Fully asymmetric backscatter communication. In *Proc. of SIGCOMM* (2015).

[11] JUNGNICKEL, V., POHL, V., NÖNNIG, S., AND VON HELMOLT, C. A physical model of the wireless infrared communication channel. *Selected Areas in Communications, IEEE Journal on 20*, 3 (2002), 631–640.

[12] KAHN, J. M., AND BARRY, J. R. Wireless infrared communications. *Proceedings of the IEEE 85*, 2 (1997), 265–298.

[13] KUO, Y.-S., PANNUTO, P., HSIAO, K.-J., AND DUTTA, P. Luxapose: Indoor positioning with mobile phones and visible light. In *Proc. of MobiCom* (2014).

[14] LEE, K., PARK, H., AND BARRY, J. R. Indoor channel characteristics for visible light communications. *Communications Letters, IEEE 15*, 2 (2011), 217–219.

[15] LI, J., ET AL. Retro-VLC: Enabling battery-free duplex visible light communication for mobile and iot applications. In *Proc. of HotMobile* (2015).

[16] LI, L., HU, P., PENG, C., SHEN, G., AND ZHAO, F. Epsilon: A visible light based positioning system. In *Proc. of NSDI* (2014).

[17] LI, T., AN, C., TIAN, Z., CAMPBELL, A. T., AND ZHOU, X. Human sensing using visible light communication. In *Proc. of MobiCom* (2015).

[18] LIU, V., ET AL. Ambient backscatter: wireless communication out of thin air. In *Proc. of SIGCOMM* (2013).

[19] NOSHAD, M., AND BRANDT-PEARCE, M. Expurgated PPM using symmetric balanced incomplete block designs. *Communications Letters, IEEE 16*, 7 (2012), 968–971.

[20] PALMER, S. E. *Vision science: Photons to phenomenology*, vol. 1. MIT press Cambridge, MA, 1999.

[21] SCHMID, S., ET AL. LED-to-LED visible light communication networks. In *Proc. of MobiHoc* (2013).

[22] SHIU, D.-S., AND KAHN, J. M. Differential pulse-position modulation for power-efficient optical communication. *Communications, IEEE Transactions on 47*, 8 (1999), 1201–1210.

[23] SUGIYAMA, H., AND NOSU, K. MPPM: a method for improving the band-utilization efficiency in optical PPM. *Lightwave Technology, Journal of 7*, 3 (1989), 465–472.

[24] WANT, R., SCHILIT, B., AND JENSON, S. Enabling the Internet of Things. *Computer 48*, 1 (Jan 2015), 28–35.

[25] XILINX, INC. *7 series FPGAs and Zynq-7000 all programmable SoC XADC dual 12-bit 1 MSPS analog-to-digital converter.* v1.7.

[26] YANG, Z., ET AL. Wearables can afford: Light-weight indoor positioning with visible light. In *Proc. of MobiSys* (2015).

[27] ZHANG, C., TABOR, J., ZHANG, J., AND ZHANG, X. Extending mobile interaction through near-field visible light sensing. In *Proc. of MobiCom* (2015).

[28] ZHANG, J., ZHANG, X., AND WU, G. Dancing with light: Predictive in-frame rate selection. In *Proc. of INFOCOM* (2015).

Privacy Mediators: Helping IoT Cross the Chasm

Nigel Davies[1], Nina Taft[2], Mahadev Satyanarayanan[3], Sarah Clinch[1], Brandon Amos[3]
[1]Lancaster University, [2]Google, [3]Carnegie Mellon University

[1]n.a.davies | s.clinch @lancaster.ac.uk,
[2]ninataft@google.com, [3] satya | bamos @cs.cmu.edu

ABSTRACT

Unease over data privacy will retard consumer acceptance of IoT deployments. The primary source of discomfort is a lack of user control over raw data that is streamed directly from sensors to the cloud. This is a direct consequence of the over-centralization of today's cloud-based IoT hub designs. We propose a solution that interposes a locally-controlled software component called a *privacy mediator* on every raw sensor stream. Each mediator is in the same administrative domain as the sensors whose data is being collected, and dynamically enforces the current privacy policies of the owners of the sensors or mobile users within the domain. This solution necessitates a logical point of presence for mediators within the administrative boundaries of each organization. Such points of presence are provided by *cloudlets*, which are small locally-administered data centers at the edge of the Internet that can support code mobility. The use of cloudlet-based mediators aligns well with natural personal and organizational boundaries of trust and responsibility.

1. Introduction

In "Crossing the Chasm" [16], Geoffrey Moore warns of a large discontinuity awaiting every new technology as it tries to expand from a small user base of "Innovators" and "Early Adoptors" (Figure 1). In contrast to those early enthusiasts, mainstream users are clear-eyed about the shortcomings of the new technology and seek a net win. Reducing the negatives will increase the chances of success.

The Internet of Things (IoT) is now approaching this chasm, as public awareness of privacy risks grow. In their June 2015 report on consumer perceptions of privacy in IoT [11], Groopman et al state that "Consumers are highly anxious about companies sharing their data: 78% of consumers are highly concerned about companies selling their data to third parties." They also state that "While older generations show higher concern, strong discomfort with the use and sale of connected device data is pervasive across all age groups, including millennials." A January 2015 report [10] by the U.S. Federal Trade Commission notes that "...perceived risks to privacy and security, even if not realized, could undermine the consumer confidence necessary for the technologies to meet their full potential, and may result in less widespread adoption." A June 2015 blog entry [25] notes that "TelecomTV also recently reported a

HotMobile '16 February 26-27, 2016, St. Augustine, FL, USA

© 2016 Copyright held by the owner/author(s).

ACM ISBN 978-1-4503-4145-5/16/02.

DOI: http://dx.doi.org/10.1145/2873587.2873600

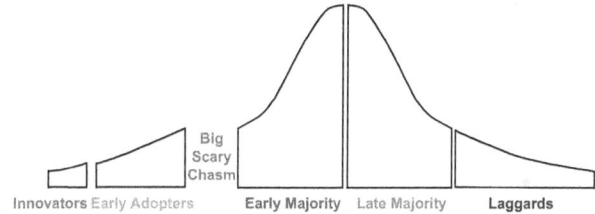

Figure 1: Technology Adoption Chasm (Adapted from Moore [16])

marked slowdown at the fluffy end of the IoT market – people have already had enough (it seems) of home IoT gadgets, so those privacy worries might already be hitting hard." Want et al [29] identify privacy and security as major concerns in IoT.

In this position paper, we put forth the view that *concern over data privacy arising from the over-centralization of IoT systems* is a critical obstacle to their growth. There is growing reluctance to expose raw sensor data to a cloud-based IoT entity. IoT deployments today are typically in silos within organisations, or in niche vertical markets. The vision of a rich ecosystem in which shared data is leveraged by a wide range of new applications is yet to be realized.

Our solution is a plug-in architecture with trusted software modules called *privacy mediators* inserted into the data distribution pipeline. A privacy mediator (or, just "mediator") performs data redaction and privacy policy enforcement *before data is released from the user's direct control*. Its platform integrity is ensured by execution on a *cloudlet* [22] in the trust domain of the data owner. This approach delivers a scalable and secure solution at the edge of the cloud, and aligns well with natural organizational boundaries of trust and responsibility. It also scales well to deployments of sensors that have high data rates (e.g., video cameras).

We make the following contributions in this position paper. First, we enunciate an important design principle: namely, that users should have the first option to control the fidelity and distribution of their data. Second, to implement this design principle, we propose an architectural framework that offers a rich set of privacy controls. In our plugin architecture, a small set of trusted third parties (privacy experts) provide the mediation code, thereby reducing the privacy burden on third party app developers. Third, we propose the use of cloudlets (rather than the cloud) to ensure the platform integrity of mediators in the user's eyes.

2. Privacy Control Requirements

Users typically develop a keen sense of what they want from a specific technology only after they have had experience using it. However, in surveys users repeatedly make comments along the lines of "I should get to decide how much of my data a service or application gets to see" and "I should get to decide who my data is shared with" [11]. Users have major angst about continuous ongoing monitoring [25] in which sensors collect measurements at small time scales (such as every minute) and can store seemingly infinite sensor history in the cloud.

Sensors are also becoming increasingly sophisticated. In the future, many of the "things" in the Internet of Things (IoT) will be video cameras. In 2013, it was estimated that there was one surveillance camera for every 11 people in the UK [5]. The report of the 2013 *NSF Workshop on Future Directions in Wireless Networking* [4] predicts that "It will soon be possible to find a camera on every human body, in every room, on every street, and in every vehicle." Such omnipresent video recorders raise significant privacy concerns. Similar concerns have already been expressed by consumers about audio recorders found in smart TVs [20], smartphones, cars, connected toys [21] and game devices. The capture of video and audio streams in private spaces without informed consent can catch consumers unaware, and lead to reputation damage when stories hit the press [20, 21].

While the IoT privacy landscape is complex, a simple principle can serve as a touchstone: *users should be able to control the release of their own data*. This translates into the following privacy control requirements for IoT.

Deletion and denaturing: Users want clear *deletion* capabilities: they need to be able to see (or hear) their data and have the option to delete segments of it. In situations where outright deletion is not required users may still wish to be able to *denature* the data: that is, obscure or modify its sensitive aspects so that it is safe to release to the outside world. For example, faces in images and videos can be blurred[24, 27], and sensor readings coarsely aggregated or omitted at certain times of day or night. Denaturing audio and video is important in many scenarios, especially those involving vulnerable participants (e.g. events involving children, political protests in totalitarian regimes).

Summarization: Providing simple summaries of data for scalar sensors is also possible. For example, a user with a watch sensor might prefer to release only the maximum and minimum heartbeat counts for a day, rather than per-minute measurements. Similarly some users may prefer to release daily or weekly totals of building energy usage rather than per-minute measurements. These are examples of *temporal summaries*. Another kind of aggregation involves *spatial summaries* such as releasing location data at the zip code level rather than raw GPS readings.

Inference: Users want control over *how* their data is used. For example, if temperature or light sensors are used to derive room occupancy as a *virtual sensor* [30], the occupants may want control over the latter sensor too. This concept of a derived virtual sensor applies to many sensors that may not appear too intrusive on their own. However regular readings from such sensors could provide significant insights into the behaviour of the occupants of the house such as their waking times, and levels of physical mobility. Over time, as these virtual sensors get exposed (via the media), users may demand control over them too.

Anonymization: Users may wish to submit data for a societal good, but may prefer to do so anonymously. Examples include data for medical research, and crowd-sourced air quality measurements from smartphones [31] used to monitor specific neighborhoods. A privacy architecture should therefore provide a capability for users to do *anonymization*.

Mobility: Users may also wish to control data flow from sensors they briefly encounter in the course of their daily life, for example, in a meeting room or public space. While not requiring new data filtering, supporting this user mobility places significant demands on any underlying architecture.

Ease of Use: Studies have shown that users often don't understand privacy controls. Although the explicit functionality listed above is needed, users are unlikely to be offered choices defined as above. Instead they would need to be shown a semantic representation of what releasing data at a given granularity could mean. For example, rather than ask users about time granularity for their temperature data, they could be asked if they agree for "room occupancy" to be computed. If they deny this option, data might only be released in a highly aggregated form (e.g. daily total). At the same time, it important not to overwhelm users with too many choices. We further discuss these issues and promising recent efforts in Section 3.5. We believe that it is important to solve the problem of making it easy for users to express and to enforce the controls they need and want.

3. Architectural Approach

The architectural solution we propose is shown in Figure 2. At its heart are *privacy mediators* – pieces of software that run on users' local cloudlets. A mediator is the first point of contact for all data produced by an IoT sensor. It is the mechanism that enforces the privacy policy specified for that sensor. Enforcement occurs in the user's own trusted domain. We describe the components of this architecture in the sections below.

3.1 Cloudlets

Key to our architectural approach is the use of cloudlets: small data centers located at the edge of the Internet, in close proximity to associated sensors and mobile devices [22, 23]. Cloudlets enable cloud services to be virtualised and then instantiated close to their point of use, rather than in the distant cloud. Multiple deployment scenarios are possible. In one option, cloudlets are physically installed in homes, schools or small businesses. It may be possible to install a cloudlet on a high-end Wi-Fi access point, or alternatively on a rack-mounted computer in a wiring closet. Performance studies need to be done to explore these options, but as we show in Section 5.2, a high-end laptop can suffice even for some demanding use cases. An alternate deployment option is for entities such as local telephone companies or cloud service providers to host cloudlets on behalf of home owners. Regardless of deployment model, a cloudlet is always logically within the trust domain of the end user.

3.2 Privacy Mediators

Mediators implement the various types of data privacy controls described in Section 2, and are an integral part of the processing pipeline for IoT sensor data prior to release. We expect mediators to be far more diverse and powerful than the types of simple reverse firewalls and outbound filtering typically deployed at the network edge of many large organizations. Mediators may be specific to a single class of IoT sensor (e.g. a temperature sensor) or may be designed to operate over data produced by many different IoT sensors.

Since sensors may produce data in proprietary formats, we

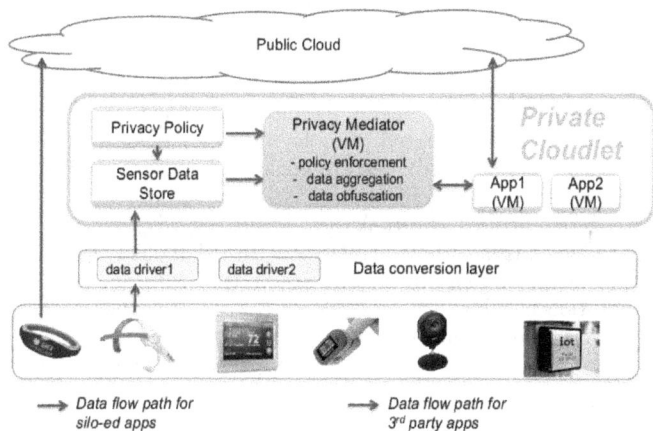

Figure 2: Privacy Architecture

expect that many sensors will require a conversion layer prior to mediation. In our architecture, sensor developers can provide *sensor drivers* (analogous to printer drivers) that convert data into standard or common formats.

Users are able to create policies that control the routing of sensor data to mediators and the configuration of individual mediators. In addition to filtering outbound data, we anticipate that in many cases it will be necessary to store local sensor data in order to perform mediation and access control. The granularity at which data is stored can also be determined by user policy and access to this storage is managed by our privacy policy component. By adhering to the good design principle of separation between policy and mechanism we gain flexibility, such as having mechanisms (e.g. video denaturing) being allowed for some apps or services, but not others.

Since cloudlets are small data centers, virtual machine (VM) encapsulation of a mediator is expected to be the norm. However, in a high-trust deployment, a lighter-weight container such as Docker may be used instead of a VM for encapsulation. The tradeoff is one of increased memory footprint and processor overhead versus superior isolation, safety and smaller attack surface. We expect most mediators to run on a cloudlet within a user's domain. However, our privacy architecture enables dynamic instantiation of mediators on other cloudlets for users that are on the move and need such functionality outside of their usual home or workplace. The use of cloudlets also enables post-mediator application-specific preprocessing of sensor data. This will be important in solving the scalability problem that metro-area networks will face when their input data rates reach excessive volumes due to the proliferation of video capture devices. The combination of mediators and cloudlets thus enables a complete solution to be deployed close to the user, with the attendant benefits in terms of trust, privacy, performance and scalability through reduced latency and bandwidth demands.

3.3 Mediators and Trust

An important design consideration is how mediators and their associated device drivers are produced and deployed. If mediators are produced by the same organisations that supply the sensors and associated cloud services then there is little for the user to gain in terms of privacy guarantees – they would still have to place total trust in the integrity of these organisations' solutions. As a result we expect that

mediators will largely be developed by independent third-parties in much the same way as virus checking software is produced today. While some may be proprietary we also expect a significant number of open source mediators to emerge that will benefit from rigorous inspection by the community. Such mediators could obtain trusted reputations by subjecting their code to organizations that give out certifications or seals of approval after inspecting and evaluating a product.

Thus a significant advantage of our architecture is that it could help spur the rich ecosystem vision in which numerous third party developers build applications on top of sensors deployed in the home. One challenge facing such developers is the need to carefully manage user data and try to minimize the occurrence of privacy incidents. Privacy incidents can occur for a variety of reasons, including leakage of private data when a service provider is hacked [28], rogue employees, one company selling data to another who in turn exposes it, communications eavesdropping when insufficient encryption is used [19], or if data gets subpoenaed. Privacy incidents can also occur when a company's transparency in their privacy policy poorly communicates what data is collected [20].

Maintaining up to date security and privacy best practices is challenging, as it requires specific skills and constant vigilance. Some companies achieve this but others do not. It thus seems prudent for less experienced companies to leave part of the privacy responsibility to those who make it a priority and obtain certifications of trust. Our approach creates a data processing pipeline that sits between third party applications and the raw sensor data. Applications obtain data by interacting with mediators via APIs. A privacy cloudlet provides a solution offering privacy functionality that developers could leverage - meaning that they wouldn't need to implement functionality such as denaturing, data aggregation, and policy enforcement, themselves.

In this model, users need to place their trust in a limited number of mediators and the privacy cloudlet service, rather than the hundreds of applications and services they are likely to use. In essence, it reduces the privacy risk surface by limiting the number of players that need to be trusted.

By interacting with user sensor data via the cloudlet, third party applications reduce their own risk and would not have any data that the users has not explicitly consented to release. Note that existing privacy policies do *not* achieve the same effect in terms of obtaining user consent since users are only given the choice to accept or decline the sharing of a particular sensor's data, i.e. today they are not given the choice to control the granularity of the data released.

3.4 Data Storage

In keeping with our basic philosophy of minimizing the threat surface for IoT data we expect that each mediator will maintain its own data buffer. Our architecture does not provide mediators with access to all IoT data on a cloudlet. Rather, mediators are connected to one or more incoming sensor streams and it is only this data that they can access. In this way rogue mediators can only compromise data that have been explicitly granted access to rather than potentially exposing a wider range of a user's IoT data.

In a system that releases only summarized sensor data, the corresponding raw data could be deleted immediately. Alternatively, it could be buffered in the cloudlet for a limited period in case it proves helpful later, e.g., video footage in a home could be useful in identifying unlawful intrusion. Simoens et al [27] show how a good balance can be achieved between privacy and performance by encrypting and storing raw video sensor data using a randomly-generated private key that is only present within the VM instance (i.e., mediator) for that sensor. Encrypted data can be decrypted on demand, with proper authorization, by the mediator.

3.5 User Policies

A key consideration in the design of our system is how users express their IoT privacy policies in a form that can be enacted using mediators. Specifying such policies has been subject to extensive UbiComp research, with many approaches having a basis in policy languages designed for managing privacy in the web (e.g. P3P and APPEL).

Myles et al. [18] explored location data management – applications wishing to access user locations submit a request that also includes a privacy policy (defined in APPEL), user-registered validators then determine if the requested information can be made available and if any transformations are needed to reduce the granularity of the data. Another policy language, Rei [13], defined four policy object types: rights (permissions an entity has to complete a specified action), prohibitions (explicit records that indicate that an entity cannot complete a specified action), obligations (actions an entity must perform), and dispensations (waivers that excuse an entity from obligations). Since [13] was mainly used for security policies, and [18] was applied only to location data, these approaches need to be explored to understand their extensibility to a broader use for privacy in IoT.

Extending policy languages for privacy in the IoT poses several key challenges, due to the scale of IoT sensors and services, and the issue that users typically struggle to engage with privacy policies in other contexts. First, the *large volume of deployed services*, means that engaging users each time they encounter a new service is simply not viable. Having policies defined per sensor rather than per app results in fewer privacy policies than the per application model we have today on smartphones. However one policy per sensor will still be too much; thus new approaches such as defining policies by class of sensor, hierarchically or other groupings of sensors, needs to be explored. Second, users may want to have *recipient-specific preferences*. A user's policy for sensors is likely to vary depending on the data recipient, and the perceived value or risk of sharing with that recipient. For example, a home owner may be willing to share detailed data with their energy supplier (for the purpose of improving the provided service or managing billing), but may only wish to share summarizations with a local government or third-party application.

To overcome these challenges and abstract over specific IoT devices and services we suggest the use of high-level privacy goals that can then be translated into mediator requests. Based on overall privacy and service goals, we propose that users maintain general profiles consisting of reusable policies that apply to classes of application or device.

However, expressing these high-level goals and profiles still requires input from users. Current privacy literature suggests two approaches for encouraging users to maintain their privacy goals and profiles. We need to determine a set of smart default privacy profiles that capture a range of opinions about privacy. In the context of permission management for Android applications, Liu et al. [15] showed

that it is possible to find a small set of (4-6) default privacy profiles that capture the preferences of many users and allow for simple customizations. Each default profile in [15] contains a list of permissions typically declined, along with those typically accepted. Employing smart default profiles means that users only need to engage when something outside of their base profile occurs. A second approach is to use an active privacy assistant [1] that advises users what to do only when things they might be concerned about arise. This work showed that when users are nudged with one privacy question per day, 60% of users were responsive and actively changed permission settings. Clearly much work remains, but the initial success of these approaches is encouraging.

4. Business Models

Our focus so far has been largely on home scenarios deploying third party applications and services. Clearly there are other business models for home services based on first party applications in which users buy a sensor directly from the service provider for a particular service - such as Opower and Fitbit. Such services can co-exist in a home deploying a private cloudlet by simply bypassing the cloudlet (as depicted in Figure 2 by the blue arrow on the left).

Our architecture is also well suited to meet the needs of businesses in which privacy policy may be delegated to administrators within a larger organization. In schools and university settings, privacy policy would likely be set by an administrator or a particular teacher. For example, elementary schools with video cameras in the classroom, might elect to release videos with the faces of children blurred - this could be useful if a school district wanted to evaluate the effectiveness of teaching tools while simultaneously protecting the privacy of individual children. Schools employ third party applications to supplement teaching materials and our architecture makes it easy for third party applications to be compliant with school privacy policies around data use.

There are many businesses from small to large that will be managing IoT sensors in buildings of a workplace. Different companies will have different sensitivities and rules. For example, medical establishments, financial establishments and law firms have different legal requirements around patient and client data. Lawyers need to be sure that accidental audio recording is not moved to the wrong place when interacting with clients. Dueling needs of hospitals are well known - they must protect patient privacy, but at the same time would like to release summarized data to improve medical research. They could instantiate our privacy cloudlet by having the storage and mediator capabilities run on a hospital's IT infrastructure and have research efforts get data via interaction with mediators.

While our architecture is able to support a range of existing IoT business models we note that it may also stimulate entirely new areas of economic activity such as the supply and validation of mediators and associated drivers.

5. Challenging Use Cases

5.1 Human Augmentation

An area of intense research interest at present is the use of pervasive technologies to augment human capabilities such as memory [9]. Cameras, microphones and other environmental sensors can be coupled with wearable devices such as lifelogging cameras to provide rich datasets relating to a user's experiences. This data can potentially be processed and then used to cue recall of memories as required. Applications range from behaviour change and increased learning capacity to support for failing memories. To understand the challenges of such systems the authors conducted the RECALL experiment in which twenty researchers, wearing a range of lifelogging devices, spent two days in an instrumented hostel to capture a test dataset for memory augmentation [7]. Fixed infrastructure cameras throughout public areas of the hostel recorded a continuous video stream and participants were equipped with wearables such as smartphones, GoPros, Narrative Clips, SenseCams and DSLR cameras. Over 280GB of data was captured including 42,959 images and 248.15 hours of video and location data.

Clearly such a scenario raises a number of significant privacy concerns with potentially very large amounts of data being captured and users interacting with a wide range of sensors in the infrastructure [9]. However, the proposed architecture begins to provide an insight into how such systems could emerge while providing user control over privacy. For example, mediators running on a local cloudlet could redact a video feed to a few still images that are used as the basis of memory cues. To support memory augmentation more generally, mediators could eventually become complex pieces of software that locally determine which few elements of the sensor data needed to be exported – enabling most of the data to remain private within the user's local cloudlet.

While our architecture offers an obvious solution for domestic and work spaces, scenarios such as memory augmentation highlight the challenge of mobile users that wish to control the capture of data relating to them as they move between instrumented spaces. Our approach of using cloudlets to support code mobility provides a robust, scalable and secure means of allowing users to dynamically instantiate mediators into spaces that they temporarily access. Clearly trust relationships still need to exist between users and the spaces themselves but this is always likely to be the case (it is not possible to prevent, for example, a space owner deploying hidden cameras). However, where such trust relationships exist cloudlets would provide a natural way to support the dynamic instantiation of one or more mediators for a user that has temporarily appropriated a physical space such as a meeting room.

5.2 Omnipresent Video

Today, most video is stored in silos close to the point of capture. In the future, we envision many use cases in which analysis of multiple video streams and fusion of extracted information offers powerful benefits to users [24]. This requires today's isolated video cameras to be integrated into an IoT framework, posing challenges for scalability as well as privacy. The high cumulative data rate of incoming videos from many cameras is a key scalability challenge.

Our privacy architecture can also solve this scalability challenge by running video analytics on cloudlets. Simoens et al [27] have shown that denaturing and video analytics at throughput acceptable for a typical home are feasible on cloudlets of modest computational power. They recommend sampling an input video stream at a lower rate than the capture rate, and to perform video analytics and denaturing only on the sampled frames. They also suggest that raw video be stored encrypted on the cloudlet, and only de-

crypted and analyzed if an explicit need to examine that video is identified. All this functionality is supported by our architecture. Shipping the extracted tags and meta-data to the cloud only requires modest bandwidth.

Denaturing has to strike a balance between privacy and value. At one extreme is a blank video: perfect privacy, but zero value. At the other extreme is the original video at its capture resolution and frame rate. This has the highest value for potential customers, but also incurs the highest exposure of privacy. Where to strike the balance is a difficult question that is best answered individually, by each user. This decision will most probably be context-sensitive. One example is to blur all faces in an image; this only requires face detection, which is a standard capability in image processing software today. A more selective privacy policy might only require the faces of certain people to be blurred. That is considerably more difficult to implement, since face recognition is a much harder computer vision problem than face detection. Fortunately, we have been successful in creating an open source implementation of face recognition using deep neural networks called *OpenFace* that provides surprisingly high accuracy [2].

OpenFace can be used as a building block for IoT services running on a cloudlet. For example, when running on a laptop such as Macbook Air, OpenFace can train to learn a new face (e.g. guests in a home) in 10-20 seconds. Subsequent recognition takes about 500 ms in our prototype. Both of these functions can thus be performed without having to offload any video to the cloud. This serves as an illustration that even complex mediators can be implemented to run in private cloudlet architectures.

6. Related Work

Protecting user privacy has been extensively explored in the UbiComp community, e.g. informing users of potential privacy threats [14] and protecting user location data [6], [8]. Our work focuses on the use of privacy mediators. The idea of a rule-based trusted intermediary that controlled the release of location information was described in [18] and a similar, though more general solution was later proposed in [17] in which Personal Data Vaults were used to filter end-users' mobile sensor data before sharing it with content-service providers. Our work differs from these rule-based intermediaries by offering a generalized cloudlet infrastructure for intercepting both mobile and (predominantly) fixed sensor data.

In [3] the use of OSGI for hosting privacy interceptors in smart environments was explored – this approach has many parallels with our architecture but focuses on enforcing privacy policies relating to contextual data when requests for information are received (and thus is similar to [18]) rather than processing outgoing sensor streams. Moreover, the choice of OSGI as an underlying platform is obviously limiting compared to the more general support provided by cloudlets. Commercial firewalls for smart homes are beginning to appear (e.g. http://www.bitdefender.com/box/) but these typically focus on protecting the home from inbound traffic rather than protecting privacy through mediation of outbound traffic from uncompromised devices.

In [26] a decentralized infrastructure for social networking is proposed where each user's configurable"butler" provides fine-grained access control and storage. In contrast, we do not address the needs of social networking, nor focus on distributed storage, nor prevent the sending of sensor data to the cloud (instead we enable the latter at a user-chosen granularity). Other work in this field includes [12] that investigates on-device sensor abstractions for augmented reality applications to prevent private data from accidentally being leaked from applications having raw sensor data access.

7. Conclusion

In this position paper we addressed the challenge of helping the IoT bridge the impending "chasm" that blocks the path to widespread adoption. We have argued that privacy is a key issue and subsequently proposed an architecture based on an essential design principal, namely that users should maintain overall control of their data and be responsible for managing its release to cloud services. Our architecture provides a framework for addressing privacy requirements in traditional IoT environments and, crucially, through the use of cloudlets and mobile code enables the support of challenging IoT scenarios in the mobile domain including human augmentation and omnipresent video. We have focused herein primarily on home scenarios because that is where the need is most urgent for IoT. In our future work, we plan to study extensions of our architecture for public space IoT applications.

Acknowledgements

This research was partially funded through the National Science Foundation (NSF) under grant number CNS-1518865. Additional support was provided by Intel, Google, Vodafone, Crown Castle, and the Conklin Kistler family fund. Any opinions, findings, conclusions or recommendations expressed in this material are those of the authors and should not be attributed to their employers or funding sources.

8. REFERENCES

[1] H. Almuhimedi, F. Schaub, N. Sadeh, I. Adjerid, A. Acquisti, J. Gluck, L. Cranor, and Y. Agarwal. Your Location has been Shared 5,398 Times! A Field Study on Mobile App Privacy Nudging. In *Proc. of ACM CHI*, 2015.

[2] B. Amos. OpenFace: free and open source face recognition with deep neural networks. http://cmusatyalab.github.io/openface/, 2015.

[3] S. A. Bagüés, A. Zeidler, C. F. Valdivielso, and I. R. Matias. Sentry@Home-leveraging the smart home for privacy in pervasive computing. *International Journal of Smart Home*, 1(2):129–145, 2007.

[4] S. Banerjee and D. O. Wu. Final report from the NSF Workshop on Future Directions in Wireless Networking. NSF, November 2013.

[5] D. Barrett. One surveillance camera for every 11 people in Britain, says CCTV survey. *Daily Telegraph*, July 10, 2013.

[6] A. R. Beresford and F. Stajano. Location privacy in pervasive computing. *IEEE Pervasive Computing*, 2(1):46–55, Jan. 2003.

[7] S. Clinch, N. Davies, M. Mikusz, P. Metzger, M. Langheinrich, A. Schmidt, and G. Ward. Collecting shared experiences through lifelogging: Lessons learned. *Pervasive Computing, IEEE*, 15(1), 2016.

[8] C. Cornelius, A. Kapadia, D. Kotz, D. Peebles, M. Shin, and N. Triandopoulos. Anonysense: privacy-aware people-centric sensing. In *Proc. of ACM MobiSys*, pages 211–224, 2008.

[9] N. Davies, A. Friday, S. Clinch, C. Sas, M. Langheinrich, G. Ward, and A. Schmidt. Security and privacy implications of pervasive memory augmentation. *Pervasive Computing, IEEE*, 14(1), 2015.

[10] FTC Staff. Internet of Things: Privacy and Security in a Connected World. Technical report, Federal Trade Commission, January 2015.

[11] J. Groopman and S. Etlinger. Consumer Perceptions of Privacy in the Internet of Things: What Brands Can Learn from a Concerned Citizenry. Technical report, Altimeter Group, June 2015.

[12] S. Jana, D. Molnar, A. Moshchuk, A. M. Dunn, B. Livshits, H. J. Wang, and E. Ofek. Enabling fine-grained permissions for augmented reality applications with recognizers. In *USENIX Security*, pages 415–430, 2013.

[13] L. Kagal, T. Finin, and A. Joshi. A policy language for a pervasive computing environment. In *Proc. of IEEE POLICY*, 2003.

[14] M. Langheinrich. A privacy awareness system for ubiquitous computing environments. In *Proceedings of the 4th International Conference on Ubiquitous Computing*, UbiComp '02, pages 237–245, London, UK, UK, 2002. Springer-Verlag.

[15] B. Liu, J. Lin, and N. Sadeh. Reconciling mobile app privacy and usability on smartphones: could user privacy profiles help? In *Proc. of ACM WWW*, 2013.

[16] G. Moore. *Crossing the Chasm*. Harpercollins, 1991.

[17] M. Mun, S. Hao, N. Mishra, K. Shilton, J. Burke, D. Estrin, M. Hansen, and R. Govindan. Personal data vaults: a locus of control for personal data streams. In *Proc. of ACM CoNEXT*, page 17, 2010.

[18] G. Myles, A. Friday, and N. Davies. Preserving privacy in environments with location-based applications. *Pervasive Computing, IEEE*, 2(1), 2003.

[19] At&t hacker "weev" sentenced to 41 months in prison, after obtaining the email addresses of 100,000+ ipad users. https://nakedsecurity.sophos.com/2013/03/19/att-hacker-weev-prison/, 2013.

[20] http://bits.blogs.nytimes.com/2015/02/10/samsung-tweaks-television-policy-over-privacy-concerns/.

[21] C. News. Talking Barbie is too creepy for some parents. http://money.cnn.com/2015/03/11/news/companies/creepy-hello-barbie/, March 2015.

[22] M. Satyanarayanan, P. Bahl, R. Caceres, and N. Davies. The case for vm-based cloudlets in mobile computing. *Pervasive Computing, IEEE*, 8(4), 2009.

[23] M. Satyanarayanan, R. Schuster, M. Ebling, G. Fettweis, H. Flinck, K. Joshi, and K. Sabnani. An Open Ecosystem for Mobile-Cloud Convergence. *IEEE Communications Magazine*, (3), March 2015.

[24] M. Satyanarayanan, P. Simoens, Y. Xiao, P. Pillai, Z. Chen, K. Ha, W. Hu, and B. Amos. Edge analytics in the internet of things. *Pervasive Computing, IEEE*, 14(2), 2015.

[25] I. Scales. Is IoT going to be squashed because of privacy concerns? http://www.telecomtv.com/articles/iot/is-iot-going-to-be-squashed-because-of-privacy-concerns-12647/, June 2015.

[26] S.-W. Seong, J. Seo, M. Nasielski, D. Sengupta, S. Hangal, S. K. Teh, R. Chu, B. Dodson, and M. S. Lam. Prpl: a decentralized social networking infrastructure. In *Proc. of ACM MCS '10*, page 8, 2010.

[27] P. Simoens, Y. Xiao, P. Pillai, Z. Chen, K. Ha, and M. Satyanarayanan. Scalable Crowd-Sourcing of Video from Mobile Devices. In *Proc. of ACM MobiSys*, 2013.

[28] Health insurer didn't encrypt data in theft. http://www.wsj.com/articles/investigators-eye-china-in-anthem-hack-1423167560, 2015.

[29] R. Want, B. N. Schilit, and S. Jenson. Enabling the Internet of Things. *IEEE Computer*, 48(1), Jan 2015.

[30] T. Weng, A. Nwokafor, and Y. Agarwal. Buildingdepot 2.0: An integrated management system for building analysis and control. In *Proc. of ACM BuildSys*, 2013.

[31] W. Willet, P. Aoki, N. Kumar, S. Subramanian, and A. Woodruff. Common sense community: Scaffolding mobile sensing and analysis for mobile users. In *Pervasive Computing Conference*, 2010.

How to Safely Augment Reality: Challenges and Directions

Kiron Lebeck, Tadayoshi Kohno, Franziska Roesner
University of Washington
{kklebeck, yoshi, franzi}@cs.washington.edu

ABSTRACT

Augmented reality (AR) technologies, such as those in head-mounted displays like Microsoft HoloLens or in automotive windshields, are poised to change how people interact with their devices and the physical world. Though researchers have begun considering the security, privacy, and safety issues raised by these technologies, to date such efforts have focused on *input*, i.e., how to limit the amount of private information to which AR applications receive access. In this work, we focus on the challenge of *output* management: how can an AR operating system allow multiple concurrently running applications to safely augment the user's view of the world? That is, how can the OS prevent apps from (for example) interfering with content displayed by other apps or the user's perception of critical real-world context, while still allowing them sufficient flexibility to implement rich, immersive AR scenarios? We explore the design space for the management of visual AR output, propose a design that balances OS control with application flexibility, and lay out the research directions raised and enabled by this proposal.

1. INTRODUCTION

Augmented reality (AR) technologies redefine the boundaries between physical and virtual worlds. Rather than presenting virtual content distinct from the physical world, AR applications integrate virtual content "into" the physical world by collecting sensory information about the user's surroundings and overlaying virtual augmentations on the user's view of the real world. These technologies are unique in their potential for immersive mixed reality (i.e., combined physical and virtual) experiences, with applications ranging from assistive technologies to driving aids and home entertainment. Moreover, sophisticated AR applications that run on immersive platforms like Head Mounted Displays (HMDs) and cars are not hypothetical—industry efforts by companies like Microsoft and BMW have demonstrated that these technologies are real and on the horizon [3, 11, 21].

Today's typical AR applications run on conventional devices (e.g., smartphones) in their own isolated contexts. For example, the smartphone application WordLens[1] detects and translates text in real time using the phone's camera. How-

[1] http://questvisual.com/

ever, as AR platforms continue to evolve and move from mobile phones to more immersive devices such as Microsoft's HoloLens [11], they can provide richer experiences by running *multiple* applications that simultaneously augment a *shared* environment. For example, a HoloLens user may wish to play an AR video game while simultaneously running Skype in the background (applications shown in Figure 1).

While AR applications have diverse potential, they also raise a number of challenging security, privacy, and safety issues [16]. Prior research efforts (e.g., [9,17]) have focused largely on addressing *input* privacy issues that stem from applications receiving unrestricted sensor access, such as the ability for applications to record videos of a user's sensitive possessions or audio of private conversations. However, little work has looked at the risks and challenges presented by unregulated, and possibly malicious, application *outputs*—for example, a buggy or malicious car application could display distracting images to interfere with the driver's focus. While ensuring the safety and security of an individual application's output is already challenging (as we will see), these issues become particularly salient with the increasingly complex interactions of multiple applications augmenting a shared environment, where applications may attempt to display overlapping content, either coincidentally or maliciously (e.g., to mount a denial-of-service attack).

In this work, we begin to address the safety and security of AR visual output. We lay out design alternatives for visual output models, and in doing so we surface challenges in balancing the flexibility of application functionality with the system's ability to control and mitigate risks from application outputs. We provide initial directions for overcoming these challenges by rethinking the role of the operating system in managing visual AR outputs. Our exploration raises directions and guidelines for future work in this space.

2. BACKGROUND AND MOTIVATION

We begin with several example AR scenarios, followed by the risks and challenges that these scenarios may raise.

2.1 Example AR Systems: The Opportunities

We first present two illustrative case studies that capture the diverse potential of AR technology: automotive AR and HMDs. We focus on these scenarios, rather than mobile phone-based AR, because they are immersive, intended for continuous use, and naturally cater to multiple concurrently running applications. However, mobile phone-based AR scenarios will also face many or all the issues we raise here.

We note that although the physical displays on which AR content is drawn—in our examples, automotive windshields and HMDs—are fundamentally two-dimensional screens, applications may display both 2D content (e.g., informational overlays) as well as content that appears visually 3D. Dis-

Figure 1: From the left — HoloLens demo showcasing multiple Windows 10 applications; HoloLens demo of a mixed-reality game that maps out the user's physical environment and displays world-aware virtual content; BMW prototype AR glasses that provide the driver with 'X-ray vision' by syncing with the car's external cameras.

played content may be static (e.g., always in the bottom of the screen) or it may need to adjust dynamically as the user moves and/or the real-world environment changes.

Automotive. Recent years have seen substantial growth in automotive AR efforts [12]. For example, technology by Continental[2] overlays 2D information (e.g., current speed limit and navigational arrows) on a car's windshield, and BMW has proposed "X-Ray Vision" (shown in Figure 1) that allows the driver to see through the body of the car [3]. Other efforts aim to display more immersive 3D augmentations. Recent work from Honda Research [23] uses 3D visual cues to aid drivers in making left turns. Honda researchers have also discussed integrating other visual elements into the car's 3D display, such as road signs or street addresses.[3]

Head Mounted Displays (HMDs). HMDs represent another class of AR platforms rapidly gaining traction. Although the idea of AR HMDs has been around for some time [20], products such as Microsoft's HoloLens and Magic Leap's AR headset are leading industry efforts to bring this technology to production. These platforms have the potential to support a range of applications — Microsoft recently showcased several HoloLens applications (Figure 1) such as an AR video player, a 3D weather app, and a video game that places virtual characters into the user's view of the real world.[4,5] These applications highlight the ability of emerging platforms, like HoloLens, to display 3D content that exists in and interacts with some model of the user's world.

2.2 The Risks and Challenges

AR applications can provide uniquely immersive experiences; however, this ability can lead to undesirable consequences if the applications are buggy or malicious. As prior work [6] notes, today's AR apps typically operate with the unrestricted ability to access sensor inputs and render augmentations. Since applications may not always be trusted by the user or by the OS,[6] this model raises a number of security, privacy, and safety issues. Even if AR platforms only allow apps from trusted developers — a policy perhaps especially reasonable for cars — it is still critical to ensure that buggy applications cannot accidentally misbehave.

Input Privacy. Unrestricted sensor access by applications

---

[2]http://continental-head-up-display.com/

[3]https://www.youtube.com/watch?v=OgsrFAe_Lgc

[4]https://www.youtube.com/watch?v=gnlIEnHIJ7o

[5]https://www.youtube.com/watch?v=3AADEqLIALk

[6]Like prior work, we assume that the OS is trustworthy and trusted by the user.

is a major privacy problem. Consider an HMD user in his or her home. Without safeguards, applications may be able to see sensitive information like medications. Prior efforts have focused on addressing visual input privacy (e.g., [9, 10, 14, 17, 22]). For example, one set of strategies leverages trusted OS modules to mediate sensor access for applications. Jana et al. propose the recognizer abstraction [9] as an OS module for fine-grained sensory access control, and Roesner et al. extend this model [17] to accommodate object- or environment-specific access control policies. The left and middle columns of Figure 2 depict the AR system pipeline from [17], which consists of system sensors, system recognizers, an input policy module, and applications. The system sensors collect information from the world, e.g., video from a camera. An OS module then recognizes objects, such as people or stop signs, and the policy module evaluates the relevant privacy (and other) policies to determine which recognized objects to communicate to which applications.

Output Safety and Security. While the above works make significant progress towards limiting the flow of sensitive sensor information *to* applications, they do not mitigate malicious or buggy outputs *from* applications. Output may take multiple forms, including visual, audio, and haptic feedback. In this work, we focus on managing visual outputs, because most of today's AR applications display visual content. We propose a new output module for the AR pipeline, shown in the right column of Figure 2. Absent defenses, a buggy or malicious application could overwrite the output of another application, display content that blocks or obscures real-world content, or display content that distracts (and possibly endangers) the user. By exploring the design space for our new output module, we establish a trajectory for defending against such threats. We consider several axes along which malicious or buggy output might occur:

- *Who* (i.e., which application) displayed particular content. Knowing this could, for example, be useful in disambiguating content generated by a phishing application or advertisement from content generated by a legitimate banking or route guidance application.

- *What* kind of content a particular application can draw. For example, should an automotive application be able to draw virtual pedestrians on the road?

- *When* an application can draw, based on the context of the user's actions or environment. For example, could an HMD texting application pop up a full-screen message when the user is doing something potentially hazardous, like walking down stairs?

- *Where* an application can draw, both on the display

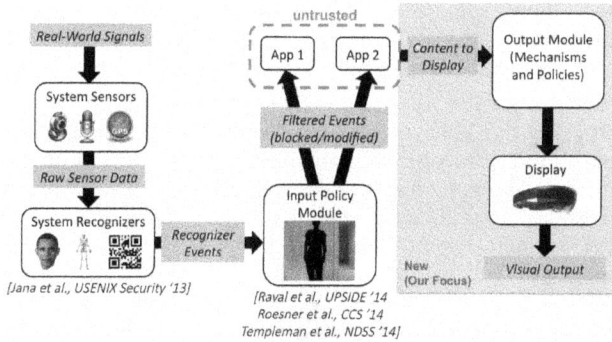

Figure 2: Pipeline for how data flows through an AR system and applications. Prior work focused on the operating system's role in processing and dispatching (possibly privacy-sensitive) input to applications. We extend this pipeline with an **output module** and explore the operating system's role in managing the visual content (i.e., augmentations) that applications wish to display.

(i.e., with respect to the user's "screen") and within the world (i.e., with respect to specific objects or 3D regions in the world). For example, could an automotive application render an ad on top of a road sign?

To our knowledge, existing research efforts and commercial systems have not explored solutions to address AR output safety and security. However, before AR systems can be widely adopted, it is critical to design mechanisms to ensure they are safe and secure, without significantly hindering the expressiveness of applications. Computer security is a form of risk management, and hence the full spectrum of adversarial actions that we discuss might never manifest. Nevertheless, our goal is to provide a technical foundation for mitigating such threats *if* they do arise.

3. DESIGN SPACE EXPLORATION

In this section, we explore several possible designs for the output module of the AR pipeline (Figure 2), focusing on visual output. The roles of the output module are: (1) to provide a mechanism for applications to specify and display visual content, and (2) to apply safety, security, and privacy policies by interposing on the rendering of this content. Our key questions in exploring this design space are: what role should the operating system play in managing visual output, and how should that role be realized? How can we design an output module to enable flexible application behaviors while mitigating risks from malicious or buggy applications? Our earlier case studies and the above-mentioned risks motivate two important design axes for managing visual AR outputs:

1. *Flexibility:* The ability of honest, non-buggy applications to display AR content. Ideally, an output module does not prevent honest applications from implementing and innovating on desirable AR functionality, including through possible interactions between apps.

2. *Control:* The operating system's ability to prevent applications from drawing malicious or undesirable AR content (e.g., "undesirable" in the automotive context may mean safety-critical distractions of the driver, or occlusion of safety-critical objects like road signs).

We now explore how these two axes play out in the design space of visual output models. We first consider two natural output models: the *windowing model* used by traditional platforms (e.g., desktops) and an alternate strawman approach in which applications can *free-draw* AR content.

(We consider these models as discrete points in a design space, though of course changes to the implementation of one model could allow it to take on characteristics of another.) We find that windowing overly constrains visual output flexibility, while free-drawing overemphasizes flexibility at the expense of control. We thus introduce a novel model based on *fine-grained AR objects* that provides better flexibility than windows and better control than free-drawing.

We assume that applications can receive input about the real world to make decisions about how and where to display augmentations, possibly dynamically updating these decisions as the user's real-world view changes. For privacy reasons, applications may receive such input with varying degrees of fidelity (e.g., raw sensor input, recognizer events [9], or information about real-world surfaces [25]), but we do not focus on the problem of input privacy in this work.

3.1 Model 1: Windowing

We first consider how the traditional desktop windowing model translates to the AR context. Under this model, the OS delegates control of separate *windows* to applications — rectangular display spaces in which they may draw arbitrary content. Windows are typically isolated from each other, so that one application cannot read content from or manipulate content in another's window. Given that this model is well established in desktop systems, it seems natural to extend it to AR — and, indeed, it appears that HoloLens utilizes such a model in running Universal Windows applications.[7]

With traditional windows, applications can display content in roughly the following manner:

1. The OS gives applications handles to separate windows corresponding to bounded regions of the display. Traditionally, windows are rectangular; in the AR context, they may represent 3D rather than 2D regions that map to the user's real-world environment. Users can typically resize and reposition these windows.

2. Applications render arbitrary content to their respective windows by calling some `draw` function that interfaces directly with graphics hardware.

Under this model, different applications cannot occupy the same display region simultaneously — if two windows overlap, only one can be in focus at a time (i.e., one window occludes the other and receives inputs). Similarly, if one application is in "full-screen" mode, in most of today's systems, this means that only it can display content. Though some windowing implementations allow transparent windows or embedded windows (e.g., iframes on the web), display region sharing with windows is limited to these features.

Control. Under this model, application outputs are isolated, and content is rendered at the window granularity. This gives the system coarse-grained control: applications can only draw inside their own windows, and they cannot autonomously reposition or resize those windows. As a result, an application cannot draw over arbitrary regions of the screen (e.g., the road viewed through an AR windshield) unless the user or the system has explicitly placed its window there. However, the system is not able to enforce finer-grained properties, like where the application can draw *within* the window. It also cannot enforce requirements on arbitrary content the application draws inside its window.

---

[7]https://msdn.microsoft.com/en-us/library/windows/apps/dn726767.aspx

47

Flexibility. The windowing model also presents flexibility challenges for multiple applications running simultaneously. While it may suffice for applications whose content fits naturally inside a bounded window, such as the HoloLens video player, it may not suit others. Consider the HoloLens game in Figure 1. If the objects and characters in the game are intended to behave like real-world objects (e.g., to move about within and interact with the user's world), the application needs to render contextually with respect to the user's world. If the application does so in full screen mode, it either prevents other applications from rendering any content at all or, if multiple applications can overlay partially transparent full-screen windows, its content may arbitrarily overlap or conflict with the content of other applications in a way that cannot be controlled at a fine granularity by the OS.

3.2 Model 2: Free-Drawing

Given the flexibility limitations of traditional windowing, we next consider a point in the design space that is intentionally flexible, allowing applications to "free-draw" anywhere within the user's view, at any time. More precisely:

1. The OS gives applications handles to a shared window corresponding to the device's full display.
2. The applications each call a `draw` function to display 2D or 3D content in this shared environment.

Flexibility. This model provides maximum flexibility for applications, which can draw arbitrarily to provide desirable AR functionality unencumbered by the assumptions embedded in the traditional windowing model. With free-drawing (and sufficient information about the user's world), applications can track and augment any objects in the user's view and visually interact with content from other applications.

Control. Unfortunately, the flexibility this model provides to honest applications also enables malicious or buggy applications to more easily display undesirable content. Without restrictions, an app could display content that disorients or visually impairs the user, or that endangers the user by occluding or modifying possibly safety-critical real-world objects. Consider the car case study. With no output restrictions, a malicious app could occlude pedestrians or road signs, potentially causing physical harm to users and bystanders. Furthermore, with multiple applications free-drawing simultaneously, applications may directly interfere with or extract information from each other's visual content. These risks are greater than with isolated windows, even if those windows are partially transparent or overlapping. Thus, while allowing applications to free-draw supports flexible rendering needs, it also provides the OS with no capability to prevent or constrain malicious behavior, nor to isolate content from different applications.

3.3 Model 3: Fine-Grained AR Objects

The above models require trading off flexibility for coarse-grained output control. We desire a visual output model that provides *both* flexibility for honest applications as well as more fine-grained output control for the system. To achieve this goal, we introduce a new AR output model based on fine-grained objects. *The key idea is to manage visual content at the granularity of **AR objects** rather than windows.* Objects are abstract representations of AR content that applications wish to place into the user's view of the world, such as 3D virtual pets or 2D informational over-

lays. In the windowing and free-drawing models, applications must manage these objects internally. Our proposed model elevates these objects to first-class OS primitives.

Flexibility and Control. Object-level granularity provides key flexibility and control benefits. Applications can create and draw objects throughout the user's view of the world; however, by making these objects first-class OS primitives, the system can enforce rich object-based constraints and dynamically manage *where* and *when* objects can be drawn, as well as how objects from different applications can interact. For example, an AR car system could prevent applications from drawing over critical objects such as road signs while still allowing applications such as navigation to display content (e.g., direction arrows) dynamically throughout the world. In some cases, the system may even be able to regulate *what* objects an application draws, to the extent that the semantics of certain objects are known to the OS. For example, the system might only allow objects that follow a certain template to overlay on top of road signs.

Concrete Instantiation. There are many possible implementation strategies — for example, one might start with a windowing model and modify the definition of a window to bound arbitrary 3D objects, or one might start from scratch. Our goal is not to propose or evaluate specific implementations or APIs, but rather to explore AR objects as first-class OS primitives. Nevertheless, we present a strawman output module design, which allows us to illustrate this idea more concretely and raise important design questions:

1. AR objects consist of visual descriptors (e.g., 3D meshes and textures) and optional "physical properties" (e.g., how the objects should respond to collisions).
2. To display content, applications request the OS to draw particular objects with certain requirements. For example, apps might request specific display coordinates or locations relative to other application or real-world objects (e.g., to display labels on real-world faces).
3. The OS processes object placement requests, along with *constraints* from a variety of parties (e.g., applications, the user, or the system itself) and contextual information about the current world state (e.g., the current speed of the car). The OS then decides which requests are permissible (or modifies requests) and renders the appropriate visual content.

This model enables several desirable properties:

OS Support for Dynamic Updates. The OS can dynamically update and redraw objects in response to user actions (e.g., head movement) or changes in the real world, rather than requiring applications to handle these changes manually.

Shared World. The OS can position application content in a shared world and manage physics-based (and other) interactions between application and real-world objects. For example, applications might register for system-based events, like collisions between objects, and define how to respond to these events. We further discuss the system's possible roles in managing these interactions in Section 4.

Subsuming Previous Models. The ability to handle a rich set of possible constraints allows an object-based model to *subsume* both the windowing model and the free-drawing model. Constraints based on logical windows, or the lack of any constraints, would emulate these models, respectively.

Contextual Tuning. Object-level granularity allows the OS

to contextually tune how strictly it applies controls, since permissible behavior may vary based on user preferences, application needs, and/or real-world context. For example, content that can safely be displayed on an AR windshield while a car is parked differs significantly from content that can safely be displayed while the car is in motion. With object-level control, and some notion of object semantics, the system can contextually tune which application outputs are controlled and how. This type of control is not achievable with a coarser-grained windowing model, which can control only where and whether an application can display.

Summary. Our key insight is that, by managing visual output at the granularity of objects rather than in windows or the full display, the OS can enable flexible application behaviors while *simultaneously* preventing them from displaying undesirable content. Instantiating such a model, however, requires rethinking rendering abstractions and interactions between applications. Future AR systems must consider these issues if they are to provide both rich experiences as well as output safety and security for users.

4. CHALLENGES AND OPPORTUNITIES

We now dive more deeply into the design and research questions that our object-based output model raises, as well as the novel opportunities it enables.

4.1 Key Design Challenges

We first consider a set of important design questions that must be addressed to realize an object-based output model.

Defining Objects and Rendering APIs. Two key considerations in supporting fine-grained, object-level augmentation control are — how should the OS define objects, and what kind of APIs should it expose to applications for displaying content? We presented a strawman API in Section 3.3, but carefully designing these APIs to minimize the burden on application developers will be critical.

Constraint Specification and Evaluation. Important object management questions we have not yet addressed are: according to what *constraints or policies* should the OS do this management, who specifies these constraints, how are they expressed, and how are they evaluated? For example, reasonable constraints in an automotive AR environment might be that applications cannot display ads or overlay objects on real-world traffic signs while the car is in motion. However, these constraints may change contextually (e.g., the car may permit ads to be shown when the vehicle is stopped). Furthermore, different parties — applications, the system, external regulatory agencies, or the user — may have conflicting preferences. Key research questions are how the OS should allow multiple parties to specify policies or constraints, how to evaluate potentially conflicting constraints in real time, and how to manage conflicts when they arise.

Managing Objects in a Shared Environment. Our object-based model allows the OS to mediate interactions between augmentations from different applications within a shared environment, though exactly what this role should be raises open questions. How much information about the real world do applications need to intelligently position (or specify constraints for the positions of) their objects? What kind of feedback should the OS provide to applications when their objects interact with each other or the physical world

(e.g., a virtual ball bouncing on the real-world floor) given that such feedback might leak private information about one application to another? How should the OS handle possibly malicious object interactions, such as one app that tries to draw over another app's object and occlude it from view? These questions highlight some of the unique challenges that immersive multi-application AR platforms may encounter.

4.2 New Capabilities

We next explore how our object-based model allows the OS to take on new roles in supporting AR applications.

OS Support for Object Semantics. Our model allows the OS to dynamically manage the interactions of application objects with each other and the real world, significantly reducing the burden on application developers to reposition objects as the user's view changes. Going one step further, the OS could *natively support* certain AR objects (e.g., people) in addition to abstract objects, by allowing applications to register objects under pre-defined classes. This design allows the OS to have a semantic understanding of certain objects and to more intelligently manage their interactions. For example, it would enable an output policy such as "applications may draw only pre-approved types of objects on top of streets while the user is driving" — a significantly more flexible policy than disallowing any drawing at all, while still maintaining safety properties. However, applications may wish to display diverse types of objects, and natively supporting all possible classes of objects is infeasible. A key question for AR system designers is thus what role, if any, the OS should take in providing native object support.

Supporting Novel Inter-App Interactions. While some amount of inter-application feedback is necessary to maintain a consistent world state within a shared environment (e.g., so applications know when their objects collide), an open question is — to what extent should applications be aware of each other? Object-level granularity raises interesting new possibilities for how applications can interact. For example, could an application take as input not only real-world objects, like faces, detected by system recognizers (as proposed in prior work [9]), but also virtual objects created by other applications? A plausible use case would be a translation application such as WordLens that takes as input not only real-world text, but also text generated by other (single-language) applications. This degree of interaction could enable powerful new AR scenarios, but it raises new challenges as well: for example, could applications manipulate their virtual objects to attack other applications that take these objects as input? Whether and how best to support such interactions must be carefully considered.

5. RELATED WORK

Researchers have explored applications and technical challenges surrounding AR for decades (e.g., [1,2,5,13,20,24,27]). However, only recently have these technologies become commercially available, and only recently have researchers begun seriously considering the security, privacy, and safety concerns associated with AR (e.g., [6,16]). Most technical work to date has focused on *input* privacy (e.g., [9,10,14,17,22]); in this paper we consider the challenge of *output* safety and security. Surround Web [25] considers both AR input and output issues, in that it limits the amount of real-world input applications need to decide where and what to display;

its techniques are complementary to ours. Some of the issues that we raise—e.g., the need to consider AR output security at all—have also been identified previously [6,16], but we expand on these directions here and make significant progress toward developing a visual output model for AR that balances OS control and application flexibility.

Related earlier efforts in the AR space have studied multi-application settings [18] and world-aware virtual objects [4]. These works do not consider security explicitly, but our object-based model could incorporate some of these earlier ideas. These works both also consider multi-user settings, which we do not consider—though we observe that they will raise interesting additional security and privacy questions.

More generally, prior work has considered display security in non-AR contexts, including secure window systems (e.g., [7,19,26]), shared cross-application UIs (e.g., iframes on the web or research proposals for smartphones [15]), and non-AR automotive displays (e.g., [8]). Though some shared issues arise in these other contexts, the complexity of AR scenarios (with virtual 3D objects and real-world interactions) raises significant new challenges.

6. CONCLUSION

Immersive AR platforms, such as Microsoft's HoloLens, are quickly becoming a reality. However, fundamental security and privacy challenges exist. Past works largely consider the privacy implications of visual *inputs* available to AR applications. We initiate a complementary investigation into the security risks of visual AR *outputs*. For example, multi-application AR systems need mitigations to prevent malicious or buggy applications from displaying content that blocks the outputs of other applications, or that occludes critical real-world objects (e.g., traffic signals or stairs). Our key technical proposal is to enable operating system control over visual output at the granularity of individual *AR objects* that are owned by applications and correspond to items with which the applications wish to augment the user's view. We provide an initial design and reflect upon how it can enable safer, diverse multi-application AR environments.

7. ACKNOWLEDGEMENTS

We thank Linda Ng Boyle and David Molnar for valuable discussions, as well as Antoine Bosselut and Suman Nath for helpful feedback on earlier drafts. This work was supported in part by NSF grants CNS-0846065, CNS-0963695, and CNS-1513584 and the Short-Dooley Professorship. This material is based on research sponsored by DARPA under agreement number FA8750-12-2-0107. The U.S. Government is authorized to reproduce and distribute reprints for Governmental purposes notwithstanding any copyright notation thereon.

8. REFERENCES

[1] R. Azuma, Y. Baillot, R. Behringer, S. Feiner, S. Julier, and B. MacIntyre. Recent advances in augmented reality. *IEEE Computer Graphics and Applications*, 21(6):34–47, 2001.

[2] R. T. Azuma. A survey of augmented reality. *Presence: Teleoperators and Virtual Environments*, 6:355–385, 1997.

[3] R. Baldwin. Mini's weird-looking AR goggles are actually useful, Apr. 2015. http://www.engadget.com/2015/04/22/bmw-mini-qualcomm-ar/.

[4] A. Butz, T. Höllerer, S. Feiner, B. MacIntyre, and C. Beshers. Enveloping users and computers in a collaborative 3D augmented reality. In *IEEE/ACM International Workshop on Augmented Reality*, 1999.

[5] E. Costanza, A. Kunz, and M. Fjeld. Human machine interaction. chapter Mixed Reality: A Survey, pages 47–68. Springer-Verlag, 2009.

[6] L. D'Antoni, A. Dunn, S. Jana, T. Kohno, B. Livshits, D. Molnar, A. Moshchuk, E. Ofek, F. Roesner, S. Saponas, et al. Operating system support for augmented reality applications. *Hot Topics in Operating Systems (HotOS)*, 2013.

[7] J. Epstein, J. McHugh, and R. Pascale. Evolution of a trusted B3 window system prototype. In *IEEE Symposium on Security and Privacy*, 1992.

[8] S. Gansel, S. Schnitzer, A. Gilbeau-Hammoud, V. Friesen, F. Dürr, K. Rothermel, and C. Maihöfer. An access control concept for novel automotive HMI systems. In *ACM Symposium on Access Control Models and Technologies*, 2014.

[9] S. Jana, D. Molnar, A. Moshchuk, A. M. Dunn, B. Livshits, H. J. Wang, and E. Ofek. Enabling fine-grained permissions for augmented reality applications with recognizers. In *USENIX Security*, 2013.

[10] S. Jana, A. Narayanan, and V. Shmatikov. A Scanner Darkly: Protecting user privacy from perceptual applications. In *IEEE Symposium on Security and Privacy*, 2013.

[11] L. Mathews. Microsoft's HoloLens demo steals the show at Build 2015, 2015. http://www.geek.com/microsoft/microsofts-hololens-demo-steals-the-show-at-build-2015-1621727/.

[12] M. May. Augmented reality in the car industry, Aug. 2015. https://www.linkedin.com/pulse/augmented-reality-car-industry-melanie-may.

[13] G. Papagiannakis, G. Singh, and N. Magnenat-Thalmann. A survey of mobile and wireless technologies for augmented reality systems. *Computer Animation and Virtual Worlds*, 19:3–22, 2008.

[14] N. Raval, A. Srivastava, K. Lebeck, L. Cox, and A. Machanavajjhala. Markit: privacy markers for protecting visual secrets. In *Workshop on Usable Privacy & Security for wearable and domestic ubIquitous DEvices (UPSIDE)*, 2014.

[15] F. Roesner and T. Kohno. Securing embedded user interfaces: Android and beyond. In *USENIX Security Symposium*, 2013.

[16] F. Roesner, T. Kohno, and D. Molnar. Security and privacy for augmented reality systems. *Communications of the ACM*, 57(4):88–96, 2014.

[17] F. Roesner, D. Molnar, A. Moshchuk, T. Kohno, and H. J. Wang. World-driven access control for continuous sensing. In *ACM Conf. on Computer & Communications Security*, 2014.

[18] D. Schmalstieg, A. Fuhrmann, G. Hesina, Z. Szalavári, L. M. Encarnaçao, M. Gervautz, and W. Purgathofer. The studierstube augmented reality project. *Presence: Teleoperators and Virtual Environments*, 11(1):33–54, 2002.

[19] J. S. Shapiro, J. Vanderburgh, E. Northup, and D. Chizmadia. Design of the EROS trusted window system. In *13th USENIX Security Symposium*, 2004.

[20] I. E. Sutherland. A head-mounted three-dimensional display. In *Fall Joint Computer Conference, American Federation of Information Processing Societies*, 1968.

[21] A. Tarantola. HoloLens 'Project XRay' lets you blast robot armies with a ray gun fist, Oct. 2015. http://www.engadget.com/2015/10/06/hololens-project-x-lets-you-blast-robot-armies-with-a-ray-gun/.

[22] R. Templeman, M. Korayem, D. Crandall, and A. Kapadia. PlaceAvoider: Steering first-person cameras away from sensitive spaces. In *Network and Distributed System Security Symposium (NDSS)*, 2014.

[23] C. Tran, K. Bark, and V. Ng-Thow-Hing. A left-turn driving aid using projected oncoming vehicle paths with augmented reality. In *5th International Conference on Automotive User Interfaces and Interactive Vehicular Applications*, 2013.

[24] D. van Krevelen and R. Poelman. A survey of augmented reality technologies, applications, and limitations. *The International Journal of Virtual Reality*, 9:1–20, 2010.

[25] J. Vilk, A. Moshchuk, D. Molnar, B. Livshits, E. Ofek, C. Rossbach, H. J. Wang, and R. Gal. SurroundWeb: Mitigating privacy concerns in a 3D web browser. In *IEEE Symposium on Security and Privacy*, 2015.

[26] J. P. L. Woodward. Security requirements for system high and compartmented mode workstations. Technical Report MTR 9992, Rev. 1 (also published by the Defense Intelligence Agency as DDS-2600-5502-87), MITRE Corporation, Nov. 1987.

[27] F. Zhou, H. B.-L. Duh, and M. Billinghurst. Trends in augmented reality tracking, interaction and display: a review of ten years of ISMAR. In *7th IEEE/ACM International Symposium on Mixed and Augmented Reality*, 2008.

A Picture is Worth a Thousand Words: Improving Mobile Messaging with Real-time Autonomous Image Suggestion

Joon-Gyum Kim
Korea Advanced Institute of
Science and Technology
kjkpoi@kaist.ac.kr

Chia-Wei Wu
University of Technology of
Belfort-Montbéliard
chia-wei.wu@utbm.fr

Alvin Chiang
National Taiwan University of
Science and Technology
M10115088@mail.ntust.edu.tw

JeongGil Ko
Ajou University

jgko@ajou.ac.kr

Sung-Ju Lee
Korea Advanced Institute of
Science and Technology
sjlee@cs.kaist.ac.kr

ABSTRACT

Text messaging on smartphones has become one of the most popular communication methods. With many smartphone chat applications, text messaging no longer is only "text"; users send emoticons to express emotions or share pictures stored on their phones. We believe that providing more visuals in chat applications by autonomously suggesting proper images from the Internet (i.e., "auto complete" with images), based on the chat content, is the next evolution of mobile messaging. Realizing this simple vision however, is a difficult task due to the intrinsic nature of mobile chat and resource limitations of smartphones. We identify these challenges and to overcome them, we suggest integrating solutions from the field of mobile computing, natural language processing, sentiment analysis, machine learning, storage, human computer interaction, networking, and systems. We present *MilliCat*, a lightweight mobile messaging service that autonomously suggests images based on chat context to improve emotion expression, nuance delivery, and information delivery of a conversation. Experimental results from our preliminary prototype implementation show promises that real-time autonomous image suggestion can provide timely, proper images while only incurring manageable networking and energy overhead.

Keywords

Mobile messaging; Image suggestion

1. INTRODUCTION

Rapid advancements in wireless communications and the wide popularity of smartphones have diversified how everyday users communicate with each other from voice-based phone calls to text messaging services and even video chat.

HotMobile '16, February 26-27, 2016, St. Augustine, FL, USA

© 2016 ACM. ISBN 978-1-4503-4145-5/16/02... $15.00

DOI: http://dx.doi.org/10.1145/2873587.2873602

Unlike short messaging services (SMS) over cellular networks, now with smartphones, using wireless data networks and a variety of text messaging applications, users can freely exchange text (and image) messages with no additional cost beyond their data plans. Such financial factors, combined with the changes in cultural aspects, have catalyzed the usage of smartphone messaging services. A recent report on the smartphone usage patterns of U.S. users show that text messaging is now the most widely used smartphone feature, exceeding the use of Internet access and voice/video calls [8].

However, when analyzing the functionalities of many messaging applications, their features are only slightly advanced than the basic SMS features of low-end feature phones. Specifically, these services are mostly based on a texting screen with minimal multimedia support. In a sense, while these applications use the wireless network to exchange text message data, they still lack the capability of connecting the users with the large amount of data available on the Internet as they exchange messages with their peers. Improved hardware resources of the smartphone allows for a user to not only "use" the wireless networks (as a communication medium), but also allows for a number of interactive services to be combined with the texting environment. As an example, based on the text message inputs of the users, a service can potentially provide real-time image suggestions to provide users with a chance to better express their feelings and deliver more visible information.

There are many text messaging applications on smartphones (e.g., native apps, WhatsApp, Google Hangouts, Facebook Messenger, Skype, SnapChat, and popular apps in the Asian market such as WeChat, Line, and Kakao Talk) but their additional features, besides texting, mostly focus on enabling video/voice chat and customizable skins. While users can share images, it's largely for pictures already stored locally on their phones. Recently, some services added new features for image sharing. Facebook Messenger for example, allows users to send trending animated memes using external applications such as GIPHY, but mostly focuses on "funny situations" and may not reflect emotions during conversations. Kakao Talk has a search feature initiated by typing "#". This feature searches the Internet for a wide variety of contents, including dictionary, music, blog, twitter, and application search. While providing some useful information, it can potentially waste energy and bandwidth

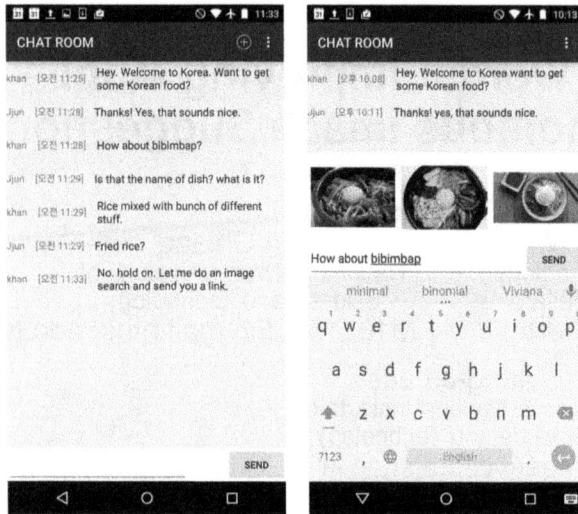

(a) Typical messaging applications usage.   (b) MilliCat usage.

Figure 1: Illustration of MilliCat operations in use compared with traditional smartphone messaging.

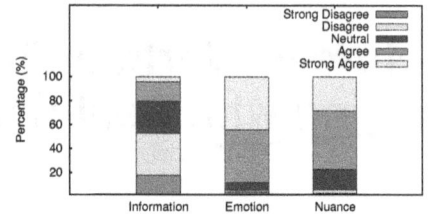

(a) Image usage purposes.

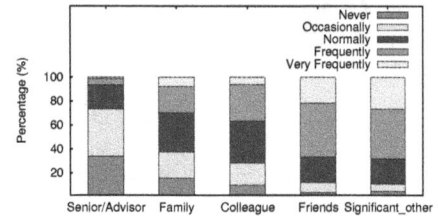

(b) Image exchanging peers.

Figure 2: Purposes of using images on smartphone messaging applications and peers to whom images are typically used.

resources by overloading users with too much information, of which, mostly, a user may not be interested in.

In this work, we present *MilliCat*, a smartphone messaging service that analyzes the messages being entered by the user to *automatically* identify a proper image on the Internet and provides the search results as real-time suggestions to the user. We can think of this as an "auto complete" with images. As we illustrate in Figure 1, with MilliCat, users get real-time image suggestions on their input text.[1] For many conversations, such a feature can benefit the overall flow of the conversation and save the user from manual external application interaction.

We start this work with a user survey conducted with 250+ active smartphone users around the world on their preferences of image usage while using text messaging applications on smartphones. Our survey reveals that regardless of the gender and age groups, users agree that images can play a key role in their conversations. Many users concur that images from the Internet can be used especially to better express their intentions and relieve any tension that pure text-based messaging might introduce.

MilliCat combines sub-modules that (i) perform sentiment analysis to identify the opinions of users' input data, (ii) process the input data using natural language processing techniques to identify the proper phrase to perform the search, and (iii) interconnect the smartphone application with prefetching and caching techniques implemented at an external server dedicated for image search and analysis. More importantly, we designed MilliCat so that it can be easily adopted and implemented as a plug-in layer for many pre-existing text messaging applications. Using the preliminary MilliCat prototype, we perform an empirical study on the additional bandwidth and battery usage on the smartphone as it performs real-time image request and fetch operations with our dedicated server. Our results show that with filtering options and text processing schemes, MilliCat pro-

---

[1]While this example is for a simple word, the core functionalities of MilliCat can be extended to more complex word phrases.

vides real-time image suggestions with latencies $< 100~msec$ and $< 50~KB$ of packet overhead per conversation.

The contributions of this work are three-fold.

- We perform a large-scale user survey to identify the needs and requirements for providing a real-time autonomous image suggestion service on mobile chat applications.

- We identify a set of technical challenges in addressing such application requirements, and list potential solutions and tools to improve the user experience in the domain of real-time autonomous image suggestion.

- Our observations lead to the design of MilliCat, a prototype implementation of a real-time autonomous image suggestion service for smartphone messaging applications, which we use to perform preliminary studies on the latency and overhead performance, and suggest guidelines for future research.

2. USER SURVEY

We start with a survey from 250+ users ranging in age groups from teens to over 50, with 11 nationalities, and different professions, including students, engineers, artists, scientists, salesmen, doctors, game designers, architects, chefs, housewives, etc. Without introducing details on the MilliCat design, we asked the participants, whom all are active smartphone users, to present their perspectives on image usage for mobile messaging. Specifically, our survey consisted of 11 questions, focusing on identifying the daily usage of smartphone messaging applications and their usage patterns on emoticons or images (typically already stored on the users' smartphones). Based on these results, we asked whether and how they thought automatically suggesting images from the Internet, based on what their input messages are, would benefit their conversations. Furthermore, we asked users on the types of images that they would like to be suggested and also the situations (e.g., conversation

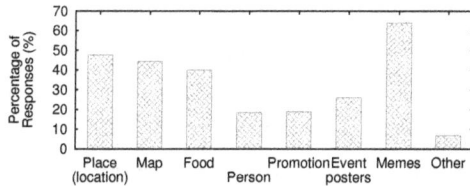

Figure 3: Preferred types of images for autonomous suggestion.

type, relationships with peer, etc.) they would prefer sharing these images in. While we omit the graphs due to space limitations, 95.7% of the survey participants answered that they often use smartphone-based messaging applications and 90% replied that they frequently use emoticons and images in their chat.

Figure 2 presents a summary of why and with whom users share images with during a smartphone messaging conversation. Notice in Figure 2(a) that most users agree that images are useful for expressing an appropriate nuance or emotions. Given that it is difficult to realize each others' "feelings" during *text* messages, users find this as an effective use-case for images. Furthermore, 20% of the participants express that images can be useful for information exchange, and the majority of these replies relate to exchanging map information or images of an unfamiliar conversation topic.

As Figure 2(b) shows, there is a trend in "when" the users prefer to use images. We notice a distinction in the usage patterns of images and emoticons with respect to the conversation peer. While widely used with friends or a significant other, the usage rate decreases significantly for colleagues, other family members (besides significant others), and senior colleagues (e.g., boss at work). This is an interesting result, and opens up opportunities for context-aware, adaptive image suggestion. Since an analysis on the contact groups or the chat history can provide hints on what category each contact belongs to, we can use this data to suggest images only when with high confidence that the images will be used when chatting with the contact.

Survey results also indicate that a high percentage (81.57%) of the participants would prefer to be autonomously suggested images from the Internet, based on the text being entered on the chat application. These results together motivate the need for further research in the domain of autonomous image suggestions for smartphone messaging applications as a way to improve the user experience.

We asked additional questions on what types of images (based on the typed text) would be beneficial if suggested autonomously during conversations. Figure 3 reveals that memes or funny images to go with the text were the most popular, followed by images of target locations, maps and food. We also notice here that there is no dominant answer to this question given that the maximum rate is ∼65%. We note that the participants were asked to select all that apply in the survey. This result suggests that an autonomous image suggesting service should not focus on a single category of images but diversify its search options.

18.43% of survey participants indicated they would rather *not* use images during their chats. Their quotes include "would take too long to find an image when connection is slow," "would it waste my data and slow down the speed?" Hence, such a new service, while providing real-time au-

tonomous image suggestions, must be lightweight enough to not excessively consume power and wireless bandwidth.

In summary, the take away messages from our user survey are the following:

- Many mobile users believe it would be useful to be able to use various images from the Internet during the chat

- Mobile users would use various images such as memes, locations, food, maps, etc., within their chat

- Users are concerned however that this service might incur excessive power and data overhead, and hence our service must be energy and data efficient.

3. SYSTEM REQUIREMENTS AND TECHNICAL CHALLENGES

Based on the observations from our user survey and prior experiences with resource limited mobile platforms, we identify a set of system-level requirements and a list of technical challenges in realizing an autonomous image suggestion module for smartphone-based messaging applications.

Below is a short-list of core system-level requirements.

- **Appropriateness of the images:** The images should be suggested only in situations when an image helps the emotion expression or nuance delivery. The suggested images hence should match the context of the users' conversation. We need to understand *what kinds* of images to show, and believe our user survey provided us with hints. Image search quality [1] is also important, and we rely on available tools as it is not the focus of our work.

- **Timeliness:** Images should be suggested at proper times with respect to *when* the user might intend to use a suggested image. For this, the system should "learn" when to send queries for an image search. As an example, based on the input of the user, the system should know whether it should search for an image on a per-character basis or per-word basis.

- **Image suggestion latency:** No matter how "appropriate" the image is, on a user experience perspective, it is important that the suggested images appear within the duration of the topic conversation. Therefore, the *latency* of image suggestions, which includes the delay for querying, image processing, wireless transmissions, and display, should be minimal.

- **Energy and resource efficiency:** One of the major concerns from our survey participants was in the energy and resource usage of our image suggestion service. Mobile phones, although recently becoming more powerful, are still considered as resource-limited platforms given that they operate on battery and over-utilizing processing power would lead to energy drain. As a result, the image suggestion service should use only minimal computational and networking resources to conserve energy.

On a practical perspective, there are a number of technical obstacles to overcome in designing a service that satisfies the requirements above.

First, the process of suggesting an appropriate, proper image is a challenging task. Specifically, the complexity of chatting sentences and the diversity of emotions complicate the estimation process in selecting the images to suggest given a specific word. We summarize some of the important tasks an image suggestion service should consider in selecting appropriate and proper images.

Sentiment analysis: Also known as opinion mining, sentiment analysis focuses on extracting underlying subjective information, such as emotions or opinions from a given text [3, 9]. It has been widely used, for instance, in analyzing consumer reviews on product websites, social media sites, blogs, and discussion forums. Existing tools such as Stanford CoreNLP [4] or the Natural Language Toolkit [5] can be integrated to provide sentiment analysis. Nevertheless, their computational complexity is high and accuracies are still in the 80% range (even with text longer than typical mobile chats) [4]. As an alternative, a list of emoticons can be used to catch first-stage opinions and extending this sentiment analysis feature remains as a major technical challenge.

Text partitioning: For proper image suggestion, the generation of a proper query message for image searching is extremely important. Given the text of a user, deciding at what point to partition the text and generate a query packet determines the quality of the image search. Partitioning can occur on a per-character basis, in words, word phrases, or in sentences. This design choice will not only impact the appropriateness of the suggested image, but also the bandwidth and energy usage of a mobile platform.

Word types: As related to text partitioning above, one could perform the query for each word. Moreover, one could limit the query to only nouns, instead of performing also for articles, adjectives, verbs, etc. However, recognizing whether a word is a noun could be difficult. For example, the word "love" in "I love you" is a verb while in "send my love" it is a noun. Also, within the nouns, there are *abstract* nouns that represent an intangible concept, such as emotions (e.g., happiness, anger), attributes and qualities (e.g., honesty, trust) that are difficult to have the right image. *Concrete* nouns on the other hand, are tangible, such as people (e.g., doctor), objects (e.g., cake), and places (e.g., island) and an image search on them would likely result in visuals that would improve the conversation. Note also that mobile users often use Internet slangs and acronyms (e.g., LOL) during smartphone chats, and are more tolerant to typos than in professional writing settings. The autonomous image suggestion service must understand this intrinsic nature of mobile chat culture to be effective.

The second technical challenge is in satisfying the latency requirement for image suggesting and display. Our experiences show that an intermediate server for image searching, fetching and caching helps ensure the fast display of images at the smartphone. However, the challenge here is in the management of this intermediate server's capabilities. Configuring the server to cache a large amount of data can benefit the latency experienced at the smartphone by minimizing the query latency, but the infrastructure cost may increase significantly. Schemes that allow the server to learn the chatting habits of individuals (and on a larger population scale) may help resolve this trade-off, but requires further research. In addition, the selection of a proper image search engine, with respect to the geographic location of the user and the server, can give a noticeable impact to overall latency performance.

Note that existing mobile prefetching techniques [2, 7] utilize users' smartphone usage pattern, for example, launching

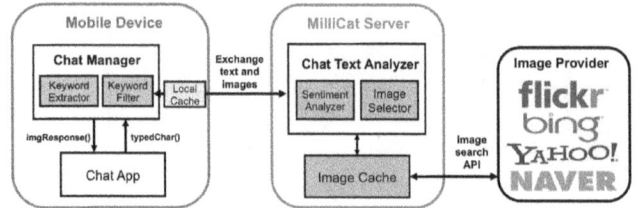

Figure 4: MilliCat system architecture.

email and news applications in the morning, to prefetch contents and images. However, applying prefetching for mobile messaging services can be challenging due to the difficulties in predicting which words would be used at which instance.

Third, minimizing the energy and bandwidth consumption is a major requirement to satisfy, and at the same time a very challenging task. A system designed for image suggestions within mobile chatting applications should intelligently manage the queries it sends to the image server, since a query not only requires energy and bandwidth to *send* the packet, but the response packet will contain the resulting images, which will consume even more resources. A tradeoff between the latency and the resource consumption must be considered. Moreover, natural language processing (NLP) schemes that suppress unnecessary queries can help maximize the efficiency at the smartphone [6].

Lastly, the design of an efficient user interface is another significant challenge. Issues such as the number of images to suggest per query or the layout of presenting the images on the screen can have high impact on both the usability and system-level performance.

4. MILLICAT

4.1 System Architecture

As a preliminary prototype to evaluate the features needed in an image suggestion service for smartphone messaging applications, we design MilliCat. The overall system architecture of MilliCat is shown in Figure 4. On the smartphone, the **MilliCat chat manager** connects to a chat application, and interacts with the **keyword extractor** and **keyword filter** to identify core terms in a text and suppress queries for common words such as article terms. The smartphone also holds a small-sized **local cache** to minimize the number of external-bound queries. Once a query reaches the MilliCat server, the **chat text analyzer** uses tools such as the **sentiment analyzer** to extract a proper search keyword. If an associated image is not in the cache, the server interacts with external databases for a proper image. The retrieved image is then cached and resized before the **image selector** validates its usefulness and returns it to the smartphone.

When interconnecting with a chat application as a plug-in, MilliCat provides APIs such as `typedChar()` and `imgResponse()` to receive the input text from the chat application and send a sequence of suggested images for the application to display. Within these APIs, we ask the application to include its own application identification along with a unique ID for each conversation for MilliCat to distinguish between different apps and conversations within. This flexibility allows MilliCat to easily interact with and improve the original functionalities of existing chat applications.

Being in the early stages of development, MilliCat currently includes most of the core features for real-time image

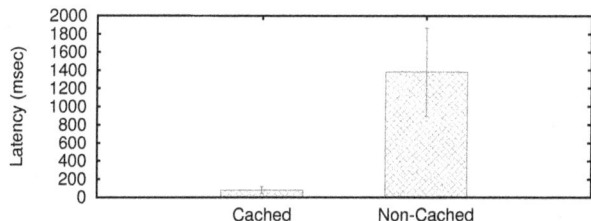

Figure 5: Image request latency with and without at-server image caching.

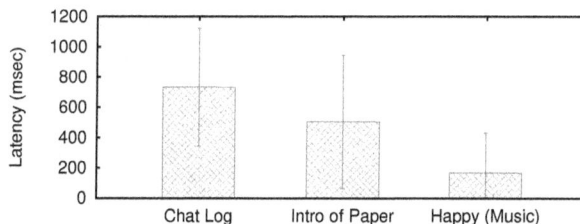

Figure 6: End-to-end image suggestion latency when queried on a per-word basis with different data sets.

suggestion as depicted in Figure 4. We are still undergoing research in providing suitable schemes for the sentiment analyzer and the keyword filter. Nevertheless, given that a major challenge is in ensuring that MilliCat does not excessively consume the smartphone's limited resources, using the current version of the system prototype, we perform a preliminary study on the bandwidth and energy overhead that real-time image suggestion introduces to traditional mobile messaging applications. Note that as our future work, we plan to evaluate the acceptability of MilliCat as part of a user study.

4.2 Preliminary Evaluations

4.2.1 Impact of Caching

First, we present in Figure 5 the latency of image suggestions with and without prior caching at the MilliCat server. Here we test for 100 different nouns and used Bing image search APIs for external image searching (e.g., non-cached images). For the cached case, we store all the images on our server and return these images directly without any external search. We see that as expected, image caching significantly reduces latency, from the query at the smartphone application to the image display, by an order of magnitude. This result shows the impact of at-server image caching for MilliCat, but we point out that image caching results in two main issues. First, as mentioned earlier, caching the images increases the storage overhead at the server. Second, without external searching, newly "trending" images may be difficult to suggest, since the server will return the images in its storage rather than performing a new search. An expiration timer for each image can resolve these issues, but the interval of image caching will become an important design choice leading to a major performance tradeoff.

Figure 6 presents the latency performance for the case where the server caches the images that were previously searched. Therefore, with commonly occurring words, the average latency of the query-reply process will reduce. We use three data sets for this experiment; the first data is a set of chat records from famous chat applications, as we detail later this section. The second data set is the first two paragraphs of this paper, and the third data set are lyrics from the song "Happy" by Pharrell Williams. Specifically, in the "Happy (Music)" data set, we see the word "happy" along with many phrases being repeated. As the results show, with more repeated data-based queries, the server gains the chance to cache related images, thus reducing the query-reply latency. Overall, these results show that with a well-configured caching server and a reasonable

amount of history data, the latency of image suggestion can fall within practically usable range ($<{\sim}100$ msec).

4.2.2 Networking & Energy Overhead

We now evaluate the packet transmission and reception overhead that real-time image suggestion systems, such as MilliCat, introduce. For our evaluations, we utilize 80 sample smartphone messaging conversations (e.g., WhatsApp, Facebook messenger, Android SMS, iOS SMS conversations) available on the Internet.[2] Each conversation has an average length of 5.95 lines with each line having an average length of 175.7 characters (or 42.175 words). Using this data, we test for five different test cases, each with different query issuing policies at the smartphone application. In the first case, a query is issued to search for a matching image at every keystroke. When typing the word "cat", in this scheme the application issues three queries; one for "c", another for "ca" and the third for "cat". The server checks if this word can be identified as a word through its local dictionary and makes a search query if the image data is not present in its cache. Potentially, we plan to use the Princeton WordNet search [10] for supporting a more robust and complete English word set. In the second case, a search query is issued for every space key entry. This case sends queries for each word typed in the text and was used for our experiments in Figure 6. Our third querying method combines the word-based querying method with the smartphone's keyword filter to suppress article terms such as "a" or "the" from being queried. In the keyword filter, we have a list of ${\sim}80$ words, which we are confident that a typical user would not request an image for. The fourth method utilizes the internal dictionary for noun-matching to only query the word if it is identified as a proper noun, and our fifth method combines this scheme with the keyword filter.

Figure 7 presents the average transmission overhead for each conversation trace. Note that when queries are sent on a per-click (i.e., per-character) basis, the transmission overhead is extremely high. As we perform word-level transmissions, local keyword filtering, and utilize the dictionary for typo filtering, the amount of transmissions drops dramatically. With the internal dictionary and keyword filter, only ${\sim}2$ KB of additional queries are generated on average for each conversation.

The result of the queries issued in Figure 7 are responses by the MilliCat server with image suggestions for the application. We plot this packet reception overhead in Figure 8. With more queries, comes more responses with images. As a result, for the per-click (per-character) case, an average of ${\sim}9.1$ MB are received for a single conversation. By changing

---

[2] We made this data available at https://goo.gl/O6k34x.

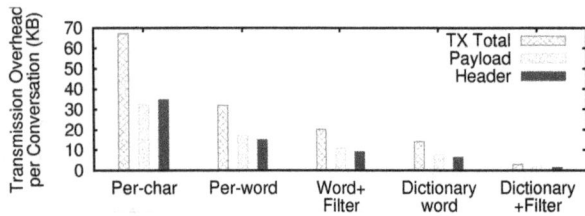

Figure 7: Chat trace transmission overhead for different querying methods.

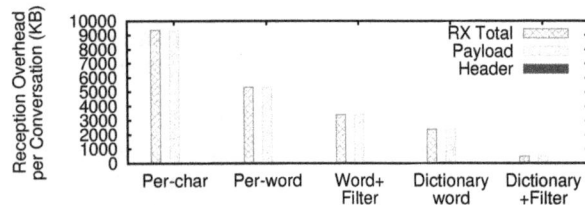

Figure 8: Chat trace packet reception overhead for different querying methods.

the querying method, we significantly reduce this overhead. This reduction also implies that the per-click case would request images less related to the actual word that the user is typing. For example, as the user types the word "catholic", the per-click case will return images for "cat" as well. Nevertheless, for the case with the internal dictionary and keyword filter, we are to expect ~47 KB per conversation. We note that for each of the search query, our current system is configured to suggest three images. This, of course, is a design choice, and lowering this will naturally reduce the reception overhead.

Finally, in Figure 9 we plot the energy used to support the operations in Figures 7 and 8, using a Samsung Galaxy SIII smartphone with Wi-Fi connections. Here, we neglect the baseline operations of the smartphone and focus on the energy spent only for MilliCat packets (e.g., queries and replies). Naturally, the trends of energy consumption are similar to that of the packet exchange overhead. We point out that with the dictionary and local keyword filter, the power usage per conversation is ~35 mW on average.

5. SUMMARY

We started this work asking ourselves, "Can we improve the user experience of smartphone messaging services using real-time autonomous image suggestions?" As of now, we have two different answers. First, our survey results show that users are willing to use such additional features as part of smartphone messaging, and our empirical results with MilliCat show that the latency and overhead of real-time image suggestions are within tolerable bounds. Therefore, real-time autonomous image suggestion for mobile chat applications holds the potential to improve mobile user experience.

On the other hand, on a technical perspective, there are still many challenges to overcome. One major challenge is in the fact that real-time autonomous image suggestions on smartphones require a combination of findings from diverse research fields: including areas such as mobile computing,

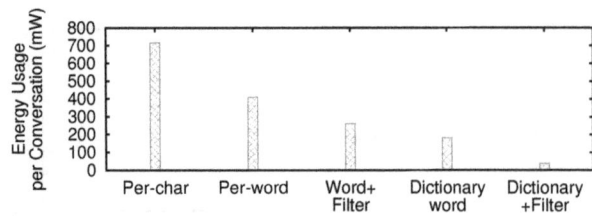

Figure 9: Overall energy overhead for different querying methods.

natural language processing, sentiment analysis, machine learning, storage, human computer interaction, networking, and systems. A key obstacle here is in compressing complex text analyzing algorithms to operate effectively with respect to the requirements of smartphone applications. For example, unlike how sentiment analysis and most text analysis tools are used today with a massive set of learning data from the Internet, chat messages are short and diverse in context. Therefore, taming existing text analyzing schemes to well-operate with smartphone chat messages is important in potentially initiating more precise queries and suppressing unnecessary queries from being sent. Nevertheless, we envision that our efforts in designing MilliCat will be the basis of realizing the next evolution of mobile messaging with more visual contents.

6. REFERENCES

[1] J. R. Bach, C. Fuller, A. Gupta, A. Hampapur, B. Horowitz, R. Humphrey, R. C. Jain, and C.-F. Shu. Virage image search engine: an open framework for image management. In *Proc. SPIE 2670, Storage and Retrieval for Still Image and Video Databases IV, 76*, 1996.

[2] B. D. Higgins, J. Flinn, T. J. Giuli, B. Noble, C. Peplin, and D. Watson. Informed mobile prefetching. In *Proceedings of the 10th International ACM Conference on Mobile Systems, Applications, and Services (MobiSys '12)*.

[3] B. Liu. Sentiment analysis: A multifaceted problem. *IEEE Intelligent Systems*, (3):76–80, 2010.

[4] C. D. Manning, M. Surdeanu, J. Bauer, J. Finkel, S. J. Bethard, and D. McClosky. The Stanford CoreNLP natural language processing toolkit. In *Proceedings of 52nd Annual Meeting of the Association for Computational Linguistics: System Demonstrations*, pages 55–60, 2014.

[5] NLTK Project. NLTK 3.0 documentation. Available at: http://www.nltk.org/, Oct. 2015.

[6] O. Owoputi, B. O'Connor, C. Dyer, K. Gimpel, N. Schneider, and N. A. Smith. Improved part-of-speech tagging for online conversational text with word clusters. In *Proc. of Conference of the North American Chapter of the Association for Computational Linguistics: Human Language Technologies (NAACL-HLT 2013)*.

[7] A. Parate, M. Böhmer, D. Chu, D. Ganesan, and B. M. Marlin. Practical prediction and prefetch for faster access to applications on mobile phones. In *Proceedings of the 2013 ACM International Joint Conference on Pervasive and Ubiquitous Computing (UbiComp '13)*.

[8] A. Smith. U.S. Smartphone Use in 2015. PEW Research Center Report. Available at: http://www.pewinternet.org/2015/04/01/us-smartphone-use-in-2015/, Apr. 2015.

[9] R. Socher, A. Perelygin, J. Wu, J. Chuang, C. Manning, A. Ng, and C. Potts. Recursive deep models for semantic compositionality over a sentiment treebank. In *Proc. of Conference on Empirical Methods in Natural Language Processing (EMNLP 2013)*.

[10] The Trustees of Princeton University. WordNet: A Lexical Database for English. . Available at: https://wordnet.princeton.edu/, Mar. 2015.

Tell Your Graphics Stack That the Display Is Circular

Hongyu Miao
Purdue ECE
miaoh@purdue.edu

Felix Xiaozhu Lin
Purdue ECE
xzl@purdue.edu

ABSTRACT

Computer displays have been mostly rectangular since they were analog. Recently, smart watches running Android Wear have started to embrace circular displays. However, the graphics stack – from user interface (UI) libraries to GPU to display controller – is kept oblivious to the display shape for engineering ease and compatibility; it still produces contents for a virtual square region that circumscribes the actual circular display. To understand the implications on resource usage, we have tested eleven Android Wear apps on a cutting edge wearable device and examined the key layers of Android Wear's graphics stack. We have found that while no significant amount of CPU/GPU operations are wasted, the obliviousness incurs excessive memory and display interface traffic, and thus leads to efficiency loss.

To minimize such waste, we advocate for a new software layer at the OpenGL interface while keeping the other layers oblivious. Following the idea, we propose a pilot solution that intercepts the OpenGL commands and rewrites the GPU shader programs on-the-fly. Through running a handcrafted app, we show a reduction in the GPU memory read by up to 22.4%. Overall, our experience suggests that it is both desirable and tractable to adapt the existing graphics stack for circular displays.

1. INTRODUCTION

Computer displays have been rectangular for a long time. This has been recently changed as wearable computers enter people's daily lives: on these computers, the display's role of content presentation is gradually giving way to the aesthetic value or human factor consideration. In embracing non-rectangular displays, smart watches are among the pioneers. Since Moto 360 sparked the trend in 2014, more than ten smart watch models have featured circular displays. The trend is burgeoning.

Compared to the fast-evolving display, the graphics stack that backs the display is mostly retaining the legacy im-

HotMobile '16, February 26-27, 2016, St. Augustine, FL, USA

© 2016 ACM. ISBN 978-1-4503-4145-5/16/02. . . $15.00

DOI: http://dx.doi.org/10.1145/2873587.2873603

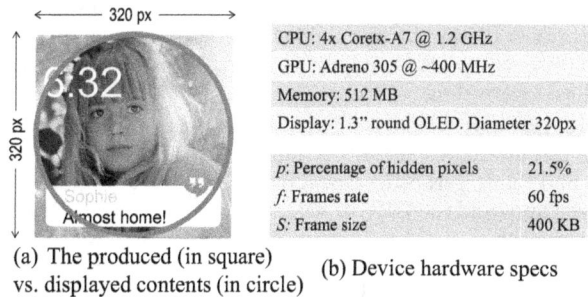

(a) The produced (in square) vs. displayed contents (in circle)

(b) Device hardware specs

CPU: 4x Coretx-A7 @ 1.2 GHz	
GPU: Adreno 305 @ ~400 MHz	
Memory: 512 MB	
Display: 1.3" round OLED. Diameter 320px	

p: Percentage of hidden pixels	21.5%
f: Frames rate	60 fps
S: Frame size	400 KB

Figure 1: The LG watch R, a circular smart watch, running the Android Wear Lollipop

plementation for engineering ease. Figure 1 shows the case of Android Wear 5.1 "Lollipop" atop the LG watch R [9], a cutting-edge smart watch featuring a round display. Despite the circular display, an app is responsible for generating contents for a virtual 320×320 square area that circumscribes the actual display as shown in Figure 1(a); in addition, all the drawing API available to apps is based on rectangular regions of configurable sizes. To ensure the UI integrity, the app developers are expected to be aware of the display shape and not to place the important UI elements off the circular boundary [5]. Underneath the apps, the graphics stack – from UI libraries to GPU to display controller – is oblivious to the circular shape of the display; they mechanically transform the app's UI contents to the pixels targeting the square area. The excessive pixels, as shaded in Figure 1(a), are only discarded at the display panel – the lowest layer of the graphics stack.

Clearly, there exists a mismatch between a circular display and the graphics stack. While this mismatch is acquiesced by today's wearable OS as-is, we seek a clear understanding of it by asking the following two questions.

1. How many resources are wasted in producing the contents that are ultimately discarded due to the circular display shape?

2. If the waste is non-trivial, how should an existing graphics stack adapt accordingly?

To answer these questions, we have examined a set of eleven typical Android Wear apps; we run them on a LG watch R and analyze the graphics stack's key layers. Through examining empirical evidence collected on the device, we have quantified the wasted resources: CPU/GPU operations, memory bandwidth/capacity, and interconnect traffic. Our findings are twofold:

- While the circular display shape does not affect an app's UI hierarchy much, it often discards a substantial portion (up to 21.5%) of background textures and rendered images.

- Accordingly, while no significant amount of CPU or GPU operations are wasted, the excessive memory and interconnect traffic – as high as 25 MBps – have led to a noticeable efficiency loss.

The findings suggest the direction towards adapting a graphics stack to a circular display: while revising the UI libraries is disruptive and unlikely to be profitable, making the textures and rendered surfaces aware of the screen shape is likely rewarding.

To this end, we explore the design space for introducing the awareness of display shape to the graphics stack; we find that interposing OpenGL, the low-level interface between apps and the GPU driver, is a viable approach. Hence, we propose to build a new software layer that rewrites the OpenGL commands and shader programs on-the-fly to fit the circular display, while keeping all other layers oblivious and unmodified. A simple prototype following this idea has reduced the GPU memory read by 21.5% and reduced the GPU cycles by up to 12%.

We have made two major contributions in this paper:

1. Through examining a set of typical wearable apps, we have quantified the resource waste due to the graphics stack's obliviousness to the circular display.

2. Towards eliminating the resource waste, we have shown that interposing the OpenGL interface is a promising approach: we demonstrate a pilot solution that rewrites the shader program and hence skips unnecessary GPU texture loading.

2. BACKGROUND & MOTIVATION

We next describe our test device, overview Android Wear's graphics stack, which inherits its overall structure from Android for smartphone, and discuss the existing system support for circular displays.

Test device. Our test device is the LG Watch R [9], one of the most popular smart watches. As summarized in Figure 1(b), the device features an LG 4237 OLED panel with a diameter of 320 pixels; it embraces a Qualcomm's APQ8026 SoC engineered towards low power. By running the STREAM benchmark [12] with all four cores at their highest frequency, we have measured the memory bandwidth as 1.8 GBps, which is much lower than smartphone memory bandwidth (often 5–10 GBps). Our prior work [10] has reported the system-level power consumption of Watch R.

Android graphics stack. In a nutshell, a graphics stack's role is to translate the app UIs to pixels shown on the display. On modern mobile devices, this procedure is heavily hardware-accelerated: multiple hardware components – CPU, GPU, and display controller – collaborate to repeat this procedure periodically, aiming at keeping pace with the display refresh rate, often 60 Hz. In the collaboration, these hardware components communicate mainly through shared buffers residing in the off-chip DRAM. Each buffer often contains information for a *rectangular* region on the display.

The graphics stack produces a frame of image in three stages from the top to bottom as shown in Figure 2. *Drawing* is done by CPU: each app transforms its hierarchy of UI elements, i.e. "view"s, to display lists, an intermediate representation of the final GPU commands. For every frame, the app translates its current display lists to OpenGL commands and sends them to the GPU driver for execution.

Rendering is done by GPU: controlled by the driver, the GPU executes the CPU-generated commands in its pipeline. It first performs vertex/primitive processing by running shader programs on the input vertices and assembling the vertices into triangles. The GPU then performs rasterization: it breaks down the triangles into fragments, runs shader programs on the fragments, and samples textures to determine each fragment's color. It finally performs pixel processing, writing back the produced pixels to the DRAM.

Composition and display are done by compositor and the display controller: once a surface is rendered by the GPU, the owner app passes it to an OS daemon called SurfaceFlinger. SurfaceFlinger blends surfaces passed from multiple apps by invoking hardware composer, which often resides in the hardware display controller. After composition, the display controller transmits the final frame to display panel for presentation.

Existing system support for circular displays. As described in Section 1, we have observed that the Android Wear OS is mostly oblivious to the circular shape of a display; as illustrated in Figure 1, it functions by assuming that the physical display is a square that circumscribes the actual circular display.

Multiple pieces of evidence support our observation: *i)* in examining the OS's UI framework source (which is fortunately open), we always see that drawable regions are specified as rectangles; *ii)* in peeking the test device's rendered surfaces or framebuffers by using Android's `GLtracer`, we always get the circumscribed square images; *iii)* the kernel's device tree specifies the dimensions of the display panel as 320×320 (shown below); this specification is the display controller driver's only knowledge about the panel.

```
// apq8026-lenok-panel.dtsi:
qcom,mdss-dsi-panel-name = "LG4237 320P OLED
    command mode dsi panel";
qcom,mdss-dsi-panel-width = <320>;
qcom,mdss-dsi-panel-height = <320>;
```

Listing 1: An exert from the Linux kernel (3.10) device tree for Watch R's circular display panel

The app developers, on the other hand, are expected to make their app UI layout "shape-aware" [5]. In particular, the developers are asked to place important UI elements in a square area called "window insets" that *inscribes* the circular display, to prevent these UI elements from being clipped by the circular display edge.

3. HOW MANY RESOURCES ARE WASTED?

We next quantify the wasted resources due to the graphics stack's obliviousness to the display shape. In the discussion,

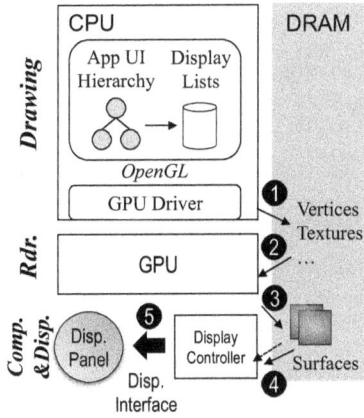

Figure 2: An overview of the graphics stack

Apps	# of UI Views			Drawing Time				Rdr. Time
	Hidden	Clipped	Total	Shader compile†	Shader link†	Texture upload†	Other cmds	
Google keep	×	×	×	8.6	1.3	4.4	2.9	4.3
Attopedia	0	9	10	8.2	1.2	25.0	2.4	4.5
Hole19	0	5	8	30.4	1.1	4.9	4.1	2.6
WearbottleSpinner	0	4	5	18.0	3.2	116.2	2.1	3.0
GridViewPager	0	6	9	23.9	4.4	2.0	2.0	2.8
Runtastic*	0	14	17	-	-	-	-	3.9
ReminderByTime*	0	13	14	-	-	-	-	3.8
Fit*	0	13	16	-	-	-	-	3.3
Weatherlive*	0	14	17	-	-	-	-	4.6
Instaweather*	0	13	16	-	-	-	-	3.8
Hangout*	0	13	16	-	-	-	-	3.7

* Wearable app "Cards" † Mostly occur upon surface creation
- Unable to determine: GLTracer unable to launch app Cards × Unable to determine: app crash
Hidden/Clipped: how many views in the UI are hidden/clipped Rdr. Time: the time of rendering an UI
Note: shader compile, shader link, and texture upload are the most expensive actions in UI drawing

Table 1: A list of studied wearable apps. All time values in ms.

Drawing (CPU)	Memory traffic: 225 KB per app bkgnd	❶
	Memory capacity: minor	
Rendering (GPU)	Memory traffic: 10 MBps	❷ ❸
	Memory capacity: 1 MB	
Composition (Disp. Ctrl & panel)	Memory traffic: 10 MBps	❹
	Display interface traffic: 5 MBps	❺
	Memory capacity: < 100 KB	

Table 2: A summary of the estimated resource waste, which is more than 3× of the inefficiency addressed in a prior wearable work [7]. Note that the wasted CPU/GPU operations are insignificant.

we use "oracle" to refer to an imaginary, ideal graphics stack tailored to the circular display: it wastes zero resource on pixels falling out of the display edge.

App study. In order to understand the UI structure of wearable apps, we studied eleven wearable apps that are popular in the app store as summarized in Table 1. These apps represent typical interactive use of smart watches and all feature image background for visual appeal. Focusing on graphics, we use Android's `Hierarchy Viewer` to examine the complexity of the UI hierarchies and how individual UI elements intersect with the circular display edge. We further measure the time spent in producing typical frames of the apps: we use `GLTracer` to measure the drawing time and use `dumpsys` to measure the CPU-perceived rendering time.

Based on the app study, we make three observations. First, a wearable app tends to have a simple UI hierarchy with a small number of views, as shown in the "Total" column of Table 1. Second, in such a hierarchy, although the views are often clipped by the circular display edge, they are rarely hidden, which is shown in the "Clipped" and "Hidden" columns of Table 1. We attribute this to the developer's consciousness of the display shape. Third, in initializing a UI surface, drawing is often expensive, as shown in the "Drawing" columns of Table 1, while in other frames it is cheap. The rendering cost is steadily moderate, as shown in the "Rdr. Time" column of Table 1.

Motivated by these observations, we next examine the graphics stack's major layers as shown in Figure 2. For each layer, we discuss the key operations and estimate how a circular display may affect the associated resource usage. Table 2 summarizes the resource waste.

3.1 Drawing

As described in Section 2, drawing is mainly done in the UI libraries and GPU driver. The associated major costs are three: *i)* transforming UI hierarchy to display lists; *ii)* compiling GPU shader code; *iii)* decoding and uploading textures to GPU. We examine these in details below.

App UI library. One app maintains a mapping between its view hierarchy and a set of Display Lists. In order to draw its UI, the app traverses the view hierarchy to update the corresponding Display Lists. When the view hierarchy is initialized or undergoes a significant change, the app has to rebuild substantial Display Lists. This is often expensive due to sophisticated UI measurement and layout [4]. However, for most frames, in particular during UI animation, existing display lists can be incrementally updated and translated to GL commands with low cost.

GPU driver. Once GL commands are ready, the app submits them to the GPU driver, which will operate the GPU accordingly. Since the GPU execution is mostly asynchronous, the cost to CPU is often minor except for two actions: compiling the GPU shader programs just-in-time and uploading textures to the GPU-owned memory region. This is shown in the "Shader compile" and "Texture upload" columns of Table 1. Fortunately, the two expensive actions often only occur upon the creation of UI surfaces; for other frames, the GPU driver execution only takes around 2–4 ms, as shown in the "Other cmds" column of Table 1.

Impact of a circular display. The circular display has little impact on the execution of app UI libraries (cost *i* above). The oracle solution is unlikely to see a reduced cost of transforming UI hierarchy: as few views are hidden by the display edge, the oracle's view hierarchy will not be any simpler. On the contrary, by catering to the circular edge, the oracle may even see an increase in the overhead of UI measurement and layout.

For the execution of the GPU driver, the oracle solution

will compile the same shader programs, paying the same cost ii. Its texture handling (cost iii), however, may decode smaller images and move fewer bytes in uploading the textures (❶). Assuming the uploaded texture has a size of T, the wasted memory traffic is $T \cdot p$. For a typical 512×512 texture used as a wearable app background, the waste is around 225 KB.

3.2 Rendering

In rendering a UI surface, the GPU processes the CPU-generated commands and data, produces triangles, rasterizes them, and fills the resultant fragments with colors from textures.

GPU execution. As shown in the "Drawing Time" columns of Table 1, the GPU execution is on the critical path of producing every frame. Given the observed simple UI hierarchy, we expect that the triangle count in each frame is low, implying light vertex/primitive processing. Furthermore, we expect much of the execution overhead comes from rasterization, in particular the entailed memory access. Since mobile GPU is backed by the off-chip DRAM, it has been demonstrated that a mobile GPU is often memory-bound and the memory access also becomes efficiency hotspots [3]. Note that due to the lack of hardware cache coherence among CPU, GPU, and display controllers, all memory sharing among them has to go through the external DRAM.

Among the memory access overheads, the following ones are tied to the circular screen shape:

Texture reading (❷): To output pixels, the GPU fragment shader loads texture and determines the pixel colors accordingly. Based on our wearable app study, the main use of textures is as the app background. Such a texture is often hundreds of KB and cannot be held in a mobile GPU's texture cache which is often a few KBs [2]. As a result, the texture access is streaming and most texture data have to be fetched from the DRAM [3]. Note this may not significantly harm the GPU performance much: the DRAM latency is hidden by massive parallelism and various optimizations such as batch fetch. Yet, the resultant excessive memory move leads to an efficiency loss.

Pixel operations (❸): The GPU produces a rendered surface by writing the final pixels back to the DRAM. To do so, it may need to first read in the pixels before writing them back, e.g. for implementing the z-order among multiple objects or a translucent effect.

To estimate resource waste, we make the following simple, conservative assumptions: for each frame, the GPU renders at least one surface, i.e. the one belonging to the on-screen app, and thus accesses the background texture that is uncompressed; in pixel operations, it writes one rendered surface exactly once. Using the notations defined in Figure 1(b), the wasted memory traffic is:

$$2 \cdot S \cdot f \cdot p = 2 \cdot 400KB \cdot 60FPS \cdot 21.5\% = 10MBps$$

Graphic buffers. The wasted graphics buffer capacity is low. The memory cost comes from two parts: the texture buffers and the rendered surfaces for individual apps. Note that each surface is often double- or triple-buffered; that is, each buffer has two to three copies.

By examining the debugging information of SurfaceFlinger,

the system daemon managing all surface buffers, we found the whole system often sees ten surface buffers, occupying about 4MB memory. As a result, the oracle solution can save at most 21%, or around 1MB, memory. This is less than 1% of the total device DRAM (512MB). We expect that the saving from the texture buffers is even lower.

3.3 Composition and Display

As shown in Figure 2, SurfaceFlinger sends multiple rendered surfaces to the display controller, which in turn composites the surfaces and directly sends the final image to the display panel over a display interface. Note that this eliminates the legacy notion of "framebuffer". These actions matter to energy efficiency: LPD [7] shows that on a similar wearable device (Samsung Gear S), the memory access and data move consume up to 14 mW or 8% of the system power.

Composition. Based on our experiment with Surface-Flingers when running various apps, it almost always composites two surfaces: one from the on-screen app and one OS surface, i.e. a black circle around the display's edge for anti-aliasing effect. As compared to smartphone, a watch has no system bar, no action bar, etc. Both surfaces are rectangular, in the same size of the circumscribed square. As a result, using the notations defined in Figure 1(b), the excessive memory traffic flowing into display controller (❹) is given by:

$$2 \cdot S \cdot f \cdot p = 2 \cdot 400KB \cdot 60FPS \cdot 21.5\% = 10MB/sec$$

Beyond the memory move overhead, we estimate that the compute demand by composition is low: the overlay engine has been specialized for bit manipulation, and the number of overlays is as small as two. Hence, the oracle solution can save little processing in composition.

Display interface traffic. Each second, the display controller sends 60 frames to the display panel (❺). Each pixel, on the interface, is still represented by four bytes. Thus, the wasted interface traffic is:

$$S \cdot f \cdot p = 400KB \cdot 60FPS \cdot 21.5\% = 5MB/sec$$

Display panel's internal SRAM. Modern display panels often use command mode [7], which holds the pixels being displayed in an internal SRAM . Although the display panel's specification (§2) presents an illusionary, 320 × 320 pixel array that takes 400 KB, it is unclear to us how its internal SRAM is organized. Ideally, it should only store pixels that will be visible on the circular display (292 KB).

4. HOW SHOULD SOFTWARE ADAPT?

Design space exploration. To reduce the resource waste, it is clear that the graphics stack should be made aware of circular displays. This raises a top design question: to which layer of the stack (shown in Figure 2) should we introduce the awareness? This design question involves a key trade-off between the entailed resource saving and software complexity.

At the very top of the stack, we may overhaul the framework API and make the app code fully aware of the display shape. In drawing their UI elements, apps explicitly confine all UI hierarchies within the circular area; they trim their

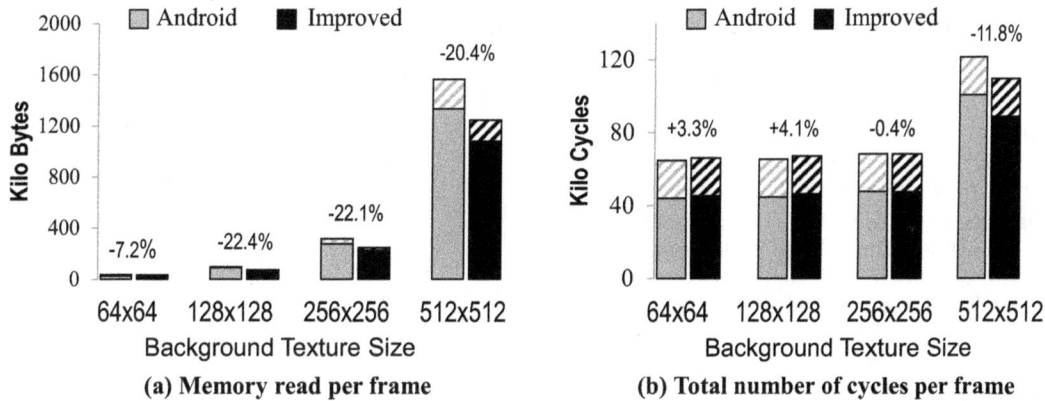

(a) Memory read per frame   (b) Total number of cycles per frame

Figure 3: The measured GPU resource consumption in rendering the benchmark app. In each column, the bottom part: the resource for rendering the background; the top part: that for all the remaining UI elements

shapes and textures so that none overflows. This approach is very similar to the oracle solution discussed in Section 3. It almost eliminates the resource waste, but puts a high burden on the app developers; even worse, wearable apps developed in this fashion are not portable across devices with different shapes of displays.

Going one layer lower, we may keep the apps oblivious but make the UI libraries aware. The apps still believe that they lay their UI hierarchies on a square display; the UI libraries keep track of the intersections between a hierarchy and the display boundary and therefore avoid producing display lists that fall out of the boundary. This approach removes developer's burden but complicates the UI libraries (which are already complicated! [4]) by exposing the display shape to them.

Going all the way down to the bottom layer, we may introduce the awareness right before all rendered surfaces are composited, making the display controller skip all out-of-boundary regions in the surfaces. This approach is similar to LPD [7]. It requires zero effort from the developers of CPU and GPU programs, but only reduces waste at ❸ and ❹; the excessive GPU-induced memory traffic (❷) has already been wasted.

Pilot solution: OpenGL interposition. In the graphics stack, we have observed that the OpenGL interface is ideal for bringing the display shape awareness: on one hand, its abstraction is low enough for granting us great control of the rendering action; on the other hand, it is still atop the GPU where the major waste occurs. To this end, we advocate for interposing the OpenGL commands and GPU shader programs before they are sent to the GPU driver. We keep the rest of the graphics stack oblivious and unchanged.

Shader program rewriting. We next showcase that a simple rewrite action of a shader program can effectively reduce GPU's memory traffic. The idea is simple: we manually rewrite the GPU fragment shader so that it checks each fragment's coordinates before coloring it; if a fragment falls out of the circular display area, the shader skips coloring it.

To evaluate the benefit of shader rewriting, we build a small benchmark app for the test wearable device; the app invokes the OpenGL API and employs GPU shaders to draw its pictorial background. We vary the size of the background's texture during benchmarking. Following the idea above, we manually rewrite its fragment shader and pro-

file the GPU resource usage with and without the rewrite. The profiling, however, faces a platform limitation: Qualcomm's GPU profiler only works with handheld devices but not wearables at the time of writing (Oct. 2015). As a workaround, we use Nexus 5 – a Qualcomm-powered smartphone – as an emulation platform: we compile the benchmark wearable app for Nexus 5 while keeping its source code, UI structure, and UI dimension exactly identical. Note that we do emulation on real hardware instead of simulation. Nexus 5 and Watch R both feature Qualcomm's Adreno GPUs from the same generation (28 nm) and only differ in the amount of physical compute resources.

As shown in Figure 3(a), our profiling results show that the rewritten shader reduces the memory read by up to 22.4%. This reduction and the resultant efficiency gain are notable: *i)* memory read is in general known as the major efficiency bottleneck in mobile graphics [2]; *ii)* the energy efficiency of a wearable device is known to be sensitive to memory traffic [7]; *iii)* the efficiency benefit applies to every produced frame, even when the UI is not updated by the app and remains still; *iv)* the gain is achieved through very low engineering effort, which is in contrast to far more sophisticated techniques, e.g., texture compression, towards the same goal.

The execution overhead introduced by the rewritten shader is low, as shown in Figure 3(b). With small to medium background textures ($\leq 128 \times 128$), the coordinates check inserted in the shader increases the total GPU cycles by less than 5%; with larger textures, the performance benefit from memory read reduction overshadows the execution overhead, leading to an up to 12% reduction in GPU cycles.

Expected Power Saving. We estimate that the pilot solution can save non-trivial power by comparing it with prior wearable study: LPD [7] saves 2.7 mW of system power by reducing the DRAM-to-display traffic by 7 MBps; assuming that the saved power is roughly proportional to the reduced traffic, our reduced DRAM traffic (❷❸) will lead to 3.9 mW of system power reduction. It is worth noting that *i)* such an amount of power matters as wearable battery is tiny; *ii)* further power saving of 5.8 mW may be harvested by novel display controller hardware that avoids the traffic waste shown in Table 2 (❹❺); *iii)* our power saving is orthogonal to LPD [7], which avoids refreshing a display region that is not re-drawn.

5. RELATED WORK

Wearables are less understood as compared to smartphones. Our own work [10] has characterized its major system aspects such as power and CPU usage; Min *et al.* [13] studies the battery usage of smart watches. However, none has studied the unique aspects of a wearable's display.

Much work has characterized mobile GPUs. For example, GraalBench [1] is a 3D benchmark suite for low-end phones and Ma *et al.* [11] has characterized the power consumption of mobile games. While their methods are inspiring, none has studied non-rectangular displays nor has examined the hardware-accelerated wearable UI.

Minimizing waste of mobile GPU resources has been a hot topic. LPD [7] reduces the memory and display interface traffic by only compositing the recently changed UI regions. Android comes with various tools to bust GPU overdraw problems [6]. DRS [8] reduces the GPU compute demand by scaling down the display resolution on-demand. Our goal is orthogonal to them: we aim to avoid producing UI regions that will be hidden by circular displays.

Memory access by mobile GPU, in particular texture memory, is a known bottleneck. Targeting power efficiency, PFR [3] improves the texture access locality by rendering two adjacent frames in parallel. While we share the goal of efficiency in GPU memory access, our approach avoids unnecessary texture memory access altogether.

6. CONCLUDING REMARKS

Limitations. Our work does not provide solution for all the discovered issues. The proposed shader rewrite technique does not reduce the identified resource waste in composition and display. To address this issue, hardware support from the display controller and panel is needed.

Our study is also limited by multiple factors. First, the immature profiling support for wearable GPU forces us to use a smartphone for emulation. The resultant measurement, while shedding lights, does not directly map to that of a wearable GPU. For instance, we have observed that the wearable GPU often causes long system-level delay, up to hundreds of ms, as the user is navigating among UI surfaces. While this implies optimization opportunity, lacking profiling support, we are unable to examine what the GPU is busy with. Second, multiple popular wearable apps crash while they are being debugged or profiled, hindering a better understanding of their internals. These even include Google's official apps and official profiler. Third, the fine-grained power model of wearables is not yet well-known, making it hard to estimate the efficiency gain in actual use. With more efforts invested by industry and academia, we expect these limitations to disappear.

High-resolution, non-rectangular display. Our study addresses the smart watch display, on which the number of pixels is small, $20-40\times$ smaller than that of a typical smartphone display. Down the road, as displays in various form factors become pervasive, we may see larger non-rectangular displays with massive pixels, e.g., a "smart" oval mirror. The implications are two: based on the discussion in Section 3, the resource waste is likely higher, making it more compelling to adapt the graphics stack; addressing the waste may warrant an introduction of the complexity to higher layers in the graphics stack, e.g., redesigning the API.

Conclusions. Our work is a first look at the implication of circular displays on system software design. We have discovered that the existing graphics stack is wasting substantial resources for contents that will never been shown due to the screen shape. To this end, we have quantified the resource waste on the LG watch R. We advocate for interposing the OpenGL commands and GPU shaders to adjust rendering activities to the display boundary. By demonstrating a benchmark app, we have shown that this approach is promising.

Acknowledgement

This work was supported in part by NSF Award #1464357. The authors thank the anonymous reviewers for their useful feedbacks. The photo in Figure 1(a) is in CC0 public domain, and is by courtesy of Pixabay.

7. REFERENCES

[1] I. Antochi, B. Juurlink, S. Vassiliadis, and P. Liuha. Graalbench: A 3d graphics benchmark suite for mobile phones. In *Proceedings of the 2004 ACM SIGPLAN/SIGBED Conference on Languages, Compilers, and Tools for Embedded Systems*, 2004.

[2] J.-M. Arnau, J.-M. Parcerisa, and P. Xekalakis. Boosting mobile gpu performance with a decoupled access/execute fragment processor. In *Proceedings of the 39th Annual International Symposium on Computer Architecture*, 2012.

[3] J.-M. Arnau, J.-M. Parcerisa, and P. Xekalakis. Parallel frame rendering: Trading responsiveness for energy on a mobile gpu. In *Proceedings of the 22nd international conference on Parallel architectures and compilation techniques*, 2013.

[4] Google. Android graphics: System-level architecture. https://source.android.com/devices/graphics/architecture.html, 2014.

[5] Google. Android wear – defining layouts, 2015.

[6] R. Guy. Android performance case study, 2012.

[7] M. Ham, I. Dae, and C. Choi. Lpd: low power display mechanism for mobile and wearable devices. In *Proceedings of the 2015 USENIX Conference on Usenix Annual Technical Conference*, 2015.

[8] S. He, Y. Liu, and H. Zhou. Optimizing smartphone power consumption through dynamic resolution scaling. In *Proc. ACM MobiCom*, 2015.

[9] LG USA. Design comes full circle. http://www.lg.com/us/smart-watches/lg-W110-g-watch-r, 2014.

[10] R. Liu, L. Jiang, N. Jiang, and F. X. Lin. Anatomizing system activities on interactive wearable devices. In *Proceedings of the 6th Asia-Pacific Workshop on Systems*, 2015.

[11] X. Ma, Z. Deng, M. Dong, and L. Zhong. Characterizing the performance and power consumption of 3d mobile games. *Computer*, 46(4):76–82, 2013.

[12] J. D. McCalpin. Memory bandwidth and machine balance in current high performance computers. *IEEE Computer Society Technical Committee on Computer Architecture (TCCA) Newsletter*, pages 19–25, Dec. 1995.

[13] C. Min, S. Kang, C. Yoo, J. Cha, S. Choi, Y. Oh, and J. Song. Exploring current practices for battery use and management of smartwatches. In *Proceedings of the 2015 ACM International Symposium on Wearable Computers*, 2015.

Tbooster: Adaptive Touch Boosting for Mobile Texting

Nohyun Jung, Gwangmin Lee, Seokjun Lee, Hojung Cha
Department of Computer Science
Yonsei University, KOREA
{nhjung,gmlee,sjlee}@mobed.yonsei.ac.kr, hjcha@yonsei.ac.kr

ABSTRACT

Current mobile devices use a touch boosting scheme to handle operations caused by user interactions with the touchscreen. The current scheme uses a predetermined DVFS step for touch boosting, regardless of user texting speed or related workloads, causing power waste due to unnecessarily high CPU frequency. In particular, the current mechanism is not optimized for power usage when the soft keyboard is used as an input mechanism. In this paper, we propose a scheme called Tbooster, which adaptively adjusts touch boosting level. The scheme reflects texting interval and texting latency, minimizing power consumption while maintaining the user's quality of experience. The scheme was implemented in Android devices and evaluated using a variety of texting applications. Our evaluation results show that the proposed technique reduces the device's overall power consumption by 4.6–13.1%, depending on texting interval and application type.

Keywords

Smartphone; Touch boosting; Soft keyboard; Texting; Power; User experience

1. INTRODUCTION

User inputs in mobile devices typically involve touch events by means of a touchscreen. User-perceived latency (the time to update the result of operations caused by the touch event) is critical and greatly affects the user's quality of experience (QoE) [1, 2]. Touch boosting is a common technique to ensure the required latency, improving QoE by instantly boosting CPU performance when a touch event occurs. This technique optimizes user-perceived latency by overriding the CPU's default DVFS (Dynamic Voltage and Frequency Scaling) governor.

Although touch boosting enhances QoE, the scheme does not always work effectively in terms of power consumption. Touch boosting normally uses a predetermined CPU frequency, regardless of features of touch events such as touch pattern and implied , workload. Although this scheme ensures high performance, the required QoE can, in some cases, be achieved with lower performance [3]. That is, the current approach to touch

HotMobile '16, February 26-27, 2016, St. Augustine, FL, USA
© 2016 ACM. ISBN 978-1-4503-4145-5/16/02$15.00
DOI: http://dx.doi.org/10.1145/2873587.2873592

boosting often causes power waste by maintaining an unnecessarily high CPU frequency in some situations.

One opportunity for optimizing current touch boosting arises when users input texts via soft keyboard. The workload due to texting is affected by two factors: (1) type of operations occurring during texting and (2) user texting speed. First, texting applications may incur diverse workloads during texting. For example, in contrast to simply outputting texts on the screen, an auto-complete feature or view update requires a non-trivial amount of workload during texting. Second, various factors such as keyboard layout, typing proficiency, and even user age can affect texting speed, which varies widely among individuals. For slow texting in particular, there are opportunities to reduce power consumption, as the related workload can be loosely processed without degrading QoE. The current approach to touch boosting does not take account of the impact of all these characteristics of texting on power efficiency.

In this paper, we describe a touch boosting system called Tbooster, which adaptively alters boosting level to reduce power consumption for soft keyboard-based texting. Our goal is to reduce power consumption while ensuring QoE by analyzing the characteristics of mobile texting. Our scheme contributes in three respects. First, we experimentally analyze the impact of touch boosting on both performance and power consumption. Second, we introduce and define the concept of Critical Texting Latency, based on an analysis of the relationship between texting latency and QoE. Finally, we optimize the touch boosting system by using an adaptive boosting control that reflects texting interval and texting latency.

2. BACKGROUND

2.1 Touch Boosting Mechanism

Modern mobile devices use the DVFS policy for the efficient management of CPU power consumption. The Ondemand governor or similar is included as a default governor in the operating system to adjust CPU frequency, based on periodic measurement of CPU utilization. For this reason, it is not optimized to handle immediate responses such as touch events. In particular, for touch events that occur at low CPU frequency in the idle state, the policy is unable to provide a satisfactory user experience. To overcome this limitation and to improve QoE for touch events, current mobile devices use a touch boosting mechanism. Figure 1 illustrates how this mechanism is implemented in an Android system. If ACTION_DOWN occurs, the system boosts performance by fixing the minimum DVFS step as defined in the touchscreen driver. If the touch event is maintained for a certain period of time, the minimum step is

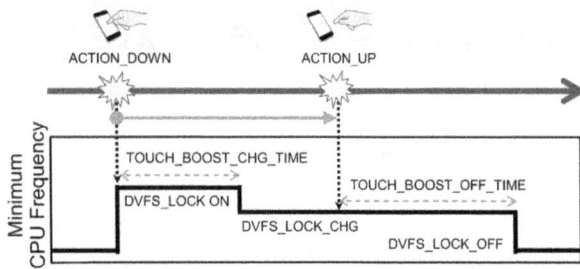

Figure 1. Touch boosting operation in Android system.

lowered. On completion of the touch event by ACTION_UP, the lock is released after a predetermined time has elapsed.

2.2 Implications for Texting

Various kinds of text input mechanisms are available for mobile devices, such as speech-to-text or Swype, but texting via soft keyboard remains the most popular [4]. Recent surveys show that, on average, users send 110 SMS messages per day [5]. Social networking applications are another modality requiring text input.

When text input occurs, the amount of associated workload varies widely, depending on the target application. For simple text output, the workload is light. However, for example, AutoCompleteTextView handle additional work for the autocomplete feature that predicts the rest of the word being typed. Additional workload varies according to the approach of the application developer. User texting speed also affects the workload incurred by texting; for faster texting speeds, the workload per unit time obviously increases. In practice, various factors such as age, keyboard layout, and proficiency can affect a user's texting speed.

3. PRELIMINARY EXPERIMENT

We conducted preliminary experiments to investigate the impact of touch boosting on both power consumption and performance.

3.1 Experimental Setup

To begin, users were surveyed to identify the categories of applications most often used for texting. Sixty people participated in the study. They were selected via Internet posting with brief interviews. 42 are in their 20's and 18 in 30's (33 male and 27 female). 36 of them were college students and 24 were office workers. The participants were using 12 different types of smartphones, and their device use was less than 1 year (33 of them), 1~2 years (16), 2~3 years (9), and more than 3 years (2). 37 of them answered they are proficient with device use, whereas rest of them were found naïvely using their devices.

The survey results are shown in Figure 2 (a). Instant Messaging (IM) applications were used by an overwhelming majority (97%) of respondents; SNS by 45%; memo by 32%; browser by 30%; and e-mail by 18%. Based on these results, ten applications were chosen from five categories (see Figure 2(a)) for the subsequent experiment. Table 1 shows the types of text-input UI (user interface) for each application—for example, Gmail type 1 is the text view used to input an email address and Gmail type 2 refers to content input.

Next, experiments were conducted to measure the general texting speed of the 60 participants. For this purpose, an application was written to log the timestamps of texting events while the participant entered short sentences. Figure 2 (b) shows the

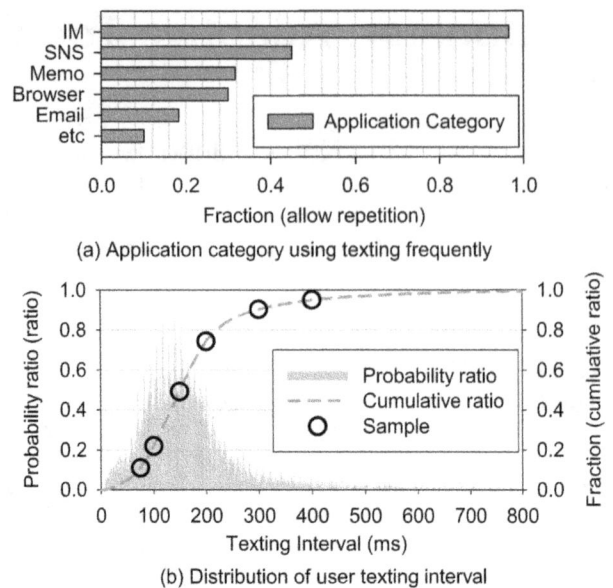

(a) Application category using texting frequently

(b) Distribution of user texting interval

Figure 2. Application category (survey results) and user texting speed (experiment).

distribution of texting intervals for 27,138 events. For one short-sentence input, the average of texting interval varied from 75 ms to 344 ms. Based on this experiment, six different texting intervals were designated: 75, 100, 150, 200, 300, and 400ms; these parameters were used for all subsequent experiments.

The target device used for experimental purposes was the Samsung Galaxy S5 (SM-G900F), running Android 4.4.2 KitKat. The device is equipped with a quad-core Qualcomm Snapdragon 801 processor and provides fifteen DVFS steps, ranging from 0.3 to 2.4 GHz. The device uses the Synaptics touchscreen, which supports touch-boosting. The DVFS step used for touch boosting is the fourth highest (1.7 GHz); 1.2 GHz is used when a touch event lasts longer than 130 ms. DVFS locking is released at 500 ms after the end of touch event. The Interactive governor is the default governor used in the Galaxy S5. It has a similar policy to that of the Ondemand governor, but more heuristics and configurable parameters are provided to enhance response time.

During the experiment, Android Monkey was used to generate a fixed interval for touch events. We noted that touch boosting occurs only if a touch event is processed by the touchscreen driver, and this does not apply to the use of Monkey. To solve this problem, we developed a kernel module specifically for Android Monkey. The module uses kprobes to detect Monkey touch events by checking the IPC data in the binder driver. Depending on the type of touch events, it calls the touch boosting function of the touchscreen driver, enabling operation as general touch boosting. Provisioning of touch boosting was controlled by enabling and/or disabling this module.

Table 1. Type of text-input UI in test applications

Application	Type 1	Type 2
IM: Telegram,WhatsApp	Search	Message
SNS: Facebook,Twitter	Search	Post
Memo: GoogleKeep,NaverMemo	Search	Memo
Browser: Chrome,Firefox	Search	WebSearch
Email: Gmail,Naver Mail	Address	Mail Subject

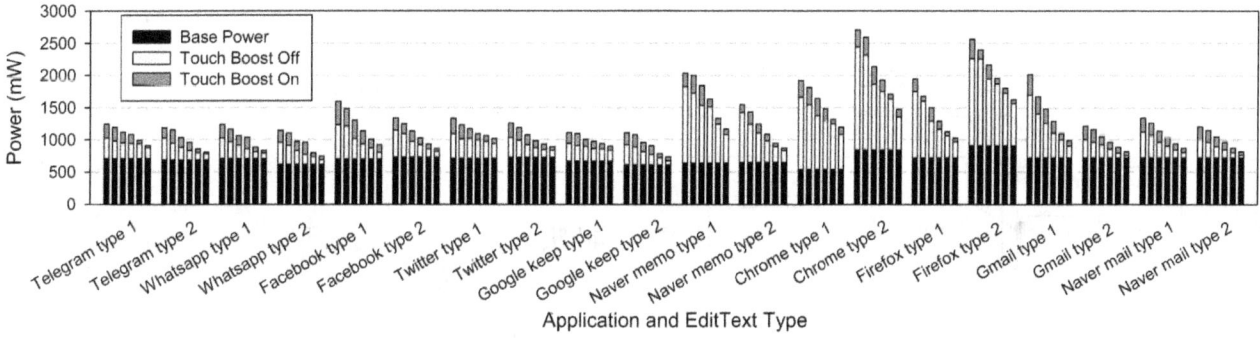

Figure 3. Average power consumption on texting (bars from left to right in each group indicate 75, 100, 150, 200, 300, and 400ms texting intervals).

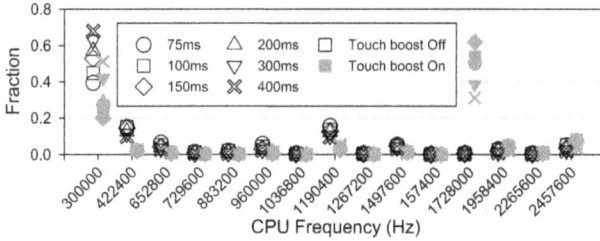

Figure 4. CPU frequency distribution when texting.

3.2 Power Consumption when Texting

To investigate the impact of touch boosting on power consumption, power consumption (with and without touch boosting) was measured while texting, using two different text-input UIs for each of 10 applications. For the experiments, the radio interface was disabled, except for Wi-Fi, which was required to provide a stable Internet connection for the browsers. The display was set to stay awake at 50% brightness, and screen auto-rotation was disabled. The target device's power consumption was measured using the Monsoon Power Monitor.

Average power consumption was measured for 100 text input events occurring at regular intervals; results are presented in Figure 3. For each text-input UI type, the input intervals used were 75, 100, 200, 300, and 400 ms (based on the results of the previous experiment in Section 3.1). In the bar chart, the interval gradually increases from left to right. Base power is the amount spent while waiting for text input. Note that base power differs for each UI type because of the characteristics of the OLED display, whose power consumption depends on usage of colors.

Figure 3 shows that power consumption increases as texting interval is shortened. This is because unit workload increases as touch events occur more frequently. There is also a difference in power consumption for each input type, as the amount of work related to texting varies with the application. For example, Gmail type 1 is AutoCompleteTextView, which requires additional work for the auto-complete feature and therefore consumes more power than Gmail type 2, which simply processes text input. Overall, without touch boosting, the device's power consumption was reduced by about 11.6% on average for the boost-on case. This is equivalent to a power reduction of 31.8% (without considering base power). The results indicate that the current approach to touch boosting significantly affects power consumption when users input texts by means of a soft keyboard.

Power consumption is caused primarily by the high DVFS step used for touch boosting. We measured CPU usage per frequency in the same environment as in the previous experiment; Figure 4

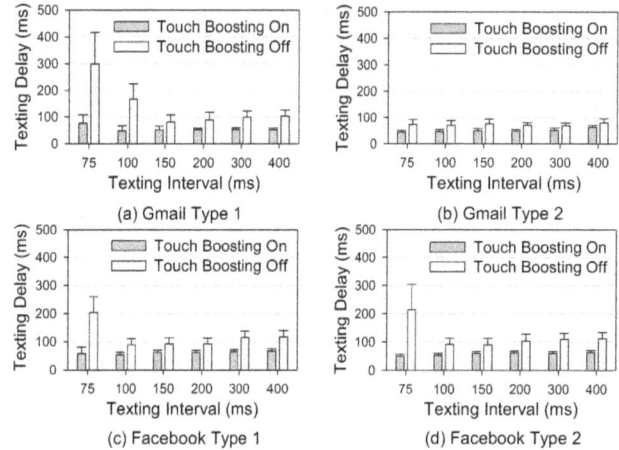

Figure 5. Texting latency versus texting interval.

shows the distribution of CPU usage. When touch boosting is disabled, the Interactive governor controls CPU frequency on the basis of CPU utilization, regardless of the touch event. The recorded usage of 0.3GHz (the lowest step) was overwhelmingly high. Usage of 1.2GHz was the second largest, but accounted for less than 20%. On the other hand, with touch boosting enabled, CPU frequency was boosted on user's touch. Since texting rapidly generates ACTION_DOWN and ACTION_UP, the DVFS_LOCK_CHG frequency is not used here. Instead, only the DVFS_LOCK frequency is used for touch boosting, and so the DVFS_LOCK frequency of 1.7GHz used by touch boosting was most frequently used; 0.3GHz came second. This result shows that enabling touch boosting maintains higher performance, resulting in higher power consumption. As touch boosting uses only one CPU frequency, this represents a good opportunity for optimization.

3.3 Texting Performance

As the purpose of touch boosting is to improve QoE, the analysis of its impact on system performance is critical. Experiments were conducted to measure texting latency (the time delay before input text is displayed on the screen) for the Gmail and Facebook applications; Figure 5 shows the results. With touch boosting enabled, texting latency varies from a minimum 43.8 ms to a maximum 75.9 ms, with an average of 56.3 ms. Texting latency does not change significantly even when texting interval is altered. However, with touch boosting disabled, texting latency is greatly affected by the texting interval. Since the power governor monitors workload periodically, there is a delay in altering CPU frequency, during which CPU performance may not be adequate

65

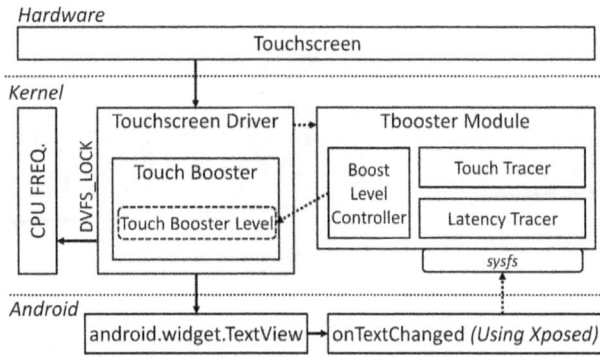

Figure 6. Overview of Tbooster.

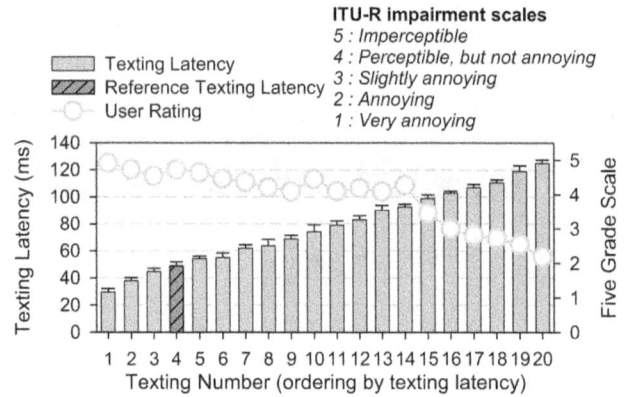

ITU-R impairment scales
5 : Imperceptible
4 : Perceptible, but not annoying
3 : Slightly annoying
2 : Annoying
1 : Very annoying

Figure 7. User QoE vs. texting latency.

for the workload. It follows that when the texting interval is very short, the delay increases because of the high workload. For a long texting interval, texting latency increases only slightly because of the small workload. Furthermore, Gmail type 1 and type 2 behave differently when touch boosting is disabled; Gmail type 1 shows a large increase in delay as texting interval decreases while Gmail type 2 does not. For Gmail type 2, texting delay also remains more or less unchanged with or without touch boosting. That is, for Gmail type 2, touch boosting maintains unnecessarily high performance and does not need any boost, as simple text viewing incurs only a very small workload in this case.

From this experiment, it can be observed that the effect of touch boosting on user experience varies according to the workload that accompanies texting, making it necessary to vary CPU frequency for touch boosting in different texting situations.

4. TBOOSTER

This section describes an adaptive touch boosting scheme that dynamically adjusts touch boosting level. An explanation of the overall architecture is followed by a discussion of critical texting latency.

4.1 System Overview

To optimize power consumption while providing adequate performance when texting via soft keyboard, we designed and implemented an adaptive touch boosting system called Tbooster. Unlike the current approach to touch boosting, which uses a predetermined CPU frequency, Tbooster alters CPU frequency dynamically, according to the texting situation. Figure 6 illustrates the overall architecture of the scheme. The system consists of three key components: Touch Tracer, Latency Tracer, and Boost Level Controller.

Touch Tracer collects texting events and timestamps for texting events. The texting interval is calculated using the timestamps, and the average recent texting interval is subsequently updated. The component uses kprobes to hook *binder_transaction*, which is the kernel function used in Android for inter-process communication. Every command transferred by binder has its own code. When a user input text via soft keyboard, we captured the command and used the code in the command to distinguish ACTION_UP and ACTION_DOWN.

Latency Tracer records the latency required to process text input for output. The component utilizes Xposed to hook the method calls and to control pre- and post-method calls in the Android platform. It hooks *onTextChanged*, which is the function of Android TextView, to obtain a timestamp when text on the screen

is changed. Based on the acquired timestamp, texting latency is then calculated.

Boost Level Controller determines the boosting level on the basis of information from both Touch Tracer and Latency Tracer. The *critical texting latency* can then be determined by comparing texting interval and texting latency for the last five touch events or for the last second (see Section 4.2. for more details). The touch boosting level of the touchscreen driver is altered by comparing critical texting latency with recent texting latency. When touch latency is greater than critical texting latency, a high level of touch boost is used (and vice versa).

4.2 Critical Texting Latency

We now define critical texting latency—that is, the texting latency required to ensure QoE during texting. The texting latency should be maintained shorter than critical texting latency.

We conducted a user study with sixteen participants to determine the effect of texting latency on QoE. For this study, CPU frequency was fixed at maximum to maintain constant performance. For the purposes of the experiment, we developed a simple application and asked users about their level of satisfaction with touch latency. In the application, twenty types of button were provided for random assignment of texting latency from 30 to 125ms. The default button had a texting latency of 50 ms, and this was used as the reference point. The testing methodology involved a double-stimulus impairment scale method, using a five-grade impairment scale as described in ITU-R BT Rec. 500 [6]. Figure 7 presents the results.

When texting latency was between 30 and 100 ms, user ratings decreased slightly, but users did not experience discomfort. The rating changed rapidly when texting latency exceeded 100 ms, as users felt uncomfortable with a texting latency above this level. A recent study [3] that classified workloads in terms of event intensity and latency found that the acceptable QoE boundary for texting is 100 ms for low event intensity (fewer events per second) and low latency (shorter execution time). Our results are consistent with those findings.

In some cases, critical texting latency should be applied conservatively. If texting latency exceeds the texting interval, the next text input will occur before completion of the previous texting operation. Because of these nested operations, texting latency can suddenly increase. Figure 8 shows the result of an experiment to measure texting latency according to touch boosting level with a texting interval of 75 ms. Boost level 12 is the CPU frequency step used in the current touch boosting system, and

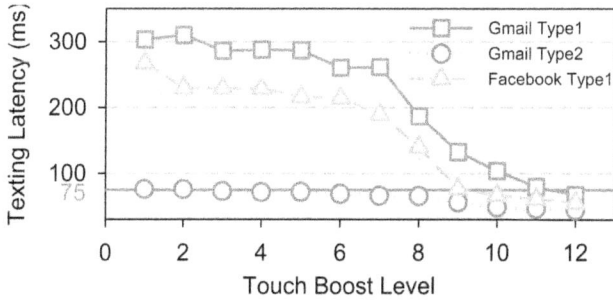

Figure 8. Relation between texting latency and boost level.

boost level 1 is the lowest CPU frequency step. If texting latency is less than the texting interval fixed at 75 ms, texting latency increases slightly even though the CPU frequency used for touch boosting is low. On the other hand, if texting latency is greater than the texting interval, texting latency increases rapidly as the CPU frequency used for touch boosting decreases. Texting interval is therefore used as the critical texting latency in this situation to prevent a rapid increase in texting latency.

Based on the results of the above experiments, a simple algorithm was developed to determine critical texting latency. When the average texting interval exceeds texting latency, user-perceived latency of 100 ms is used as the critical texting latency. Conversely, when the average texting interval is less than the texting latency, texting interval is used as the critical texting latency. Here, user-perceived latency is the latency at which users began to experience discomfort in the previous user study. Based on this critical texting latency, we adaptively control the touch boost level to provide adequate QoE for diverse workloads.

5. EVALUATION

Tbooster was evaluated to validate its effectiveness for power saving, texting quality, and overhead as implemented on a Samsung Galaxy S5 running Android KitKat.

5.1 Power Saving

Experiments were conducted to measure power consumption both before and after applying Tbooster. The 20 texting cases used in Section 3.2 were benchmarked for the purposes of the evaluation. Figure 9 shows the overall effect of power reduction as compared to the current touch boost approach. Power saving effectiveness was found to be dependent on texting interval. As Figure 9 shows, the shortest touch interval of 75 ms leaves little room to lower the touch boost level, as workload per unit time is high and the critical texting latency is 75 ms. Thus power saving at 75 ms is reduced by only 4.6%, with an average of 74.8 mW. Second, for 300, and 400 ms, the power savings are 7.2 and 5.9%, respectively. As shown in Figure 3, touch boosting has less impact

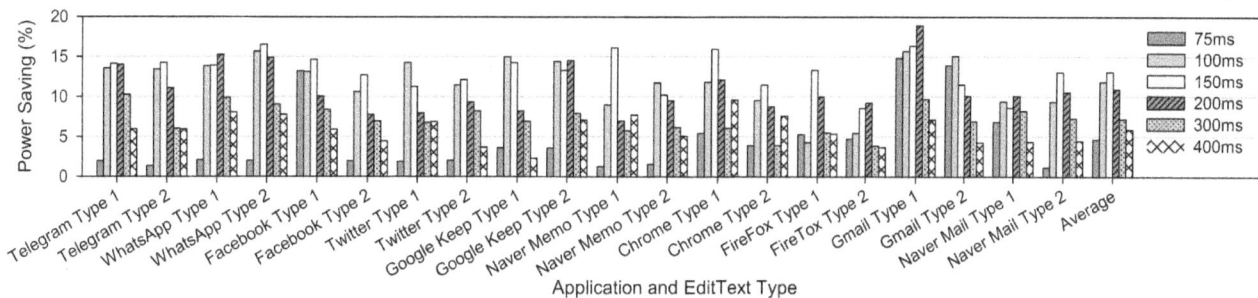

Figure 10. CPU frequency distribution using Tbooster.

on power consumption as texting interval increases, and the reduction of power consumption is small, with averages of 72.6 and 57.3 mW. Finally, at 100, 150, and 200 ms texting intervals, power savings of 11.8, 13.1, 10.8%, respectively, were observed. This is meaningful because, according to the user study on texting intervals in Section 3.1, these account for most of the distribution of users' texting interval. In this range, texting latency is smallest when touch boost is turned off, representing a good opportunity to lower CPU frequency for effective touch boosting. The average power saving for the entire texting interval is 8.9%, and the effect of touching boosting itself (excluding base power) is approximately 25.6%.

To further analyze the power saving effect, experiments were conducted to measure CPU usage by frequency. Figure 10 shows the distribution. Usage of 1.7 GHz (the frequency used for current touch boosting) is considerably reduced by the use of Tbooster. In the case of frequencies lower than 1.7 GHz, CPU usage increases in every case while decreasing for frequencies higher than 1.7GHz; this is because touch boosting level was adaptively adjusted on the basis of texting latency and texting interval. CPU usage, which was concentrated at 0.3GHz and 1.7GHz, is now seen to be evenly distributed across other CPU frequencies.

The above evaluation was done in controlled environment for the exact analysis of the efficacy of the proposed mechanism. In fact, many factors in real use scenario influence the energy consumption of device, and mobile texting would constitute a fraction of the overall portion. Here, one critical question would be how much does this optimization improve day-to-day battery life? The answer is hard to get since the overall energy savings should be measured for typical users under long-term and duplicative use scenarios. Leaving this for future work, we in this work conducted a rough evaluation on the gross effect of Tbooster, with ten apps (Figure 9) plus two more messenger apps - Kakao Talk and Line. Each application was used for 30 minutes under *normal application use*, i.e., no controlled setup, and the energy consumption was measured with and without Tbooster. We observed that during this period device energy is saved 1.9~13%, and 6% on average. As predicted, WhatsApp, Kakao Talk, and Line were most effective since text input is the primary

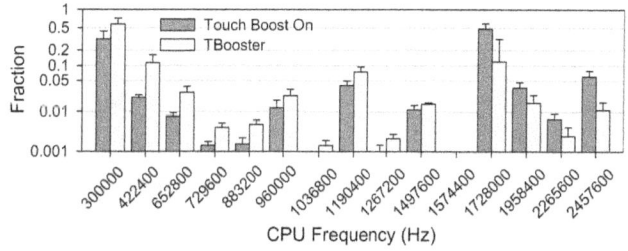

Figure 9. Effect of Tbooster on power consumption.

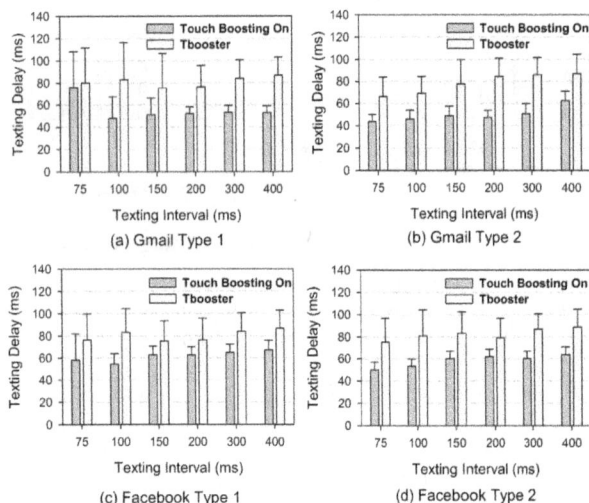

Figure 11. Tbooster: texting latency vs. texting interval.

functionality of the applications. Considering that typical users are frequently using messenger apps for a considerable amount of time in daily basis, we believe that the effect of Tbooster should be meaningful in real world scenarios.

5.2 Texting Quality

Texting latency was measured to investigate any possible degradation of texting quality by Tbooster. Figure 11 shows that for current touch boosting, texting latency is about 55.7 ms, which is far shorter than the acceptable QoE measure of 100ms. Using Tbooster, the average texting latency is 79.6 ms, an increase of 43% above the baseline. However, Tbooster maintains an average texting latency lower than the critical texting latency when texting interval is increased from 100 ms to 400 ms. At 75 ms, texting latency is slightly greater than the critical texting latency, but because it is still lower than the acceptable QoE measure, the quality of user performance is not significantly reduced.

5.3 Overhead

For overhead analysis, we measured the additional power consumption when using Tbooster. For the experiment, the Boost Level Controller was deactivated to render touch boosting identical with that of the default state. Power consumption with the deactivated Tbooster was then compared to current touch boosting. At texting intervals of 75, 100, 150, 200, 300, and 400ms, there was additional power consumption of 0.93, 0.62, 0.33, 0.22, 0.14, and 0.13%, respectively. When the texting interval was shortened, overhead increased because the computation overhead for Tbooster increases as touch events occur more frequently. Nevertheless, even at the shortest texting interval of 75 ms, the power overhead for Tbooster was 0.93%, which is negligible.

6. RELATED WORK

Recent studies have considered user experience and user interaction in relation to managing the power consumption of smartphones. SmartCap [7] showed that a neural network-based inference model is useful in deciding minimum acceptable frequency without degrading user experience. The technique proposed in AURA [8] effectively determines CPU frequency for each interactive session by classifying applications according to intensity of user interaction. A power optimization framework

based on user-perceived response time analysis was proposed in [2], and [4] characterized and compared energy consumption for three text input modalities: type, talk, and Swype. In similar vein, the present study investigated touch boosting for soft keyboard input and suggested improvements.

7. CONCLUSION

Current touch boosting systems use a predetermined CPU frequency step that takes no account of factors such as user texting speed, types of texting view, or workloads associated with texting applications. This commonly results in unnecessarily high performance demands, and as a consequence, power is wasted. Here, we have proposed an adaptive touch boosting system for texting that dynamically adjusts touch boosting level on the basis of texting latency and texting interval. Tbooster has been shown to reduce power consumption during texting while maintaining texting latency below critical texting latency. Using real applications, our evaluation shows that Tbooster reduces overall device power consumption by 4.6 to 13.1% (depending on texting interval) while satisfying user-perceived latency.

8. ACKNOWLEDGEMENTS

This work was supported by Samsung Research Funding Center of Samsung Electronics under Project Number SRFC-TB1503-02.

9. REFERENCES

[1] Ravindranath, L., Padhye, J., Agarwal, S., Mahajan, R., Obermiller, I., and Shayandeh, S. 2012. AppInsight: Mobile App Performance Monitoring in the Wild. *OSDI* 12, 107-120.

[2] Song, W., Sung, N., Chun, B. G., and Kim, J. 2014. Reducing energy consumption of smartphones using user-perceived response time analysis. *Proc. 15th Workshop on Mobile Computing Systems and Applications*.

[3] Zhu, Y., Halpern, M., and Reddi, V. J. 2015. Event-based scheduling for energy-efficient QoS (eQoS) in mobile web applications. *Proc. IEEE 21st International Symposium on High Performance Computer Architecture (HPCA)*.

[4] Jiang, F., Zarepour, E., Hassan, M., Seneviratne, A., and Mohapatra, P. When to Type, Talk, or Swype: Characterizing Energy Consumption of Mobile Input Modalities.

[5] Nielsenwire. 2010. US teen mobile report: Calling yesterday, texting today, using apps tomorrow [blog post]. http:/fblog. nielsen. com/nielsenwire/onlirte_rnobile/us-teen-mobile-report-calling-yesterday-texting-today-using-apps-tomorrow.

[6] BT.500-13 ITU-R Recommendation, "Methodology for the subjective assessment of the quality of television pictures", *Tech. Rep. BT.500-13*, ITU, 2012.

[7] Li, X., Yan, G., Han, Y., and Li, X. 2013. SmartCap: user experience-oriented power adaptation for smartphone's application processor. *Proc. Conference on Design, Automation and Test in Europe*.

[8] Donohoo, B. K., Ohlsen, C., and Pasricha, S. 2011. AURA: An application and user interaction aware middleware framework for energy optimization in mobile devices. *Proc. IEEE 29th International Conference on Computer Design (ICCD)*.

Toward Extrapolation of WiFi Fingerprinting Performance Across Environments

Filip Lemic
Technische Univesität Berlin
lemic@tkn.tu-berlin.de

Vlado Handziski
Technische Univesität Berlin
handziski@tkn.tu-berlin.de

Giuseppe Caso
Sapienza University of Rome
caso@newyork.ing.uniroma1.it

Pieter Crombez
Televic Health Care NV
p.crombez@televic.com

Luca De Nardis
Sapienza University of Rome
lucadn@newyork.ing.uniroma1.it

Adam Wolisz
Technische Univesität Berlin
awo@ieee.org

ABSTRACT

Out of the plethora of approaches for indoor localization, WiFi-based fingerprinting offers attractive trade-off between deployment overheads and accuracy. This has motivated intense research interest resulting in many proposed algorithms which are typically evaluated only in a single or small number of discrete environments. When the end-user's environment is not part of the evaluated set, it remains unclear if and to what extent the reported performance results can be extrapolated to this new environment. In this paper, we aim at establishing a relationship between the similarities among a set of different deployment environments and parameterizations of fingerprinting algorithms on one side, and the performance of these algorithms on the other. We hypothesize about the factors that can be used to capture the degree of similarity among environments and parameterizations of the algorithms, and proceed to systematically analyze the performance of two fingerprinting algorithms across four environments with different levels of similarity. The results show that the localization error distributions have small statistical difference across environments and parameterizations that are considered similar according to our hypothesis. As the level of similarity is decreased, we demonstrate that the relative performance of the algorithms can still be preserved across environments. For dissimilar environments, the localization errors demonstrate larger statistical differences.

Keywords

Indoor localization; indoor positioning; fingerprinting; performance extrapolation; radio frequency; WiFi.

1. INTRODUCTION

Radio Frequency (RF)-based localization, specifically WiFi Received Signal Strength Indicator (RSSI)-based fingerprinting, is one of the promising candidates for an ubiquitous indoor localization service [ ]. Consequently, performance evaluations of such algorithms in different environments are becoming publicly available [,]. Thus, the interested users are able to get insights in the performance of various algorithms in different environments through these standardized benchmarks. However, it is still unclear if the performance results, in terms of localization errors, achieved in one environment and for one parameterization of an algorithm, can be representative for another environment and parameterization of the same algorithm.

The extrapolation of the performance of fingerprinting algorithms across environments would be beneficial from two perspectives. From the technological and research perspective, it would allow categorization of algorithms based on their suitability for different types of environments. From the users' perspective, the extrapolation would give them the possibility of speculating about the performance of different algorithms for a particular environment without the need for extensive experimentation. Collection of such measurements is particularly problematic for buildings that are usually not accessible for an extensive experimentation (e.g. hospitals or buildings under construction).

The possibility of performance extrapolation for different systems has been addressed in various research domains. For example, in network experimentation the need for having realistic experimentation conditions in testbeds has been addressed in [ ], while for evaluation of artificial intelligence the question of extrapolation of results achieved in testbeds to reality has been addressed in [ ]. Moreover, in [ ] the authors aim on predicting the performance of GPU applications by correlating them to existing benchmarks, while in [ ] the authors qualify the similarity of computer systems and then use this similarity for predicting the performance of a new application. However, in the domain of WiFi fingerprinting, the question of performance extrapolation is, to the best of our knowledge, still open.

In this paper, we systematically analyze the performance achieved by a set of WiFi RSSI-based fingerprinting algorithms in a set of environments with different characteristics. Our goal is to establish a link between the similarities among environments and parameterizations of algorithms in these environments, with the possibility to extrapolate the performance of such algorithms across environments. Our contributions include a hypothesis about the extrapolability of the performance of WiFi fingerprinting algorithms across environments, demonstrating the feasibility of the hypothesis, and outlining a methodology for its further evaluation.

This paper is structured as follows. In Section 2, we formulate our hypothesis about the possibility of performance extrapolation of fingerprinting algorithms across environments. We characterize the similarity among environments

HotMobile'16, February 23–24, 2016, St. Augustine, FL, USA

© 2016 ACM. ISBN 978-1-4503-4145-5/16/02...$15.00

DOI: http://dx.doi.org/10.1145/2873587.2873588

by looking at two aspects: physical shape and setup, and RF propagation characteristics. In Section 3, we describe the physical shape and experimental setup in all environments used in the evaluation. In Section 4, we introduce a model used for calculating propagation characteristics of different environments. In Section 5, we overview the evaluated algorithms and provide the evaluation scenarios and approaches, while in Section 6 we discuss the obtained results. Finally, in Section 7, we outline directions for further evaluation of the given hypothesis and we conclude the work.

2. EXTRAPOLATION HYPOTHESIS

For the accurate extrapolation of the performance of fingerprinting algorithms across environments one has to be careful to select both environments and parameterizations of an algorithm that can be characterized as "similar". One of the important parameters in accessing the similarity of two environments pertains to their physical shape, *w.r.t.* their outer size, as well as the sizes of their inner spaces. We further hypothesize that similarities in the parameters of propagation in different environments are important factors for characterizing the similarity among environments.

Apart from the environments *per-se*, we hypothesize that the parameterizations of a fingerprinting algorithm in these environments have to be similar for being able to extrapolate the performance of an algorithm across environments. This pertains to the type of algorithm used, the number, density and deployment locations of Access Points (APs), their transmission powers and operating frequencies, the number of measurements taken at each measurement point, and the number and density of training points. Given that the parameterizations of an algorithm in two environments are comparable and the environments are similar, we hypothesize that a reliable extrapolation of the algorithm's performance across environments is possible.

We evaluate the hypothesis by comparing the performance achieved by two fingerprinting algorithms in a baseline, real-life hospital environment with their performance in three other environments with different levels of similarities to the hospital environment. The performance results of fingerprinting algorithms in these additional environments are publicly available [8], and they serve as standardized benchmarks of the performance of fingerprinting algorithms. Our similarity characterization yields that one environment is highly similar to the hospital baseline, in both physical and propagation characteristics, while the other two environments have increasing dissimilarities with the baseline.

3. ENVIRONMENTS: PHYSICAL SHAPE AND EXPERIMENTAL SETUP

In this section, we present the physical shape and the experimental setup in the four used environments, with the relevant environment related parameters given in Table 1.

Hospital: The hospital serves as a baseline environment for which we would like to extrapolate the performance of fingerprinting algorithms. The measurement campaign was performed in the "chirurgic day" ward of the Sint-Jozefskliniek Izegem in Belgium, with footprint depicted in Figure 1a). For the measurement collection the end section of a corridor was used, while the rest of ward was in "normal operation", meaning people were present in the hospital. In the given environment, six IEEE 802.11g APs (WNDR 4300) were deployed, one in each room in the environment of interest, with

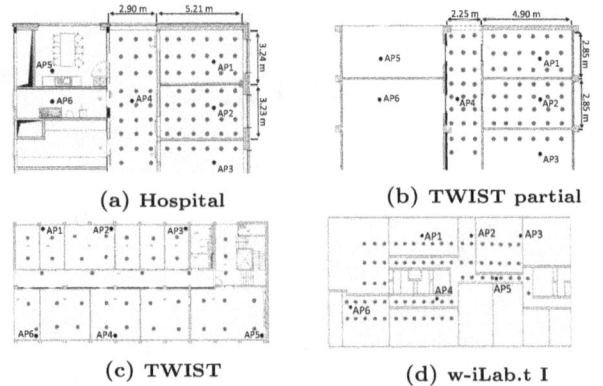

(a) Hospital   (b) TWIST partial

(c) TWIST   (d) w-iLab.t I

Figure 1: Footprints of the four environments

their locations indicated in the figure. The APs were configured in beaconing mode, with beacon transmission period of 100 ms. The transmission power of each AP was set to 20 dBm. The APs 1, 3 and 4 were operating on WiFi channel 6, while for the others (AP 2, 5 and 6) the operational channel was WiFi channel 11. In the environment of interest, which included three rooms and a hallway, a total number of 73 measurement points were defined in a relatively dense grid with cell size equal to 1 m, as indicated by the red dots in Figure 1a). In each of the defined points, the wireless environment was sampled for WiFi beacon packets using a laptop with external wireless adapter (TL-WN823N). At each location, four scans of the wireless environment were performed, meaning that at each location, from each visible AP, at most 4 beacon packets could be obtained. Due to a limited availability of the environment and in order not to interrupt the normal hospital activities, the measurement campaign was constrained in both size and duration. However, it represents one of the first publicly available datasets that capture a realistic hospital environment for the purpose of evaluation of WiFi-based fingerprinting.

TWIST partial: The standardized benchmark obtained from this environment, which is a part of the TWIST testbed in Berlin [9], has high levels of similarity with the hospital environment, *w.r.t.* similar sizes of the offices/rooms, outer sizes, and similar activities as in the hospital (people moving in the testbed premises, since it is an office building). We believe that this environment mimics the hospital environment to the level that is practically possible, as shown in Figure 1b). In this part of the environment, six WiFi APs were deployed at similar locations as for the hospital. The APs were configured as in the hospital, although they were of a different type (TP LINK N750). Similarly, 73 measurement points were selected and in each point the wireless environment was scanned four times, same as for the hospital, but using an Airport Extreme network interface card.

TWIST: The TWIST testbed environment in its entirety is an office environment, with room sizes slightly bigger than the hospital environment and with an outer dimensions of roughly 30x15 m^2. Also in this environment, six dedicated WiFi APs were deployed with their locations shown in Figure 1c). They were configured to operate in beaconing mode with beacon transmission period of 100 ms and transmission power of 20 dBm. In this environment, 41 measurement points were defined and in each of the points four scans of the wireless environment were performed.

w-iLab.t I: The w-iLab.t I testbed is an office environment with outer dimensions of roughly 45x 17 m^2. In comparison to the TWIST testbed, in this environment the office sizes are less similar to the hospital, as shown in Figure 1d). For this measurement campaign also six "dedicated" WiFi APs were deployed with the same configuration as in the TWIST environment. For the measurement campaign 69 measurement points were defined and in each of them a scan of the wireless environment was performed. In this environment also four measurements per point were taken.

Table 1: Parameters of the environments

Parameter	Outer size	Mean room size	Wall type
Hospital	8.1 x 7.4 m	15.0 m^2	plywood
TWIST partial	7.2 x 6.8 m	12.5 m^2	concrete
TWIST	30.0 x 15.0 m	27.0 m^2	concrete
w-iLab.t I	45.0 x 17.0 m	51.0 m^2	plywood

4. PROPAGATION CHARACTERISTICS

For further understanding of the similarities among environments, we modeled the RF propagation parameters by leveraging the collected measurements. The applied propagation model is the COST 231 multi-wall model for indoor radio propagation [ ]. The applicability of this model for indoor localization purposes has been demonstrated in [ ]. The first attenuation contribution in the model is a well-known one-slope term that relates the received power to the distance. Two parameters influence the attenuation in this term: the constant l_0 (the path-loss at 1 m distance and at the center frequency of 2.45 GHz) and the path-loss exponent γ. The second attenuation contribution is a linear wall/obstacle term. The number of obstacles in the direct path between transmitter and receiver is counted and for each type of obstacle an attenuation contribution is assumed. Given the model and the site-specific measurements from different environments, we leveraged a least square fitting procedure that allows minimizing the cost function between the measured received power and the modeled one.

Table 2: Parameters of the propagation model

Parameter	l_c [dB]	γ	l_w [dB]
Hospital	57.38	1.46	2.60
TWIST partial	58.36	1.25	2.78
TWIST	53.73	1.64	4.51
w-iLab.t I	60.23	1.29	1.12

The parameters to be optimized are the constant l_c related to the least square fitting procedure, the γ path-loss exponent, and the wall attenuation factor. Although $\gamma = 2$ is a usual assumption for the propagation in the free space, coming from Friis equation, due to the obstacles in our environments we also estimate γ. Moreover, we do a set of prediction tests on (rolling) 10% of sampling points using a model fitted on the remaining 90%, to be sure that we do not have unexpected interactions between the linear constant and the γ. The modeled averaged propagation parameters are given in Table 2, since small discrepancies are obtained by performing the rolling tests. As indicated in the table, for all environments l_c and γ variables have comparable values. Furthermore, in terms of wall attenuation, the similarity between the hospital and the partial TWIST environments is high, while smaller similarities are observed between the hospital, TWIST and w-iLab.t I environments.

5. EVALUATED ALGORITHMS, SCENARIOS AND APPROACHES

This section gives an overview of the fingerprinting algorithms, scenarios, and approaches used in the evaluation.

5.1 Fingerprinting Algorithms

Euclidean distance of averaged RSSI vectors: This simple, yet popular fingerprinting algorithm [ ] computes an average value of the RSSI measurements obtained from each AP used for localization. The fingerprint is a vector of average values of the RSSI measurements obtained from all APs used for localization in both training and runtime steps, where K is the length of the vector. Let $\overline{\boldsymbol{X}}_{t,m} = [\overline{RSSI}_{t,1}, ..., \overline{RSSI}_{t,k}, ..., \overline{RSSI}_{t,K}]$ be the vector of averaged RSSI values $\overline{RSSI}_{t,i}$ from each AP i obtained in training step at point $m \in 1, ..., M_t$, i.e. training fingerprint. In the same manner, let $\overline{\boldsymbol{X}}_r = [\overline{RSSI}_{r,1}, ..., \overline{RSSI}_{r,k}, ..., \overline{RSSI}_{r,K}]$ be the vector of averaged RSSI values $\overline{RSSI}_{r,i}$ from each AP i obtained in runtime step, i.e. runtime fingerprint. The pattern matching procedure uses Euclidean distance between a training fingerprint at the cell m and the runtime fingerprint:

$$D_E(\overline{\boldsymbol{X}}_{t,m}, \overline{\boldsymbol{X}}_r) = |\overline{\boldsymbol{X}}_{t,m} - \overline{\boldsymbol{X}}_r|. \tag{1}$$

Training fingerprints with the smallest distance D_E are then used in a post-processing procedure.

Pompeiu-Hausdorff distance of RSSI quantiles: A recently proposed procedure [ ] uses a vector of q quantiles of the RSSI values from each AP as fingerprints, which are calculated in two steps. First the Cumulative Distribution Function (CDF) of the RSSI measurements from each AP is computed. Second, the quantiles, i.e. RSSI values with probabilities $k/(q - 1)$, where $k = 0, 1, ..., q - 1$, are calculated. The result of the quantile calculation in both training and runtime steps is a quantile matrix $Q_{K,q}$, where K is the number of APs visible at the given location and q is a number of quantiles. The pattern matching procedure of this algorithm uses the Pompeiu-Hausdorff (PH) metric for capturing similarities between training fingerprints and a runtime fingerprint, with $d(x_{t,k}, x_{r,k})$ being the Euclidean distance between elements of the runtime fingerprint $\boldsymbol{X}_r$ and training fingerprint $\boldsymbol{X}_{t,m}$ at point m:

$$D_{PH}(\boldsymbol{X}_{t,m}, \boldsymbol{X}_r) = \max_{x_{t,k} \in \boldsymbol{X}_{t,m}} \min_{x_{r,k} \in \boldsymbol{X}_r} d(x_{t,k}, x_{r,k}). \tag{2}$$

5.2 Evaluation Scenarios

To create multiple scenarios for evaluating the possibility of performance extrapolation across environments, for both algorithms we filtered the collected raw data (i.e. we used different parameterizations of algorithms) as follows. Firstly, we evaluated the localization errors in case measurements from all APs were used as inputs to an algorithm (including the APs that we have not deployed and using both 2.4 and 5 GHz Industrial, Scientific and Medical (ISM) frequency bends). Secondly, we used only measurements from the 2.4 GHz ISM frequency band. Thirdly, we used only measurements from "dedicated" APs, i.e. the six APs we deployed for localization purposes. Furthermore, we filtered measurements from only some dedicated APs to evaluate if the performance degradation due to a removal of particular APs is consistent across environments. Our decision on which AP to include was not driven by the goal of optimizing the APs deployment, but merely to increase the diversity of evaluation scenarios.

However, in case the environments are less similar, the feasible questions that can be addressed, under the assumption that the relative difference in performance results across environments is preserved, are more limited. According to that limitation, we designed our evaluation scenarios. In the first scenario, we used only six dedicated APs. In the following scenario, we used the APs 1, 2 and 4, which corresponds to a scenario in which two APs are on one side and one AP is in the center of the other side of an environment. In the third scenario, we used the APs that are all on one side of an environment. Finally, in the last two scenarios, we filtered one AP from the corner and from the center of an environment, respectively. The goal is to evaluate the possibility of preserving the relative difference in performance across environments for different scenarios, despite the fact that differences in environments and parameterizations exist.

5.3 Evaluation Approaches

The localization errors in fingerprinting generally have two aspects: spatial and temporal [13]. The temporal one is related to changes of measurements in time domain, which usually causes inconstancies between training and runtime fingerprints. The spatial aspect is related to a particular environment and respective algorithm's parameterization. We aimed on removing the temporal aspect and focusing on the spatial one, so we do not clearly differentiate between the training and runtime phases of fingerprinting, i.e. we use measurements from the same measurement campaign in both phases. We leveraged two approaches to obtain the split between the training and runtime phases. Firstly, we used first three RSSI measurements from each AP at each location for training, while the fourth measurement was used in the runtime phase. In the reminder of this paper we will refer to this approach as "evaluation approach 1". Secondly, while a given measurement point was evaluated, measurements from all other points were used for training, and we will refer to this approach as "evaluation approach 2". Two approaches were selected to increase the number of evaluation scenarios, thus increasing the reliability of our findings.

6. EVALUATION RESULTS

In this section, we present the results of evaluating the possibility of extrapolating the performance of fingerprinting algorithms across environments. Given the observations from Section 3 and Section 4, we classify one environment and algorithms' parameterization as "similar" (TWIST partial), while the other two are "less similar" to the baseline hospital environment (TWIST and w-iLab.t I).

6.1 Extrapolation in Similar Environments

The distributions of localization errors for the two used algorithms in similar environments are given in Figure 2 and Figure 3 for the evaluation approaches 1 and 2, respectively. As visible in the figures, for both algorithms and for both evaluation approaches the localization errors in similar environments show small statistical differences. The results show that it is possible to give a statement about the performance of fingerprinting algorithms in one environment by using the performance results from another, similar environment. The results also validate the statistically repeatable performance of the used algorithms across similar environments.

Furthermore, we evaluated the similarities in distributions of localization errors across environments using Pearson's Chi-Squared tests. The results yield that, for all evaluation scenarios, both evaluation approaches, and both algorithms, the hypothesis of localization error distributions across environments being statistically comparable is true with the

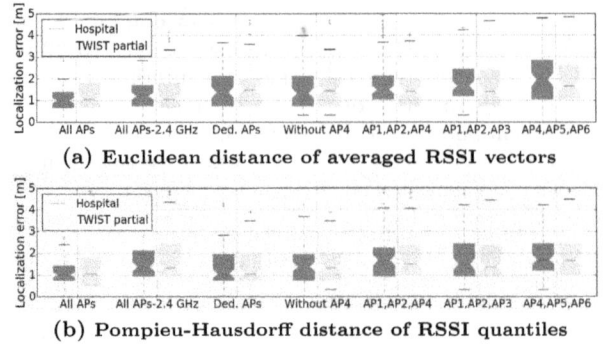

(a) Euclidean distance of averaged RSSI vectors

(b) Pompieu-Hausdorff distance of RSSI quantiles

Figure 2: Comparison of localization error distributions for similar environments - evaluation approach 1

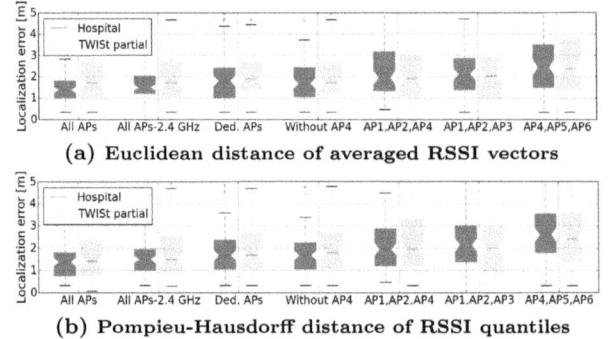

(a) Euclidean distance of averaged RSSI vectors

(b) Pompieu-Hausdorff distance of RSSI quantiles

Figure 3: Comparison of localization error distributions for similar environments - evaluation approach 2

probability of more than 95%. Finally, we used the Cohen's d tests to evaluate the magnitude of the difference of mean localization errors across environments. The result of a Cohen's d test is Cohen's d value, which is a scale-free indication of the size of an effect between two observations [14]. As a rule of thumb, Cohen's d values smaller than 0.2 represent small effect, values smaller than 0.5 represent medium size effect, while higher values than 0.5 represent high effect size. Specifically, in our evaluation Cohen's d values represent the magnitude of the effect that the change of an environment has on the achieved localization errors. Table 3 gives the Cohen's values for localization error distributions achieved by the two used algorithms for different evaluation scenarios across two similar environments. As visible in the table, the calculated Cohen's values are smaller than 0.2, meaning that the change of environments in this case has a small effect on the localization errors. Higher Cohen's d values are obtained in case all APs in the environments were used in the evaluation ("All APs" and "All APs-2.4 GHz"), since in these scenarios also uncontrollable APs (e.g. visible APs from neighboring buildings) were used as inputs to the algorithms, which resulted in a higher effect size that a change in environments has on the achieved localization errors.

In order to get a clearer view on the possibility of performance extrapolation of fingerprinting algorithms across environments, in Figure 4 we depict the localization error distributions achieved by the used algorithms in different rooms in two similar environments. Furthermore, in Table 4 we present the Cohen's d test results for the distributions of localization errors per room for different evaluation scenarios across similar environments. Due to lack of space, we present only results obtained by leveraging the evaluation approach 1, and this will be followed through the rest of

Table 3: Cohen's d test results achieved in similar environments for different evaluation scenarios and for both evaluation approaches (approach 1/approach 2)

All APs	All APs 2.4GHz	Dedicated APs	Without AP4	AP1,AP2,AP4	AP1,AP2,AP3	AP4,AP5,AP6
		Euclidean distance of averaged RSSI vectors				
0.45/0.58	0.06/0.39	0.03/0.18	0.09/0.06	0.11/0.12	0.08/0.07	0.09/0.07
		Pompieu-Hausdorff distance of RSSI quantiles				
0.16/0.35	0.14/0.34	0.02/0.19	0.06/0.24	0.02/0.02	0.07/0.12	0.06/0.03

Table 4: Cohen's d test results for the localization errors per room achieved in similar environments for different evaluation scenarios - evaluation approach 1 - (room 1/room 2/room 3/hallway)

Dedicated APs	Without AP4	AP1,AP2,AP4	AP1,AP2,AP3	AP4,AP5,AP6
	Euclidean distance of averaged RSSI vectors			
0.11/0.07/0.38/0.09	0.19/0.01/0.29/0.15	0.01/0.11/1.15/0.12	0.22/0.07/0.79/0.09	0.23/0.16/2.79/0.11
	Pompieu-Hausdorff distance of RSSI quantiles			
0.17/0.15/0.85/0.03	0.12/0.22/0.60/0.11	0.05/0.09/2.00/0.08	0.16/0.11/1.30/0.19	0.21/0.16/2.91/0.14

the paper, since the results, except for the values of the obtained localization errors, are consistent for both evaluation approaches. The rooms in Figure 4 are labeled with "1", "2", "3" and "Hall", and those are respectively the rooms where APs 1, 2 and 3 are deployed and the hallway (Figure 1a, Figure 1b). It is clear from Figure 4 and Table 4 that the change of environments has a small effect on the achieved localization errors per room, except for the errors achieved in the room labeled with "3".

The reason for this trend lies in the fact that only 6 measurement points have been defined in the room labeled with "3". Due to that, no meaningful statistics about the localization errors in this room could be extracted. In other words, it is not our intention and we believe it is not possible to extrapolate the localization errors for a single measurement point from one environment to another. The reason why a single evaluation point is not sufficient lies in the instability of the RF-based indoor localization algorithms and solutions, which is related to an intrinsic randomness in each wireless environment. This means that, even for the same environment and exactly the same measurement point, if a localization estimate is requested twice, these estimates are usually not the same. On the contrary, we believe it is only possible to accurately extrapolate the statistics of errors, and for obtaining a statistic a meaningful number of samples has to be used. This requirement is not fulfilled for the samples in the room labeled with "3", thus the performance of algorithms is not statistically comparable in this case.

6.2 Extrapolation in Less Similar Environments

In case less similar environments are used for the performance evaluation, the results are depicted in Figure 5. Despite a smaller level of similarity between those environments and the hospital, we aim on evaluating the possibility that the relative difference between the achieved localization errors for different parameterizations of algorithms can be preserved. Note that for this case we do not evaluate scenarios in which all measurements are used, but only scenarios where measurements from the six dedicated APs are leveraged. The reason is that, due to larger sizes of these environments in comparison to the hospital, the number of visible APs is expected to be increased, which could lead to wrong conclusions about the extrapolation possibility.

As visible in Figure 5, the evaluation results show that a relative difference between various parameterizations of algorithms is preserved for the TWIST environment, while for the w-iLab.t I environment that is not the case. More specifically, it is visible in the figure that, for the hospital and the TWIST environment, higher localization errors are achieved in case APs from one side of the environment are used as

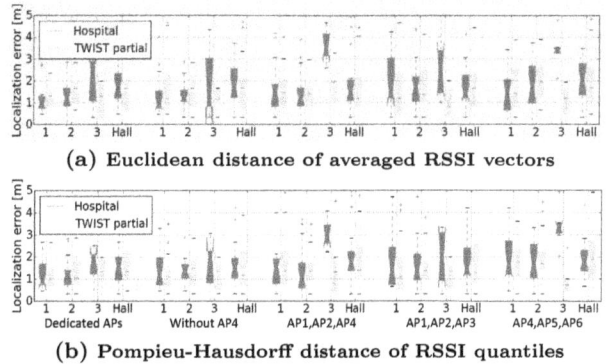

(a) Euclidean distance of averaged RSSI vectors

(b) Pompieu-Hausdorff distance of RSSI quantiles

Figure 4: Comparison of localization error distributions per room for similar environments - evaluation approach 1

anchors for location estimation (AP1,AP2,AP3 in figure), in comparison to the scenario when two APs are used on one side and one anchor on the other side of the environment (AP1,AP2,AP4). This observation, however, does not hold for the w-iLab.t I environment, since in this case the localization performance is better when only APs from one side of the environment are used. Similarly, for both algorithms, and for both hospital and TWIST environments, comparable localization errors are achieved in case an AP from the center of an environment is not used for the localization purposes (Without AP4), in comparison to a case when an AP from the corner of an environment is not used (Without AP1). As it can be seen in the figure, in this case the ranking is again not preserved for the w-iLab.t I environment. Similar observation can be made from Table 5, since Cohen's d values are similar across different evaluation scenarios in case the hospital is compared to the TWIST environment, while they have larger discrepancies in case the hospital is compared with the w-iLab.t I environment.

Clearly, the hospital environment and the two other, less similar environments differ in the outer sizes, as well as in the number of inner walls. However, the hospital and TWIST environments have comparable room sizes, while that is not the case for w-iLab.t I environment. Furthermore, the wall attenuation factor is different for all three environments. This factor is much higher for the TWIST environment, in comparison to the hospital, while for the w-iLab.t I this factor is much smaller than for the hospital environment. A relatively high wall attenuation indicates that a wireless environment has higher spatially distinguishable features, which benefits fingerprinting in general [13]. This is possibly a reason for substantially smaller localization errors in TWIST, in comparison to w-iLab.t I environment, in case a small number of APs is used. In all three environments, the same number and configuration of APs are used, although their deployment locations and densities are different. Finally, the number and density of measurement points differ, while the number of measurements taken at each point is the same for all three environments.

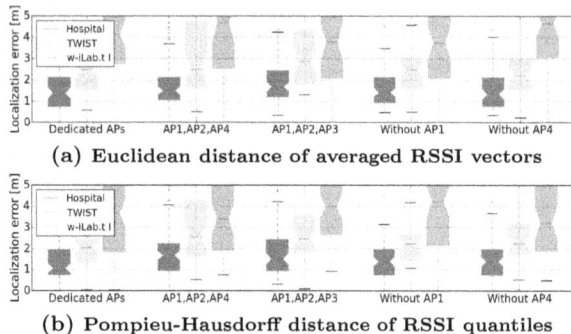

(a) Euclidean distance of averaged RSSI vectors

(b) Pompieu-Hausdorff distance of RSSI quantiles

Figure 5: Comparison of localization errors for less similar environments - evaluation approach 1

Table 5: Cohen's d test results achieved in less similar environments - evaluation approach 1

Ded. APs	AP1,2,4	AP1,2,3	No AP1	No AP4
Euclidean distance of averaged RSSI vectors				
0.68/1.41	0.69/1.04	0.64/1.39	0.79/1.67	0.84/1.32
Pompieu-Hausdorff distance of RSSI quantiles				
0.74/1.56	0.72/1.27	0.77/1.04	0.82/0.47	0.72/1.84

7. CONCLUSION AND FUTURE WORK

In this paper, we postulated a hypothesis for the extrapolation of fingerprinting algorithms' performance across environments, given that the environments and the parameterizations of fingerprinting algorithms in these environments are similar. We demonstrated that the performance of a set of fingerprinting algorithms in one environment has a small statistical difference to their performance in a similar environment, in terms of the absolute values of localization errors. We have also shown that, even in case environments and parameterizations of algorithms are less similar, the relative performance of fingerprinting algorithms can be preserved. In other words, we demonstrated that the performance extrapolation across environments is a feasible concept, which depends on the similarities among environments.

While we have demonstrated that the performance extrapolation of fingerprinting algorithms across environments is possible, at this point we cannot make any final conclusions on how similar the environments and respective algorithm's parameterizations have to be. In order to give a reliable answer, insights from additional environments and algorithms are necessary. Our future work will be oriented toward this goal, but we also seek support form the community. The envisioned contribution from the community is twofolds. Firstly, the interested parties can contribute by extending the available datasets with data from additional environments. These data-traces can be provided and used in a simple way through a set of publicly accessible web-based services. Secondly, the interested parties can contribute by evaluating their fingerprinting algorithms using the offered data-traces and provided evaluation services, as described in [8]. By increasing the number of environments and evaluation results, more insights in the correlation between the similarity of environments and parameterizations of algorithms, and the similarity between the achieved performance of such algorithms will be gained. These insights

will serve to evaluate with higher confidence our hypothesis about the possibility of extrapolating the performance of fingerprinting algorithms across environments. Furthermore, it will serve to assess the change in the performance of fingerprinting algorithms due to changes in some of the detected important factors for characterizing the similarities between two environments and parameterizations of algorithms.

In this paper, we have focused on RSSI-based fingerprinting, while future work will also be oriented toward capturing other environment parameters that are influencing the performance similarity of different localization approaches. Our aim is to identify a smaller number of environmental similarity parameters that have a broader impact on the extrapolability of different localization approaches across environments. One clear drawback of our approach is that, at the moment, we have based the assessment of the similarity in a manual way, through the physical shape and propagation characteristics of different environments. To scale the approach we will resort to automatizing it. We are considering to use the SWAT (Stanford Wireless Analysis Tool) [15] for collecting low-level wireless network measurements and using them for automatized quantification of the similarity metrics of different environments.

8. ACKNOWLEDGMENTS

This work has been partially funded by the EU Commission (FP7-ICT-FIRE) within the project EVARILOS (grant No. 317989). The author Filip Lemic was partially supported by the DAAD (German Academic Exchange Service).

9. ADDITIONAL AUTHORS

Tom Van Haute (Ghent University, tom.vanhaute@intec.ugent.be)
Eli De Poorter (Ghent University, eli.depoorter@intec.ugent.be)

10. REFERENCES

[1] P. Bahl et al., "RADAR: An In-building RF-based User Location and Tracking System," in INFOCOM'00, 2000.
[2] D. Lymberopoulos et al., "A Realistic Evaluation and Comparison of Indoor Location Technologies: Experiences and Lessons Learned," in IPSN'15, 2015.
[3] F. Lemic et al., "Experimental Evaluation of RF-based Indoor Localization Algorithms Under RF Interference," in ICL-GNSS'15, 2015.
[4] A. Bavier et al., "In VINI Veritas: Realistic and Controlled Network Experimentation," in SIGCOMM'06, ACM, 2006.
[5] J. Hernández-Orallo et al., "On More Realistic Environment Distributions for Defining, Evaluating and Developing Intelligence," in Artificial General Intelligence, Springer, 2011.
[6] S. Che et al., "BenchFriend: Correlating the Performance of GPU Benchmarks," High Performance Computing Apps, 2013.
[7] S. Phansalkar, Measuring Program Similarity for Efficient Benchmarking and Performance Analysis of Computer Systems. ProQuest, 2007.
[8] F. Lemic et al., "Web-based Platform for Evaluation of RF-based Indoor Localization Algorithms," in ANLN'15, 2015.
[9] F. Lemic et al., "Infrastructure for Benchmarking RF-based Indoor Localization under Controlled Interference," in UPINLBS'14, 2014.
[10] E. Damosso et al., COST Action 231: Digital Mobile Radio Towards Future Generation Systems. EUR Series, 1999.
[11] G. Caso et al., "On the Applicability of Multi Wall Multi Floor Propagation Models to WiFi Fingerprinting Indoor Positioning," in FABULOUS'15, 2015.
[12] F. Lemic et al., "Experimental Decomposition of the Performance of Fingerprinting-based Localization Algorithms," in IPIN'14, 2014.
[13] V. Honkavirta et al., "A Comparative Survey of WLAN Location Fingerprinting Methods," in WPNC'09, IEEE, 2009.
[14] J. Cohen, "A Power Primer," Psychological bulletin, 1992.
[15] K. Srinivasan et al., "SWAT: Enabling Wireless Network Measurements," in ACM Sensys'08, ACM, 2008.

A Wireless-Based Approach for Transit Analytics

Lei Kang   Bozhao Qi   Suman Banerjee
Department of Computer Sciences
University of Wisconsin-Madison
{lkang, bozhao, suman}@cs.wisc.edu

ABSTRACT

We propose Trellis — an in-vehicle WiFi-based tracking system that passively observes mobile devices and provides various analytics for transit operators. Our infrastructure is fairly low-cost and can be a complementary, yet efficient, mechanism by which such operators collect various information, e.g., popular original-destination stations of passengers, waiting times of passengers at stations, occupancy of vehicles, and more. A key challenge in our system is to efficiently determine which device is actually inside (or outside) of a transit vehicle, which we are able to address through contextual information. While our current system cannot provide accurate actual numbers of passengers, we expect the relative numbers and general trends to be still fairly useful from an analytics perspective. We have deployed a preliminary version of Trellis on two city buses in Madison, WI, and report on some general observations on transit efficiency over a period of four months.

Keywords

In-Vehicle Systems; Mobile Computing

1. INTRODUCTION

Public transit systems carry millions of users in their daily activities throughout the year and are, sometimes, an important part of public infrastructure provided by local governments. Like all systems, public transit has always looked for mechanisms that allow them to improve their services for people in terms of, say, what new routes or stops should be introduced, how do peak and off-peak behaviors be handled, and much more. Traditionally, these decisions are often based on limited surveys — the local Madison Metro Transit would use infrequent volunteers ask people about their transit preferences. However, just as mobile devices have transformed crowd-sourced data collection in a whole range of domains, we believe that transit systems can also benefit significantly from it. In this paper, we advocate a fairly

HotMobile '16, February 26-27, 2016, St. Augustine, FL, USA
© 2016 ACM. ISBN 978-1-4503-4145-5/16/02. . . $15.00
DOI: http://dx.doi.org/10.1145/2873587.2873589

low-cost and simple system through which a transit operator can gather significant user and usage analytics about its operations at a scale and form never possible before.

Examples of transit analytics and Trellis: Transit systems typically need to learn about a lot of usage characteristics. What are the most popular stops at different times of the day; what are wait times for its passengers; how long do they wait at exchange points waiting for the next vehicle; how occupied are different vehicles at different times of the day; and so on. Some of these questions are significantly related to funds allocated to them — in particular, operators sometimes receive government funds based on how many *passenger-miles* they carry annually [11, 3, 14]. Today, these operators use a number of low fidelity methods to collect such information. For instance, farecards swiped inside inside buses may allow the operator to know the stations at which passengers get on (although they might not be able to infer where the passengers get off). Similarly, optional surveys (either in person or over the phone) allow them to collect other statistics. Approaches such as the above tend to provide incomplete data or data with fairly low fidelity.

Our proposed system, Trellis, takes advantage of widely available mobile devices and the popular notion of crowd-sourcing from many passengers to quickly gather such information at a significantly larger scale. Wi-Fi-based monitoring system has been widely used in many related scenarios, such as understanding network performance [8], estimating vehicle trajectories [16], and tracking human queues [18]. Trellis is based on similar principles and is fairly simple — it uses a low-end Wi-Fi monitoring unit mounted on the vehicle to determine when a certain passenger gets on and off the vehicle. The approach relies on the fact that many mobile devices typically have their Wi-Fi function turned on, which makes them sufficiently trackable. Obviously systems such as Trellis will miss accounting for passengers who travel without mobile devices or those with their Wi-Fi function turned off, but our experience shows that we can still track general trends in transit behavior quite effectively [1]. We recommend our current version of Trellis to track relative trends in transit systems, as opposed to using them for exact and absolute counts. (We note that in Trellis, we maintain user privacy by simply using consistent hashes on MAC addresses, and not the actual MAC address itself; the latter is dropped immediately.)

---

[1] Techniques such as randomized MAC addresses may lead to inaccuracies, but we should be able to systematically eliminate all devices that do so, while still keeping *relative* counts somewhat accurate.

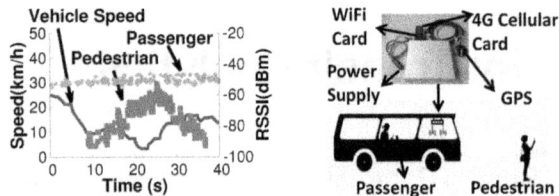

Figure 1: Different RSSI patterns between passenger and pedestrian, and the Wi-Fi monitor installed on vehicle.

We believe a simple and low-cost infrastructure such as Trellis mounted on public transit vehicles can be used to perform transit analytics for a wide range of questions effectively. For the purpose of this paper, we demonstrate how such a system maybe used to answer one specific question (just as an example) – *what are the origin-destination pairs of the user population and how does the popularity of these origin-destination pairs vary for different stations, at different locations, and at different times of the day.* Through our work, we demonstrate how we can build an origin-destination matrix to understand passenger travel patterns using Trellis, which can often identify alternative bus scheduling or routing to improve passenger travel times.

In the end, Trellis provides yet another approach to collect transit information in real-time and can potentially be combined with other existing or complementary approaches.

Trellis approach, some challenges, and preliminary implementation: We implement the Trellis system using off-the- shelf embedded platforms equipped with Wi-Fi interfaces and have deployed it to operate on two city buses in Madison, WI (in collaboration with our partners — Madison Metro Transit). In particular, our functionality is built into an existing system that provides a free Wi-Fi service, called WiRover [13], that is available on these city buses. Given that Wi-Fi services on transit systems are a growing phenomenon, the ability to add a system such as Trellis may not even require new hardware to be installed on these vehicles.

Many aspects of the design of Trellis is fairly intuitive. However, there are some specific challenges that we needed to address. One of them is to reliably determine whether an individual is actually located inside the vehicle (passenger) or outside of it (pedestrian). While one may consider existing localization techniques as that use mobile device Received Signal Strength Indication (RSSI) to infer this information, we have a much simpler mechanism to solve this issue. When a vehicle is moving, typically the signal strength of a passenger's mobile device observed by a vehicle-mounted observer will stay somewhat stable, while that of a pedestrian will fluctuate and eventually disappear (Fig. 1). Hence, by observing device signal strengths coupled with either vehicle location changes or speed of movement, one can easily discern who is inside the vehicle and who is not. This capability is a key building block in the Trellis system.

Contributions. We present, Trellis, a low-cost in-vehicle wireless monitoring system that can track station-to-station passenger movements to assist transit operators for transit user analytics. We develop various simple heuristic algorithms to separate passengers from pedestrians and identify where passengers get on or off a vehicle. To test the efficacy of our system, we have deployed this on two city buses in Madison, WI, over a period of four months and have evaluated how it can be used to infer popular original-destination stations of passengers over time and space. As we continue to work with our partners from Madison Metro Transit (our local transit operator), we continue to evaluate how such a system can be used to identify where to add new bus routes, or when to add faster (non-stop) services between various stations throughout the city at different times of the day and over different days of the week.

2. TRELLIS SYSTEM DESIGN AND IMPLEMENTATION

In this section, we discuss the system design, implementation and deployment.

2.1 System Design

Our system uses a front-end sniffing module to collect Wi-Fi devices' signals and transit GPS information, and uses a back-end modeling module to reconstruct transit schedules and human mobility patterns. The sniffing module collects the data from mobile devices and stores the data into local database. Meanwhile, the sniffing module can send calculated passenger number to remote server in real-time through cellular link, i.e., for the purpose of real time monitoring. Although our system supports real-time communication, we use separated program to send the data from databases to remote back-end server. The back-end server reconstruct public transit schedules and human mobility patterns from the collected data. It further aggregates the data from multiple transit sniffing system instances to provide a more complete view of the transit schedules and human mobility patterns. On top of the abstraction and aggregation modules, we construct origin-destination matrix to analyze transit efficiency in spatial and temporal domains.

2.2 System Implementation

We operate the Wi-Fi monitoring system on the Ubuntu 14.04.1 64bit distribution (with linux kernel version 3.19.0-28-generic), that runs on PC Engines APU platform [1]. APU platform is a mobile embedded platform that is equipped with 1GHz dual core CPU and 4G DDR3 DRAM. We use multi-thread program written in C/C++ to conduct the sniffing tasks. One thread is used to collect the Wi-Fi packets from the specified wireless interface. It also includes a module to check the correctness of received packets by validating the Cyclic Redundancy Check (CRC). Another thread is used to collect the GPS location information from the GPS module. All the data is stored in SQLite database files. There is another thread to send packets back to the data analysis modules, e.g., the number of passengers on bus for real-time demo. There are also bash scripts written to keep the cellular card and sniffer system running when the bus starts or the system aborts due to software or hardware failures. The data analysis modules are written in Java. Each data analysis module performs difference tasks, e.g., transit schedule reconstruction, automatic passenger counting etc.

2.3 System Deployment

We deploy our Wi-Fi monitoring system in two city buses. The bus route is illustrated in Fig. 2. The bus route covers the main campus of the University of Wisconsin-Madison (bottom right) as well as a residential area (top left) accommodates graduate students and visiting scholars. The

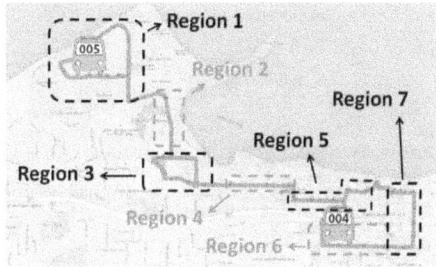

Figure 2: Bus route with labeled bus stops. The map size is around 1.5 mile × 2 mile. Each route traversal takes 45-50 minutes and covers about 8 miles. We divide the route into seven adjacent regions for easy analysis.

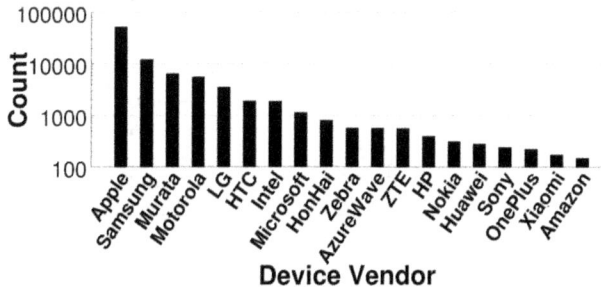

Figure 3: Distribution of devices by vendors in log scale.

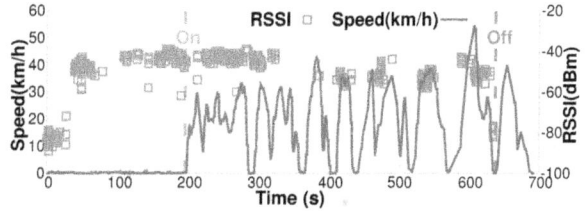

Figure 4: Identify where the passenger get on or off the bus.

city buses are operated by one local bus company. Based on our observation, the scheduling of each city bus is relatively random and the on-road or maintenance dates of each bus is unpredictable. There are usually multiple buses on the same route, while each bus is separated by 7 to 20 minutes based on the time of the day.

2.4 Statistical Properties

We collect data from both buses for around 90 days and 12 hours per day. In total, both buses travel more than 10,000 miles. Among the collected traces, we find 114,227 unique devices. By looking at the Organizationally Unique Identifier (OUI) of the MAC address (the first three octets), we are able to compare the distribution of various vendors. As shown in Fig. 3, Apple dominates all other vendors. Starting from iPhone 5s and iOS 8, Apple introduces randomized MAC address in probe requests under certain settings to protect user privacy. MAC randomization happens only in sleep mode (screen off) where the probe request with randomized MAC sent out roughly every 2-3 minutes. This feature certainly overestimates the number of iPhone users, but it exposes limited impact on statistical transit analytics.

3. PASSENGER TRACKING

In this section, we describe how to reconstruct bus schedules and passenger riding patterns.

3.1 Transit Schedule Reconstruction

For the purpose of public transit analytics, e.g., route design, scheduling, evaluation etc., it is important to track and record public transit when it passes each station. To reconstruct the public transit schedule from collected data, we extract the bus routes and stations from the transit operator's

website [5]. Each bus station is labeled by an index, GPS location information and direction. By matching the GPS information of the bus stations and that of collected from the sniffing system, we can know when the buses pass each bus station. Location information is not sufficient to accurately localize the bus at any specific time, because there are bus stations that are paired across street as dual way stations. To address this issue, we also need to match the heading direction of bus station with that of calculated from collected GPS. This module essentially provides when the bus arrives each station and how long it stays at that station. This information is important for transit operator to compare the actual operations of the bus with the ideal schedules. It can also be used to accurately identify when one passenger get on/off the bus.

3.2 Passenger Tracking

3.2.1 Onboard Detection

To track the passengers, we need to identify when and where they get on and off the bus. The most challenging task is to extract useful information from collected data. First, the RSSI readings are inaccurate and highly fluctuating. Therefore, we cannot use RSSI alone as the indicator to identify if one passenger is on bus. Second, the Wi-Fi signals are opportunistically received. The Wi-Fi signals from mobile device are based on user activities, e.g., screen on or off etc. Even worse, users may turn off Wi-Fi function to save power, which make some applications more challenging, e.g., automatic passenger counting etc.

To identify when and where one particular passenger get on and off the bus, we use multiple RSSI readings at different locations to track the position of the passenger. Essentially if there are consistent high RSSI readings after the bus traveling a certain distance, this device is on the bus with high probability. We will discuss how to find such a RSSI threshold δ in later section.

In Fig. 4, we illustrate the RSSI patterns and the time when the passenger get on and off the bus. We use similar logic to identify the bus stations where the passenger get on and off. We divide the entire bus trip into continuous road segments and each road segment is between two logically nearby bus stations. We identify if the passenger is on bus during this road segment by probing the RSSI readings of received packets. If there is at least a portion of α packets have RSSI readings higher than δ, then this device is on bus in this road segment. For each on bus passenger, it may travel with bus for one or more road segments. The starting bus station of the first such road segments is recognized as the bus station where the passenger get on the bus. The ending bus station of the last such road segments is recognized as the bus station where the passenger get off

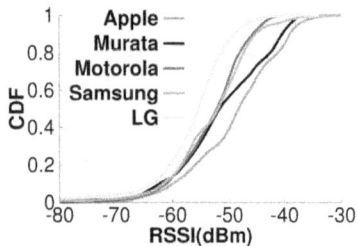

Figure 5: The CDF of on-bus mobile device Wi-Fi signals' RSSI readings.

the bus. It should be noted that we only use this method to identify the bus stations where the passenger get on and off the bus, if there is no packet received during some road segments in between, we still recognize this passenger is on the bus during the trip.

3.2.2 Parameter Selection

After we recognize the road segments the passenger is on bus, we collect the RSSI readings from different devices of various vendors. The cumulative distribution function (CDF) of on-bus RSSI readings are summarized in Fig. 5. This indicates that different thresholds δ should be assigned based on different vendors. Interestingly, the mobile devices from various vendors have huge difference on emitted power (10dB), presumably passengers (no matter what device he is using) are sitting randomly on the bus.

3.3 Origin-Destination Matrix

Another abstraction we build is the origin-destination matrix, which essentially records how many passengers ride from one bus station to another. Let S denotes this matrix and s_{ij} denotes each element in the matrix. s_{ij} refers to the number of passengers get on at bus station i and get off at bus station j. This matrix only builds the spatial relationships between bus stations, while temporary information is also important for transit analytics. We divide the 47 bus stations into seven geographically adjacent regions for easy analysis, i.e., as illustrated in Fig. 2. In the seven regions, there are 11,4,6,7,7,5 and 7 bus stations, respectively. Based on this matrix, we can analyze the region-to-region movement of the passengers. We may also add another dimension, i.e., time domain, to analyze passenger riding patterns in different periods of the day.

4. TRANSIT ANALYTICS

4.1 Automatic Passenger Counting

After reconstruct the transit schedules and passenger riding patterns, we conduct automatic passenger counting to record how many (essentially which) passengers getting on and off at each bus stations. This information is important for transit operators to make transit plans, improve the transit efficiency and seek government funding.

There are several popular methods that current transit operators are using to do this task. First, they are using ticketing system combined with human labor manual counting method. However, most ticketing systems only record how many passengers (assuming they are using traceable tickets instead of cash) get on buses, and cannot record how many passengers get off buses. Human labor counting is expen-

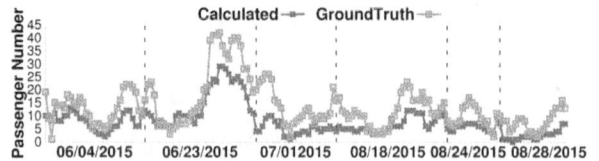

Figure 6: Automatic passenger counting results and ground truth.

sive and time consuming. Second, they are using camera or infrared sensors. But these systems are very expensive and not easy to deploy. Also existing methods are not able to track individual passenger.

Table 1: Ground Truth Data

Date	Time	Duration(mins)	Corr.
06/04/2015	12:15	42	0.72
06/23/2015	11:14	51	0.92
07/01/2015	15:28	48	0.71
08/18/2015	14:26	63	0.62
08/24/2015	11:26	38	0.88
08/28/2015	13:44	49	0.69

Our system provides a low-cost approach to assist or even replace existing counting methods. We evaluate counting accuracy by calculating the correlation between estimated passenger numbers and ground truth. The ground truth data is collected by volunteers who take the bus and count the number of passengers getting on/off the bus at each bus station. We collect the ground truth data in six trips on six different dates. The start time and duration of each trip is illustrated in Table 1. We mannually count the number of passengers getting on/off each bus station and record the numbers in a customized Android app. The Android app is used for recording the number of passengers only and does not serve any other purposes. The ground truth data is then synchronized with the data collect by the sniffing system based on time and GPS location. The date, time and calculated correlation are summarized in Table 1.

While the estimated passenger numbers are strongly correlated with actual passenger numbers (with average of 0.76) the correlation can be lower than 0.62 in some cases. We further analyze this particular case by looking into the actual passenger riding patterns. We summarize the calculated passenger numbers and the ground truth passenger numbers in Fig. 6. Each point in Fig. 6 refers to the number of passengers at each bus station. The difference between calculated and ground truth is the estimation error of our passenger counting system. It is shown that the low correlation is due to some passenger burst, probably caused by students finish one class together and with phone turned off. This present little effects on long term statistical analysis since the burst is short and the group of students get off the bus after only few bus stations.

4.2 Bus Stop Statistics

The strong correlation between estimated passenger numbers indicates our method is sufficient for statistical analysis. For example, our method show that passenger riding is periodic during weekdays. We summarize the average number of

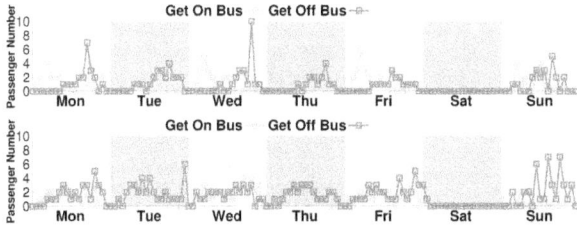

Figure 7: Bus stop in the residential area (top) and the main campus (bottom).

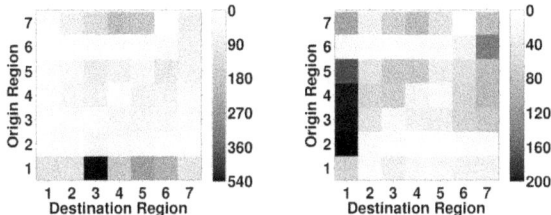

Figure 8: Passenger statistical riding patterns at morning hours (7am-9am), and evening hours(17pm-19pm)

passengers getting on and off two specific bus stations during each hour of one week in Fig. 7. The top one shows the passenger riding patterns in a residential area and the bottom one is in main campus. In residential areas, people are going out for work in the morning and going back home in late afternoon, there are obvious peak in those hours. In main campus, students and staffs are coming for work in morning hours and going back home in late afternoon. Further, undergraduate students live on campus. They travel between dormitories and teaching buildings for different classes during the day, so there are peaks in the number of passengers getting on and off the bus.

4.3 Transit Scheduling Analytics

Transit operators need to make scheduling decisions based on passenger volume and transit occupancy. By analyzing the origin-destination matrix, we can evaluate the transit efficiency and provide suggestions if the transit operators consider to adjust schedules.

We summarize the passenger region-to-region movements during morning hours and evening hours in Fig. 8. Each box in the color map is the number of passengers travel from (seven) different regions to that region. The darker the color, the more the passengers. As can be seen from the figures, nearly half of the passengers travel from region 1 are going to region 1-3 in morning hours(Fig. 8 left). This observation indicates that the bus route can be separated into two segments, while some buses can travel between region 1 and 3 and the rest follow the old schedule but less stop frequency. This can reduce the waiting time of the passengers want to go to region 3 due to lower duty cycle (the route is much shorter) while the rest passengers can have better riding experience due to less travel time. Meanwhile, the cost of the transit operators are reduced as well due to the improved efficiency and less frequent stops. In the evening rush hours(Fig. 8 right), most of the passengers get on the bus from different regions and are riding back to region 1, which means passengers are going back home. This indi-

cates the origin schedule during evening hours is reasonable and efficient.

5. RELATED WORK

5.1 Passenger Counting

Transit operators are required to submit passenger statistics to national transit database [4], so they collect passenger numbers either by manual counting or expensive sensor systems. [7] uses video processing to count the number of passengers getting on/off each bus station. [11] uses passive, non-radiating infra-red technology to detect and count people moving through a door or gate. These system can detect number of passengers are passing a door, but they require expensive hardware and are not able to track individual passengers that are riding between each pair of stations. Meanwhile, the bus passengers are required to tapping IC card when get on and get off the bus in some Asian cities [2, 20]. These system does not count the passengers who are paying by cash. More importantly, tapping the key card when get off the bus may cause extra delays and queues at each bus station. Trellis does not require passenger operations.

5.2 Human Mobility Study

Understanding human mobility [6] enables many applications such as traffic engineering and urban planning. [19] infers human mobility based on multiple data resources, e.g., cellphone and transit data, to avoid baised judgement by single data resources. [12] claims that human trajectories show a high degree of regularity by tracking smartphone locations. [10] infers human mobility by using taxicab location traces. Our work falls in the same category and proposes new applications by performing passenger tracking. However, we propose novel way to conduct public transit analytics by deploying Wi-Fi sniffers on city buses, which separate our work from existing ones.

5.3 Human Tracking by Wi-Fi

[9] uses one pair of fixed Wi-Fi devices to estimate the total of people walking in an area based on power measurements. [18] tracks human queue length by using received Wi-Fi signal features and analyzes the waiting time in the queue. However, it requires customers' smartphones connecting with APs and generating traffics. [16] estimates the trajectory of smartphone holders by using multiple monitors on the road. [17] use mobile phone sensors to estimate people's trajectory, which is fundamentally different from our approach that is using Wi-Fi sniffer to track bus passengers.

6. DISCUSSION

In this section, we discuss the limitations of our system and propose other potential applications.

6.1 Limitations

First, the accuracy of passenger tracking is limited by some unpredictable factors. For example, some passengers are not using smartphones or the Wi-Fi is turned off etc. In these cases, the sniffing system is not able to detect the presence of the passenger. Also, some passengers may use multiple smart devices, e.g., a tablet and a smartphone. In this case, the sniffing system may overestimate the number of passengers. Second, some Apple devices are using randomized MAC address that we are not able to identify. Since randomized MAC address, if triggered, is sent out sparsely in time domain, which makes little effects on our system. But if it actually happens, we may over count the number of Apple users (not our focus though) and may fail to identify the passenger. Our work focuses on providing statistical analysis on transit efficiency to assist public transit operators instead of tracking every single passengers. These limitations exposes challenges for our tasks, but do not affect the practicability of our system.

6.2 Other Applications

Although we focus on transit analytics in this paper, some other applications are possible given the rich data set and well designed abstraction. For example, our system can be used to predict the riding route of individual passenger. Some smartphone applications can use these information to schedule cellular traffic based on link qualities at different locations along the route. Some Wi-Fi related applications can also benefit from accurate predication of passenger's presence [15].

7. SUMMARY AND FUTURE WORK

Our work proposes a passive crowd-sourced approach to infer how passengers use transit systems. The system follows the popular paradigm of tracking mobile devices as identifiable by vehicle-mounted Wi-Fi observers. While our preliminary system demonstrates both feasibility and preliminary usefulness, numerous challenges remain. They include: (i) mechanisms to improve device identification accuracy in the vehicle context; (ii) identification of different analytics capabilities that such a system can provide efficiently; (iii) performing a more rigorous privacy analysis in such vehicular scenarios, even when MAC addresses are obfuscated; and (iv) evaluating other complementary techniques to achieve similar goals and how they can either complement or enhance our proposed system.

8. ACKNOWLEDGMENTS

We would like to acknowledge the anonymous reviewers and our shepherd Dr. Kaushik Veeraraghavan, whose comments helped bring the paper into its final form. This research project is supported in part by the US National Science Foundation through awards CNS-1405667, CNS-1345293, CHE-1230751, CNS-1343363, CNS-1555426 and CNS-1525586.

9. REFERENCES

[1] Apu platform. *http://www.pcengines.ch/apu.htm.*
[2] Ic card in hong kong transit. *http://www.octopus.com.hk/home/en/.*
[3] Infodev automatic passenger counting. *http://www.infodev.ca/vehicles/counting-passengers.html.*
[4] National transit database. *http://www.ntdprogram.gov/.*
[5] Route 80, madison, wisconsin. *https://www.cityofmadison.com/Metro/schedules/Route80.*
[6] F. Asgari, V. Gauthier, and M. Becker. A survey on human mobility and its applications. *arXiv preprint arXiv:1307.0814*, 2013.
[7] C.-H. Chen, T.-Y. Chen, D.-J. Wang, and T.-J. Chen. A cost-effective people-counter for a crowd of moving people based on two-stage segmentation. *Journal of Information Hiding and Multimedia Signal Processing*, 2012.
[8] Y.-c. Cheng, M. Afanasyev, P. Verkaik, P. Benkö, J. Chiang, A. C. Snoeren, S. Savage, and G. M. Voelker. Automating cross-layer diagnosis of enterprise wireless networks. In *In Proc. of ACM SIGCOMM*, 2007.
[9] S. Depatla, A. Muralidharan, and Y. Mostofi. Occupancy estimation using only wifi power measurements. *IEEE Journal on Selected Areas in Communications*, July 2015.
[10] R. Ganti, M. Srivatsa, A. Ranganathan, and J. Han. Inferring human mobility patterns from taxicab location traces. In *Proceedings of the 2013 ACM international joint conference on Pervasive and ubiquitous computing*. ACM, 2013.
[11] H. E. Gerland and K. Sutter. Automatic passenger counting (apc): Infra-red motion analyzer for accurate counts in stations and rail, light-rail and bus operations. *INIT GmbH Innovations in Transportation.*
[12] M. C. Gonzalez, C. A. Hidalgo, and A.-L. Barabasi. Understanding individual human mobility patterns. *Nature*, 2008.
[13] J. Hare, L. Hartung, and S. Banerjee. Beyond deployments and testbeds: experiences with public usage on vehicular wifi hotspots. In *Proceedings of the 10th international conference on Mobile systems, applications, and services*. ACM, 2012.
[14] T. Kimpel, J. Strathman, D. Griffin, S. Callas, and R. Gerhart. Automatic passenger counter evaluation: Implications for national transit database reporting. *Transportation Research Record: Journal of the Transportation Research Board*, 2003.
[15] J. Manweiler, N. Santhapuri, R. R. Choudhury, and S. Nelakuditi. Predicting length of stay at wifi hotspots. In *INFOCOM, 2013 Proceedings IEEE*. IEEE, 2013.
[16] A. Musa and J. Eriksson. Tracking unmodified smartphones using wi-fi monitors. In *Proceedings of the 10th ACM conference on embedded network sensor systems*. ACM, 2012.
[17] A. Thiagarajan, L. Ravindranath, K. LaCurts, S. Madden, H. Balakrishnan, S. Toledo, and J. Eriksson. Vtrack: accurate, energy-aware road traffic delay estimation using mobile phones. In *Sensys*. ACM, 2009.
[18] Y. Wang, J. Yang, Y. Chen, H. Liu, M. Gruteser, and R. P. Martin. Tracking human queues using single-point signal monitoring. In *Proceedings of the 12th annual international conference on Mobile systems, applications, and services*. ACM, 2014.
[19] D. Zhang, J. Huang, Y. Li, F. Zhang, C. Xu, and T. He. Exploring human mobility with multi-source data at extremely large metropolitan scales. In *Proceedings of the 20th annual international conference on Mobile computing and networking*. ACM, 2014.
[20] P. Zhou, Y. Zheng, and M. Li. How long to wait?: predicting bus arrival time with mobile phone based participatory sensing. In *Mobisys*. ACM, 2012.

Ephemeral Apps

Ketan Bhardwaj
Georgia Institute of
Technology
North Ave NW
Atlanta, GA, USA
ketanbj@gatech.edu

Ada Gavrilovska
Georgia Institute of
Technology
North Ave NW
Atlanta, GA, USA
ada@cc.gatech.edu

Karsten Schwan
Georgia Institute of
Technology
North Ave NW
Atlanta, GA, USA
schwan@cc.gatech.edu

ABSTRACT

Despite a tremendous increase in the number of mobile apps, coupled with their popularity with consumers, there exists a wide gap in app availability vs. their use. Recent trends suggest that this gap will further widen in the future. *Ephemeral apps*, proposed in this paper, lower the barrier for end-user app acceptance by removing the app installation step when 'trying out' new apps, without requiring modifications to current apps or any additional programming efforts by app developers. We estimate the resulting reduction in time-to-use for apps to be a factor of 10x by leveraging the emerging 'edge cloud' tier of the Internet.

1. INTRODUCTION

The number of apps available in the Google play store neared 1.5 million by the end of 2014. The fast pace and momentum achieved by the native app eco-system is evident in Figure 1.(b), which shows the number of new apps per month during 2014. While new apps abound, a wide gap exists in app availability and their acceptance. In fact, only 15% of total available native apps are downloaded more than 5,000 times, as shown in Figure 1.(a)[1]. The app discovery gap is likely to widen with the impending explosion of new apps prompted by the wearables, on-demand interactions in Internet-of-Things, situation-specific apps, etc.

The resulting quandary is that while end users prefer native apps over web apps or other browser-based interactions [1, 2], due to their faster performance, seamless access to device features, security, etc., a wide gap will continue to exists in app availability vs. their actual use. Simply put, with so many available apps, how can users search, install, and try them, even if they might benefit from or like them? This is particularly the case for apps with a transient usage model, i.e., those used only in contexts users experience infrequently. For a developers thriving on innovation and quick rollout of new apps, this poses a grave concern, as it creates a high barrier for acceptance of their apps.

---

[1]Data source: http://www.appbrain.com/stats/

HotMobile '16, February 26-27, 2016, St. Augustine, FL, USA

© 2016 ACM. ISBN 978-1-4503-4145-5/16/02. . . $15.00

DOI: http://dx.doi.org/10.1145/2873587.2873591

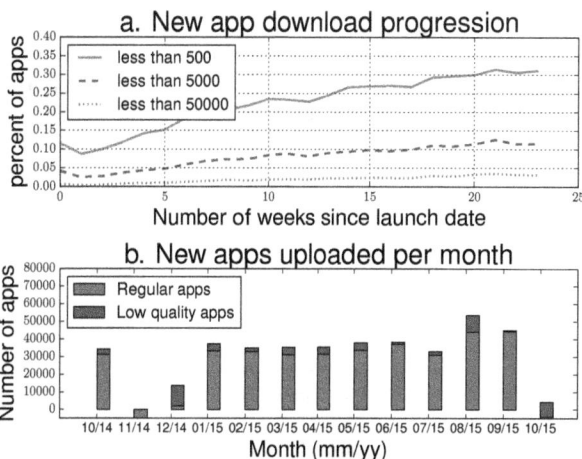

Figure 1: (a) App downloads in weeks after launch with more than 500, 5k, and 50k downloads (b) No. of apps uploaded to the Google Play store in 2014.

App discovery can be seen as two problems: (i) *contextual app selection* which refers to classifying and presenting relevant apps to users based on their current context, history of used apps etc., and (ii) *barriers to app's first use* which refer to effort on the end user's part to install and try out an app for the first time. This work focuses on the latter – reducing the barriers in app's first use by end users. For contextual app selection, we rely on existing mechanisms employed by app stores, e.g., recommendation engines, user reviews, etc., and addressing that problem is not the focus of this paper.

Specifically, we argue for *Ephemeral Apps* as new types of apps that (i) 'pop up' instantaneously on end-user devices in appropriate contexts, (ii) are transient, in that they can completely disappear including the state they might have created from the device once the end-user leaves the context, (iii) do not require any additional effort from app developers, (iv) do not need to change user behaviour of how they use apps today and finally, (iv) offer similar levels of performance, access to device features and security as native apps.

Ephemeral apps make it easy for users to 'try apps out' before deciding to install them permanently, hence reducing barriers in app discovery; or they can use them only within their current contexts, then discard them, expecting to experience an updated app next time in the same context, prompting the use of new available apps by end users and aiding with app discovery. This eliminates not only the need to explicitly install apps that may only be of temporary interest to a user, but also 'de-clutters' end user devices from too many apps and avoids device pollution from their persistent on-device state. It also reduces the need for users to deal with managing their app updates and seeing notifications for seldom used device-resident apps [4].

Achieving those goals, however, requires both infrastructure, and systems software support in Mobile OSes.

In terms of infrastructure, ephemeral apps benefit from the emerging 'edge cloud' tier infrastructure situated beyond the last mile of Internet, including wireless access points and routers, low-power microservers, and similar. Prior work has shown such *eBoxes* – short for 'edge boxes' – to be suitable for accelerating the delivery of mobile app services, for caching and streaming [4, 3], support for personal clouds [7, 5], for app acceleration, offload or aggregation via cloudlets [8], etc., and we believe this trend will continue due to increases in eBoxes' capabilities. We make another important observation that most apps turn on the network to access Internet anyways: out of top 5000 popular apps in the Google Play Store, we inspected, 98.9% of apps require Internet permissions. This highlights that using networked nearby resources for ephemeral apps puts minimal overhead on mobile devices.

In terms of system support, Ephemeral apps require the following:

- Mobile OSes - Android
  1 *Ab-initio app streaming support:* so that devices can directly run streamed apps, without requiring their installation,
  2 *Invisible app ephemerality support:* to keep device clean of the apps and the associated state created on device without any app specific modification,
- *eBox based app streaming server* to allow efficient app streaming server capabilities on eBoxes, while maintaining performance at par with native apps.

Our previous work showed how to fetch app components from a remote server and presented an efficient design of app streaming server [4] to manage app updates that can lead to potentially better app loading performance for streaming apps, subject to wireless connectivity. However, it assumes that apps are installed on end client devices before app streaming can occur. We also already explored mechanisms to maintain app cache on eBoxes [3]. In this work, we build on our previous work but are exploring (i) ab-initio app streaming support, i.e., streaming without any prior app and/or configuration on the device, and (ii) invisible app ephemerality, i.e., system level garbage collection, to purge the app along with its created/modified state, targeting Android devices. However, it is important to note that ephemerality is a weaker property than forensic deniability as proposed in [6] and therefore can be supported with much lower overheads on device side. The clear benefit of this approach is the elimination of the efforts involved in searching and installing apps. Stated quantitatively, while search time vs. the time required to identify some ephemeral app is hard to estimate, the time taken to download, install, and start using an app has a quantifiable lower bound. Figure 2 shows the time taken to simply install an app on an Android phone (Nexus 5) from a PC connected via USB cable using Android debug bridge (ADB), measured for 5000 apps - the top 100 in each category dowloaded from the Google Play store. Our preliminary investigation suggests

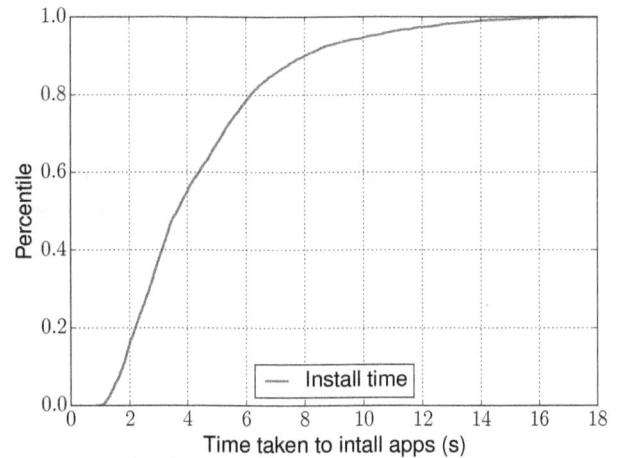

Figure 2: Showing CDF of the lower bounds on time spent during app installation.

that with ephemeral apps, this delay can be reduced by a factor of 10x, bringing the time required to try an app below 5 seconds.

2. MOTIVATION

The following factors motivate ephemeral apps:

Convenience: Interaction on-demand
With so many available apps for multiple devices owned by an user, it is very inconvenient for a user to search, install, and use those apps. Ephemeral apps can reduce this inconvenience, by providing apps to users based on their connectivity to an eBox. An important angle of looking at ephemeral apps is in context of the IoT market: it would be cumbersome to search and install apps for each such possible 'thing'.

Performance: Efficiency of native apps
End user preference for native apps is, in part, due to their faster response times or better performance vs. that seen for web apps and their consistent user interfaces mandated by the mobile OSes. Ephemeral apps can keep these characteristics, by making it possible for native apps to be streamed from eBoxes and run on devices with the efficiency of native apps.

Seamless access to device features
End user preference for native apps is also driven by apps being able to seamlessly access device features for better user experience. Ephemeral apps can preserve the benefits of native apps, and address web apps' limitations on access to device features, while maintaining the same levels of security as native apps.

3. GOALS

Ephemeral apps must have the following characteristics from which we derive the design goals:

Instantaneous: Ephemeral apps must be able to appear instantaneous in that a single ephemeral app should be able to appear on end-user devices within 300 ms. This rules out pushing full app installs on devices automatically and/or on-demand as the user goes from one context to other.

Transient: Ephemeral apps and the state that they create on end user's device must completely disappear from the device once the end-user leaves the context. Important to clarify is that the intent is to keep device clear rather than removing the trace of its execution as was the goal of earlier work like [6].

No additional effort from app developers: Making ephemeral apps must not be different from creating native apps. This is important from a practical standpoint of their acceptance by developer community.

No change in user behaviour: Using ephemeral apps must not present a learning curve for end users to use them i.e., users must be able to use them in same way as they use native apps installed on device.

Performance and device features: Ephemeral apps must be able to perform at same level as native apps and have access to device hardware on existing devices under existing permission models.

4. DESIGN CHOICES

We briefly present the available design space to support ephemeral apps in Android:

4.1 System layer for app streaming

Our goal is that functionality required to support ephemeral apps must leverage the existing app model supported on client devices. Modern devices with 'tall' mobile OS stacks are shown in Figure 4, and 'thinner', well packaged mobile apps on top. We posit that since the majority of system level functionality required by apps is abstracted by the app framework APIs, runtime, etc., provided by the mobile OS, it is possible to hide the complexity associated with app streaming and ephemerality completely from app developers, while providing efficient app execution leveraging devices' capabilities. On the eBox side, this also allows to leverage system level information like the order of app components to optimize streaming performance [4].

4.2 Streaming from cloud vs. eBox

Mobile devices are subject to well-understood constraints, such as power consumption. Using remote resources not subject to those constraints can, enhance user experiences on devices. Concerning the use of such remote resources for ephemeral apps, we argue the relative advantage of eBoxes vs. remote data centers in terms of (i) increasingly fast wireless networks, (ii) cheap storage at eBoxes to house app repositories and low access latency due to lower network distance.

4.3 Ephemeral vs. Native, web, thin client apps

Currently, most mobile OSes like Android, iOS etc. support the following app models:
- Native app: specifically designed to run on a device's OS, uses features exposed by platform via APIs and is constrained by OS semantics.
- Web app: the entire app or its parts are downloaded from the web during execution. It can be accessed from any web-capable mobile device without requiring operating system-specific customization.
- Hybrid apps: most native apps utilize web connectivity, and web apps provide offline modes. The resulting form of apps are referred to as hybrid apps.
- Thin client apps: require a remote access app, e.g., VNC client on device while actual execution happens remotely.

We posit that *Ephemeral Apps* can potentially obtain native app user experience in terms of responsiveness, access to device features, security, efficient operation than thin client apps with central management capabilities of web apps by allowing on-demand streaming of the native app components needed for execution, via eBoxes.

5. FEASIBILITY AND CHALLENGES

We are using Android to prototype ephemeral apps. The simplified interaction between the modified Android modules and an eBox-based ephemeral app server are depicted in Figure 4. Presented below are the technical challenges that need to be solved to support the ephemeral apps:

Handling diverse app Anatomy and Execution

A typical Android app is comprised of AndroidManifest.xml (app config file), classes.dex (JAVA classes), .arsc file (binary resource file), assets, res folders (static resources e.g., icons, strings etc.), native libraries, and miscellaneous components (certs, HTML help files etc), referred as app components which are needed during installation and/or execution. In Android, an app executes as an instance of the Android Runtime (ART) in which Android framework libraries are preloaded during fork of the Zygote process, and platform features are exposed via APIs. To make apps ephemeral, these components must be made available on demand, via streaming, in a way that does not hurt app performance. With the current architecture of mobile OSes (specifically, Android), it is a daunting task because each of these app components is handled in a different subsystem, e.g., classes.dex are loaded by the ART runtime, .arsc files are accessed using the asset manager, whereas resource in res or asset folder may be read explicitly. To makes matters worse, these system components can be used in different ways, e.g., app can use either a URI and/or binary buffer mode to load static assets. This also highlights an important point that existing mechanisms like on-demand class loading or JAVA reflection do not suffice for mobile app streaming.

Ensuring app Integrity, Sandboxing and Permissions

App integrity is established by downloading apps only from trusted app stores with self-signed certificates from developers. For ephemeral apps, since there is no installation step, the mobile OS and ephemeral app servers collaboratively need to make available app components and establish their integrity. We propose to use certificate based verification of the ephemeral app server as a valid provider of apps. The certificate may be provided by app stores or any other trusted third party and implement a merkel tree of signatures which can be used to verify individual app components as opposed to full app during installation.

Permissions required by apps are prompted to the user for approval on installation, at which time each app is assigned a UID, GID. These are then used to enforce permissions to access hardware features and inter-app communication using Binder IPC at linux kernel layer. Android application sandbox using Linux's discretionary access control (DAC) and SEAndroid mandatory access Control (MAC) to isolate an app data and code execution from other apps. For ephemeral apps, Android needs to support lazy allocation of UIDs, GIDs and handle app permissions at runtime - a feature introduced in Android M. We also need to define appropriate SEAndroid policies for ephemeral apps to ensure security guarantees during their execution.

Managing App State

Android provides no guarantees to apps about their state and expects them to manage it explicitly via state machine callbacks. This is consistent with our vision of ephemeral apps where we propose to capture their app state and clean it up. However, two types of persistent state are typically associated with an Android app:

System State:

By system state, we refer to the information Android maintains about or on behalf of apps during installation e.g., its package, (uid, gid) pairs, etc. and during execution e.g., web caches, cookies, data journals, per app shared data, app private files etc.

App State:

- *On-device state* refers refers to the state needed for app start or resume, created by an app during execution. e.g., shared document-like content handled by Android on devicesâĂŸ local storage and the content of internal state, like user preferences, handled using the APIs, etc.
- *Remote app state* refers to state explicitly committed to a cloud-based backend, e.g., saved game progress. This is consistent with our ephemeral app vision and requires no special treatment for ephemeral apps.
- *Content based state:* refers to the content used by an app during its execution that is not part of the app-specific content cache. Apps may fetch it from some back end service, their own network-based storage, or some third party, e.g., mobile ads, etc.

Ensuring app performance. Compared to web apps, while both app models require network interactions to fetch the app components, we posit ephemeral apps would perform better because of the number and size of web app components (JavaScript, HTML, CSS, etc.) vs. native app components that need to be fetched, and the additional processing in web apps launching a browser, creating DOM objects, handling dependencies and rendering those on device which would not be required for streamed native app components. Comparing to thin clients, these entail aggressive use of network to fetch screen contents, send user inputs, sync on-device sensors with remote thin client server for every user interaction, while rendering of the screen contents on end user device. In contrast, streamed native app components would require less use of network because of reduced payload to be fetched and the possibility of reuse of fetched app components (classes, UI images, etc.) during an ephemeral app session. This leads us to believe that ephemeral apps can be more responsive and would require less power than other alternatives for their execution.

Integration with app stores: Figure 3 depicts our vision of how ephemeral apps can be made available via collaboration by app stores and eBoxes, i.e., without app developers to buy into something new. We believe this is important to continue to leverage auditing capabilities of app stores that check apps for security before making them available to authenticated end users, and for continuing to support developers using pay per use model for ephemeral apps. However, this doesn't rule out alternate delivery channels where app stores can deliver apps to vendor equipment that they expose as ephemeral apps to end users. An additional interaction between eBoxes and app store is required to provide eBoxes with valid certificates that they can present to end user devices to verify their integrity as trusted app providers.

Maintaining user trust model: Ephemeral apps blur

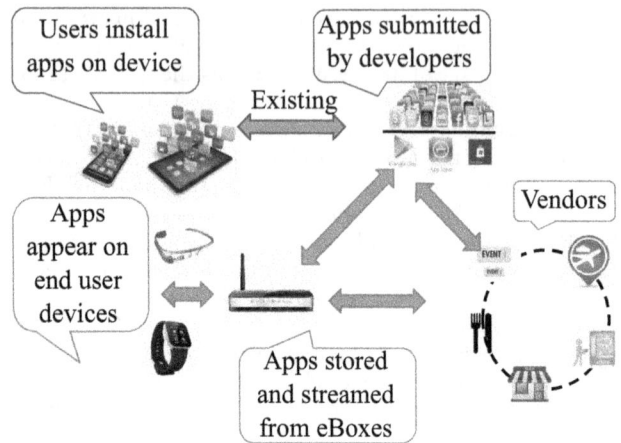

Figure 3: showing an overview of ephemeral app ecosystem and its potential integration with existing app stores.

the distinction between web apps and native apps. A subtle point in introducing ephemeral apps in the app ecosystem is that users trust apps downloaded from app stores but the same is not true for web apps. This requires careful consideration of the trust model being used to distinguish end user's interaction with ephemeral apps from web app or native apps. We posit that the app store integration proposed above and the runtime permission model introduced in Android M in combination can be used to provide a workable trust model, where only apps verified by app stores will be provided to eBoxes or vendors that they can make available as ephemeral apps. The end user devices only show ephemeral apps being made available by trusted ephemeral app providers which is verified by certificate presented by an eBox. For apps that are shown in end user devices, users would be prompted for specific permissions as they continue using an ephemeral app, a feature that we developed but is also introduced in Android M.

Preserving user privacy: Streaming ephemeral apps raises privacy concerns because with knowledge about which app components are fetched during execution, it is possible to infer what a user is doing with it. To address that, we plan to implement a differential privacy techniques while fetching app component to reduce these risks. We believe it would be an interesting proposition if we can actually leverage these extra requests to fetch somewhat related app components.

6. PROPOSED DESIGN

Ab-initio App streaming: support in Android is designed to work seamlessly for existing apps. It is designed to operate in two phases (i) *Conjuring phase* and (ii) *Execution phase*. The rationale behind the two phase-design of the ephemeral app life cycle is to (i) not require installation of apps on device and (ii) ensure faster app discovery by decoupling presentation of an app from its launch and execution. *Conjuring phase* starts when a user invokes his ephemeral home screen referred to as Stage - a new launcher app on users' device connecting to an eBox. Stage requests for list of available ephemeral apps; on receipt of the response, a certificate based verification is done to establish the integrity

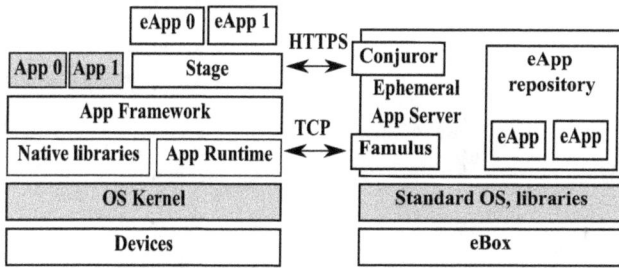

Figure 4: Showing the co-existence of existing and the proposed ephemeral app ecosystem.

of an eBox/app server as a valid app provider; If the user trusts it, Stage starts fetching icons of the available apps to populate the end user's screen/Stage. In addition to the icons, the response includes top level hashes from merkle trees of available ephemeral apps and information needed to launch an app, e.g., activity name or first class to be loaded. *Execution phase* starts when a user decides to launch an ephemeral app. It is proposed as a new API in Android app framework which asks the activity Manager to start a new app runtime (ART) instance. Before forking an instance of the app runtime, the activity manager asks the package manager to assign a virtual blanket of permissions and to assign ephemeral uid, gid, that belong to a separate range from existing uid ranges used in Android, and which can later be used to handle permission exceptions to provide runtime permission approvals for ephemeral apps (e.g., if an app requires more than already assigned blanket permissions). To keep app sandboxing guarantees for ephemeral apps while also ensuring availability of storage for caching app components fetched during app streaming, we plan to implement a new SEAndroid security context and associated policy: ephemeral app domain. During execution, app streaming is designed to work seamlessly for existing apps by intercepting calls to the runtime's class loader, native library loader and the app framework's Asset Manager, and redirecting those to a remote (e.g., eBox-based) ephemeral app server via a Streaming Client embedded in the ephemerality manager discussed next. This ensures that even when the apps are not installed on a device, the running apps are offered the same runtime environment as if they are installed. Concerning state created by apps, which normally is stored in app specific folders on the device's local storage, ephemeral apps are assigned new location which also helps in providing system level app ephemerality discussed next.

App ephemerality: To track app's system state without support from apps, we plan to (i) route all ephemeral app component requests through a system wide ephemerality manager and (ii) add hooks in all app relevant framework APIs to capture app private state which can then explicitly logged on-device. Since, ephemerality manager requests the needed app components, it also checks each received app component for its integrity using the ephemeral app's top level hash, thereby ensuring runtime app integrity. Briefly, the ephemerality module must expose a native and JNI interfaces which can be used by the Android app framework APIs and by individual system services to request app components and log app state when apps use those APIs. These logs are the key to enabling system level ephemerality guarantees. Asynchronously saving, discarding and/or syncing of

apps and their states can be supported in order to minimize ephemerality-related overheads on the system. The ephmerality module allows processing of the logs under different policies, each of which is derived from end user preference about the app state. For instance, if a user indicates that he wants to discard app state then, on app exit, the ephemerality manager can access the logs to gather app state generated by that app and deletes them followed by removal of the logs from the database. Similarly, if an end user chooses to sync state to an eBox, the Ephmerality Manager sends app state to an eBox before deleting the logs.

In our incomplete prototype, we support on-demand loading of app-specific classes, assets, etc. but requires a stub app (stage app) to be installed. Complete implementation of support for ab-initio app streaming and handling app ephemerality in Android is currently in progress. We discuss the proposed design below:

Stage - a new ephemeral apps launcher app: Stage app communicates with eBox based app streaming server for available apps. Before populating Stage with app icons, it established the integrity of eBox using certificate-based authentication.

App framework support for ephemeral apps

Package Manager: The package manager is modified to provide information to the app framework about available ephemeral apps, for assigning UID, GID in a different range than installed apps, and for creating app specific directories for their use in caching and/or for ephemeral app state at launch time.

Activity Manager: The enhanced activity manager supports the launch of apps in ephemeral mode i.e., launching new activity for ephemeral apps without interfering launch of with installed apps. At launch time, the developer signature attached with the app is checked. Additionally, we plan to implement a checksum verification for the app executable and components between device and app stores before start of actual streaming.

Lazy Permission handler: We added a new permission exception handler to the ActivityThread which is basically linux level thread running the application. When the exception handler is invoked when an ephemeral app incurs a permission that hasn't been assigned to it. This give rise to a permission grant dialog in similar ways the Android framework issues the 'application not responding' (ANR) dialog.

Asset manager: The framework's asset manager is modified to facilitate loading assets like icons, xmls by redirect ephemeral app's asset requests to an eBox vs. its own file system.

Android app runtime - ART

The following components of ART need to be changed to support ephemeral apps:

Ephemeral Class linker: We added a new class in ART that behaves similarly to existing class linker excepts that it searches and streams the requested app-specific classes from an eBox vs. the device's local storage.

Native library loader: Similarly, ART's interaction with the native library loader streams app-specific native libraries from the eBox vs. the device's local storage.

App Ephemerality support in Android

To seamlessly support ephemerality for unmodified android apps, we added a core library libephemeralutils which performs all network operations needed for streaming of app components from the Android app framework and ART runtime on behalf of ephemeral apps. By doing this, it seamlessly facilitates logging of fetched app components. Additionally, it also provides support - native and JNI APIs - for explicit logging of any state or change in file created by an ephemeral app on phone's file system. We plan to instrument Android APIs that are used by apps to write to phones file system to create a per app log in form of a SQLite database. These logs are then used to clear device of any app state or changes made by an ephemeral app.

eBox-based ephemeral app server
The ephemeral app server consists two subsystems:
Conjuror: an HTTPS server establishing the integrity of an eBox as a valid app provider during connection time; it pushes apps to the end user device, i.e., app metadata and TCP port, which will be used for actual streaming of app components by a client. It is also responsible for maintaining an app repository on a SSD attached to it via USB 3.0 and performs app preprocessing when the apps are added or updated. Preprocessing includes extracting app metadata for app push, streaming app components.

Famulus: a TCP socket server handling on-demand streaming of app components for a single app; it implements the logic to translates app-specific URIs to entries on its own file system generated by conjurer, which contains uncompressed apps conforming to the same directory structure as would be on device with installed app.

7. PRELIMINARY EVALUATION

Experimental Setup: We used a Nexus 5 phone running Open Source Android v5.0.1.3 for device side evaluation. The phone is connected to eBox prototyped using Linksys WRT1900ac 802.11ac Wi-Fi router running OpenWRT. The same router with an attached SSD of 20GB is used to prototype the eBox based app streaming server.

Feasibility: We report that we have been able to run native existing apps as 'Ephemeral apps' via app streaming and app ephemerality on Android without requiring any changes in those apps.

Time to use: Figure 5(iii) shows the lower bounds of time to to start using an app when installing it from app store vs. using ephemeral apps. In addition, Figure 5 shows upto 10x reduction in time to use compared to installation and launch time of top 40 apps which include the top app in each category downloaded from Google Play Store. Also, important to note is that, launching app via app streaming doesn't lead to delay in app launch time and hence, leading us to believe responsiveness is comparable to native installed apps.

8. SUMMARY

We propose 'ephemeral apps' as a solution to address the gap in app availability vs. end-user acceptance, evaluated with a prototype implementation on Android. Future work will complete their implementation and perform additional evaluations with realistic multi-tenant loads.

Acknowledgement

We would like to thank our shepherd, Kaushik Veeraraghavan, for his insights during the preparation of the final version of this paper. This work is partially supported through research grants from Intel, VMware, and NSF CNS1148600.

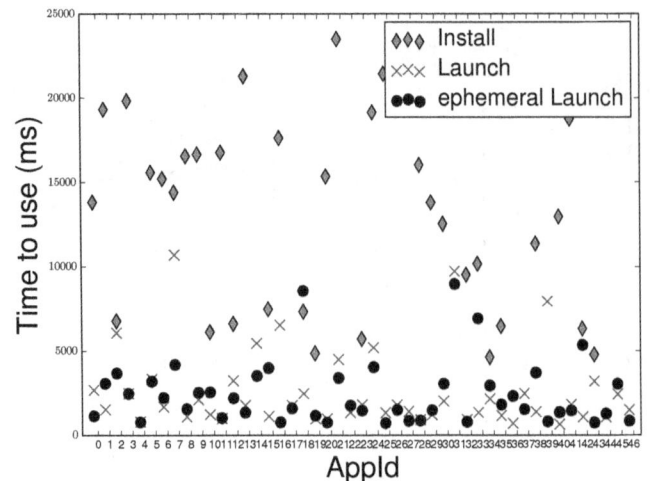

Figure 5: Comparing time to use of ephemeral apps made available from a nearby eBox vs. lower bounds of install and launch time for top 40 apps.

9. REFERENCES

[1] Apps solidify leadership six years into the mobile revolution - Flurry @ http://www.flurry.com/bid/109749/Apps-Solidify-Leadership-Six-Years-into-the-Mobile-Revolution.

[2] Mobile apps overtake pc internet usage in u.s. - cnn money @ http://money.cnn.com/2014/02/28/technology/mobile/mobile-apps-internet/.

[3] K. Bhardwaj, P. Agarwal, A. Gavrilovska, and K. Schwan. Appsachet: Distributed app delivery from the edge cloud. In *7th EAI International Conference on Mobile Computing, Applications and Services*, MobiCASE '15, 2015.

[4] K. Bhardwaj, P. Agarwal, A. Gavrilovska, K. Schwan, and A. A. Appflux: Taming mobile app delivery via app streaming. In *2015 Conference on Timely Results in Operating Systems (TRIOS 15)*, Monterey, CA, USA, 2015. USENIX Association.

[5] K. Bhardwaj, S. Sreepathy, A. Gavrilovska, and K. Schwan. Ecc: Edge cloud composites. In *Proceedings of the 2014 2Nd IEEE International Conference on Mobile Cloud Computing, Services, and Engineering*, MOBILECLOUD '14, pages 38–47, Washington, DC, USA, 2014. IEEE Computer Society.

[6] A. M. Dunn, M. Z. Lee, S. Jana, S. Kim, M. Silberstein, Y. Xu, V. Shmatikov, and E. Witchel. Eternal sunshine of the spotless machine: Protecting privacy with ephemeral channels. In *Presented as part of the 10th USENIX Symposium on Operating Systems Design and Implementation (OSDI 12)*, pages 61–75, Hollywood, CA, 2012. USENIX.

[7] M. Jang, K. Schwan, K. Bhardwaj, A. Gavrilovska, and A. Avasthi. Personal clouds: Sharing and integrating networked resources to enhance end user experiences. In *INFOCOM, 2014 Proceedings IEEE*, pages 2220–2228, April 2014.

[8] E. Koukoumidis, D. Lymberopoulos, K. Strauss, J. Liu, and D. Burger. Pocket cloudlets. *ACM SIGPLAN Notices*, 47(4):171, June 2012.

Better Performance Through Thread-local Emulation

Ali Razeen, Valentin Pistol, Alexander Meijer, Landon P. Cox

Duke University

ABSTRACT

Mobile platforms are shifting away from managed code and toward native code. For example, the most recent versions of Android compile Dalvik bytecodes to native code at install-time, and apps frequently use third-party native libraries. The trend toward native code on mobile platforms calls us to develop new ways of building dynamic taint-tracking tools, such as TaintDroid, that achieve good performance. In this paper, we argue that the key to good performance is to track only when necessary, e.g., when an app handles sensitive data. We argue that *thread-local emulation* is a feature that captures this goal. In this paper, we discuss the motivation for thread-local emulation, the software and hardware techniques that may be used to implement it, results from preliminary work, and the many challenges that remain.

1. INTRODUCTION

Dynamic information-flow analysis (i.e., *taint-tracking*) underlies a wide range of experimental mobile services, including secure deletion [19], protecting user privacy [9], and attesting to data authenticity [11]. TaintDroid [9] is the most widely used implementation of taint-tracking for mobile platforms, and it owes much of its success to good performance.

TaintDroid tracks tainted data by interposing on bytecodes within the Dalvik virtual machine, which is a managed-code runtime like the Java Virtual Machine (JVM) or Common Language Runtime (CLR). Because managed code typically runs more slowly than native code, integrating taint-tracking logic into the Dalvik virtual machine introduces little additional slowdown. However, not only do apps increasingly rely on their own fast native code, but with the introduction of the Android Runtime (ART), Android now compiles developer-supplied Dalvik bytecodes into native code at install time [1]. Both trends have rendered TaintDroid's approach to tracking obsolete, and raise an important question: is it possible to build a practical implementation of taint tracking for mobile platforms dominated by native code?

Prior work on taint tracking native code is not promising. These systems typically deliver prohibitive slowdowns of between 10 and 30x compared to untracked native code [7, 15]. However, we observe that apps may not spend much of their time handling tainted data. For example, a blogging app may handle a user's password only while authenticating and not after. Similarly, relative to the time spent pulling and displaying friends' content, a social media app may spend little of its time processing and uploading images taken by the device's camera. Thus, if one were only interested in tracking passwords or images taken with the camera, then perhaps the system could taint track only during the initial login process or when the camera is used. By taint tracking *selectively*, the performance penalty may be made proportional to the number of instructions that handle tracked data.

Nearly a decade ago, the Xen team described a trap-and-emulate approach to selective taint tracking that uses page protections to identify when a program accesses tainted data [13]. Unfortunately, relying on page protections alone to implement selective taint tracking is insufficient on mobile platforms. Mobile apps are inherently multi-threaded and run on devices with multi-core CPUs. Since all threads in a process must adhere to the same page protections, when any thread handles tainted data, all of the app's active threads must also be emulated.

Thus, for modern mobile systems, we believe that practical native taint tracking requires *thread-local emulation*. Thread-local emulation allows threads that do not handle tainted data to run at full speed, while slowing down only those threads that handle tainted data. Thread-local emulation is particularly important for mobile apps, in which the primary UI thread must not be slowed by taint-tracked background threads. In this paper, we argue that thread-local emulation would offer significant benefits to mobile systems, and we explore some potential ways to implement it.

The rest of this paper is organized as follows. In Section 2, we provide background on taint tracking. In Section 3, we describe why a simple trap-and-emulate approach to selective taint tracking is insufficient for Android. In Section 4, we describe several ways to implement thread-local emulation. In Section 5, we present results from our preliminary work. In Section 6, we speculate about how to integrate taint tracking into Android without relying on the Dalvik VM. Finally, in Section 7 we present related work, and in Section 8, we provide our conclusions.

HotMobile '16, February 26-27, 2016, St. Augustine, FL, USA

© 2016 ACM. ISBN 978-1-4503-4145-5/16/02...$15.00

DOI: http://dx.doi.org/10.1145/2873587.2873601

2. BACKGROUND: TAINT TRACKING

Taint tracking records data dependencies between program storage, such as individual memory addresses and registers, and one or more taint sources, such as a device's GPS sensor or the network. Each storage location has an associated taint label indicating whether its current value depends on a taint source. Because taint labels are not part of the physical- or virtual-machine interface, a taint-tracking system must update labels through *emulation*. That is, the system must interpose on any operation that transfers information from one storage location to another, such as a virtual-machine bytecode or physical-machine instruction. For example, TaintDroid maintains a 32-bit label for each object field and program register and updates fields' and registers' labels whenever a Dalvik bytecode executes.

For many years taint tracking was most commonly used to detect and defeat malware [15, 23], but many recent systems demonstrate that it is a generally useful technique for addressing a range of problems. For example, YouProve [11] uses taint tracking to attest to the authenticity of sensor data generated by a smartphone, such as audio or images, even if the data is compressed or cropped. Pebbles [19] uses taint tracking to logically group data items that are scattered across disparate parts of a storage system into higher-level units, such as an email or expense report. Grouping related data items into logical units allows the system to securely delete sensitive emails and other documents that span multiple databases and files. CleanOS [20] uses tracking to record where sensitive data resides in a device's memory and filesystem, so that this data can be evicted to the cloud if the device is lost or stolen. Finally, taint tracking has helped monitor how apps use private data [9], verify the security of point-of-sale apps [10], and improve apps' energy efficiency [18].

For nearly all of these systems, efficient taint tracking is crucial. The extra work required by emulation, i.e., interposing on each operation to update taint labels, imposes an inherent performance penalty. However, if the additional work is small relative to the time required to perform the original operation, then the overall performance penalty will also be small. This is precisely how TaintDroid achieves good performance; the Dalvik bytecodes on which it interposes are slow compared to native ARM instructions. At the same time, the poor performance of Dalvik bytecodes has led app developers to use more native code, and recent versions of Android compile bytecodes to native instructions at install time. This move to native code has had the unfortunate side effect of inflating the cost of taint tracking. Taint tracking native code typically costs between 10 and 30x, whereas TaintDroid's overhead is less than 20%.

One way to make taint tracking practical again is to do it selectively. In particular, apps may only rarely handle tainted data, and thus it may be possible to pay the price of emulation only when required. For example, if a system is only interested in tracking data from the GPS sensor, then apps that do not use location data will not pay a performance penalty. Or if an app uses location data, then it will only slow down while processing location data. Of course, for apps that make heavy use of tracked data, then the slowdown will be severe and unavoidable. However, we expect that many interesting apps will spend little time, relative to their lifetimes, handling tracked data. A major part of our ongoing work is testing this hypothesis.

For the rest of this paper, we concern ourselves with only explicit information flows, and we ignore implicit flows, e.g., information flows triggered by a program's control flow. The impact of this limitation depends on the use case. Prior work on implicit flows has shown that for certain applications and data types, implicit flows can be tracked at a reasonable cost. For example, SpanDex [8] quantifies and limits the amount of password information leaked through a malicious app's control flow. A general solution to the problem of implicit flows is unlikely to emerge anytime soon, but tracking implicit flows is unnecessary for many systems. For example, in YouProve, an app using implicit flows to leak information does not undermine the system's goals. YouProve will not attest to the authenticity of sensor data leaked through implicit flows, which defeats the reason for using it in the first place.

3. SELECTIVE TAINT TRACKING

To begin, we will assume that a mobile app consists of Dalvik bytecodes executing within a Dalvik VM and native libraries executing on the bare metal. TaintDroid provides taint tracking for bytecodes, but does not handle native code.

To implement selective taint tracking of native code, we must capture transitions from Dalvik to native code. Android apps are written in Java and use the Java Native Interface (JNI) to invoke native methods. Thus, we must first modify the JNI bridge and use the `mprotect` system call to disallow read and write access to memory pages containing tainted data when a native method is called from Dalvik.

As long as native code does not access tainted data, it will run at full speed. However, if native code tries to access tainted data, the operating system will raise a segmentation fault (`SIGSEGV`). The fault handler will transfer control of the thread to taint-tracking and emulation software running in the thread's address space. The emulator executes the program's instructions and performs dynamic taint tracking based on instructions' semantics. For example, suppose the emulator encounters the instruction `add r0, r1, r2`, which computes the sum of `r1` and `r2` and stores the result in `r0`. In addition to updating the value of `r0`, the emulator will update `r0`'s taint label using `r1`'s and `r2`'s labels: `Taint(r0)` ← `Taint(r1)` ∪ `Taint(r2)`, where ∪ represents the union of two taint labels. The emulator executes native code in this manner until (1) it returns to Dalvik via the JNI bridge, or (2) all register labels are taint free[13].

While this approach works well for single-threaded programs, it creates a dilemma for apps that have threads executing in parallel. First, to emulate the faulting instruction, the fault handler must access tainted data. However, when the handler executes, it is still bound by the protections that caused the original fault. Accessing tainted data with these protections in place will trigger a new fault, leading to an unending series of faults and no forward progress. At the same time, allowing the fault handler to remove page protections to avoid an infinite loop would allow non-emulated threads to access tainted pages without trapping.

To prevent this, we could force all threads to run in emulated mode anytime a thread accessed tainted data. Placing each thread in emulation mode would allow us to safely disable page protections and rely on threads' emulation layers to protect tainted data. The downside of emulating all threads is that every thread would pay a significant performance penalty, even when they do not access tainted data. This is particularly problematic for mobile platforms like Android, on which the main UI thread must remain fast to ensure good responsiveness. An ideal solution would only taint track the threads that access tainted data.

4. THREAD-LOCAL EMULATION

Thread-local emulation ensures that a thread will only pay the performance penalty of emulation if it accesses tainted data. Implementing thread-local emulation requires a way to protect tainted data from non-emulated threads while simultaneously granting emulated threads access. In this section, we discuss possible software and hardware techniques that may be used to do so.

4.1 Software Techniques

Reading Memory with the Kernel: Each process in the Linux kernel can access its own address space through the kernel by reading and writing /proc/self/mem. As the reads and writes take place in kernel space, they succeed without being restricted by page protections. Hence, the emulator can use it to access tainted data. Before emulating an instruction, it has to check if the instruction uses a memory location located in a protected page. If so, it has to perform the access via the kernel interface.

Multiple Virtual Page Mappings: The emulator can also use a technique proposed by Appel and Li [3]. For each page with tainted data, the emulator can create new entries in the process's page table that map to the same physical page, but with relaxed protections. Using these new mappings, the emulator can access tainted data without turning off page protections. Since the non-emulated threads will not be aware of the page table entries created by the emulator, they will not be able to freely access tainted data.

4.2 Hardware Techniques

We may also use hardware-specific features to implement thread-local emulation. Although this usually means a more complex implementation, hardware acceleration also gives us good performance. In this section, we focus on features provided in the ARM ISA. Although this limits the generality of the implementation, we consider it acceptable since most mobile devices use an ARM processor.

ARM Domains: The ARMv7 ISA has a feature known as memory domains. It allows each 1 MB region of a process's address space to be classified under different logical sections known as domains. There are a maximum of sixteen possible domains and each domain has one of three permissions associated with it. The domain permissions are set in a per-core CPU register known as the *domain control register*, which means that they are set on a per-thread basis. On an access to a memory location, the CPU core checks the running thread's permission for the domain of that location. If the permission is set to CLIENT, the core relies on page protections to decide if the access should be allowed. If it is set to NONE or MANAGER, access is unconditionally denied or allowed, respectively.

Memory domains may be used to implement thread-local emulation in the following manner. First, we define a new domain, TAINT. When a page contains tainted data, the surrounding memory region is classified under the TAINT domain. By default, a thread has CLIENT permissions for TAINT. The emulator, however, is given MANAGER permissions

over TAINT. This means that even though the emulator runs in the same address space as the process, it can directly access tainted memory since its permissive MANAGER domain overrides page protections. Other threads will continue to be governed by page protections because they use the CLIENT permission.

Exposing Privileged CPU Features To User-Level Code: The inclusion of virtualization features in modern CPUs provides us with interesting opportunities. For instance, Belay et al. proposed Dune [5], a method of exposing privileged CPU features to user-level applications. In Dune, virtualization hardware features are used to allow applications to perform user-level page-table management. Applications can easily write their own page table entries and switch between different page tables. This is useful as our emulator can create its own page table mappings to freely access tainted data without also allowing non-emulated threads to do so. Unfortunately, Dune is not immediately usable in our work on smartphones for two reasons. First, Dune is implemented for the x86 ISA and not ARM. Second, as the authors of Dune admit, their page table management feature is not thread-safe. They state that this limitation is a matter of implementation but it is unclear how much work it would take to make it thread-safe in the context of ARM.

5. PRELIMINARY WORK

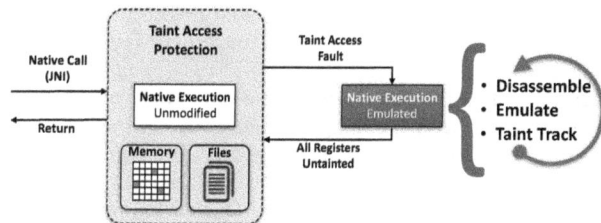

Figure 1: Overview of selective native code taint tracking with thread-local emulation.

In this section, we present results from our preliminary work on thread-local emulation for Android. A high-level overview of our system is illustrated in Figure 1. It follows a design similar to the one outlined in Section 3 and is currently implemented on Android 4.1.1.

Taint tracking at the bytecode level is done by TaintDroid. When an app uses the JNI, a taint protection layer ensures that memory pages containing tainted data are protected. If a thread attempts to access tainted data in native code, a taint access fault (a SIGSEGV) is triggered, which starts the emulator. The emulator disassembles each instruction, emulates its behavior, and performs taint propagation. When the CPU registers are no longer tainted, emulation ends and the thread executes natively.

To test the performance of our system, we developed a custom microbenchmark application, fully written in native code. This benchmark reads extended JPEG metadata (EXIF) from a tainted JPEG file using the libjhead native library and writes the metadata to standard out. It was developed based on our observations of the Instagram app. We found that it processes pictures taken with the camera in native code. During the processing step, it extracts the

EXIF data using the `libjhead` library and then applies a custom image filter.

We ran the benchmark on a Galaxy Nexus smartphone, and measured the time taken for it to complete, with and without taint tracking enabled. When taint tracking was enabled, we performed a full emulation of the benchmark and tried reading tainted memory with both the kernel and ARM domains. Our goal was to measure the amount of slowdown imposed by native-code taint tracking. Each experiment was conducted a hundred times. We report the median numbers below.

When the emulator reads tainted data through the kernel, the slowdown was 1,048x. In other words, the benchmark is over a thousand times slower when taint-tracking is enabled. As one might have predicted, trapping to kernel space each time we need a data item from a protected page is prohibitively expensive. When the emulator reads tainted data using ARM's memory domains, the slowdown is just 22x. We noticed similar levels of improvement in other data-heavy microbenchmarks.

Note that although a 22x slowdown is still significant, this is the slowdown of a microbenchmark that performs a single task. It does not reflect the amortized performance we expect with a third-party app that processes primarily untainted data.

5.1 Discussion

While implementing thread-local emulation, we noticed several issues that need to be addressed before we can have a practical system. In this section, we discuss each of them in detail.

Exiting Emulation Mode: We only want to emulate a thread while it is handling tainted data. Although it is safe to exit emulation when none of the CPU registers contain tainted data, it is not efficient to do so. Suppose we reach a state of untainted registers. Due to temporal locality, the next instruction may load tainted data again. Hence, it is wasteful to exit emulation as soon as the registers are untainted. We noticed this overhead due to unnecessary switching between native and emulation execution in our experiments. If we run our JPEG benchmark under selective taint tracking while using ARM domains, the slowdown is over 100x. Recall that the slowdown with full emulation is 22x. Our results are consistent with the observations made by Ho et al. in their selective taint-tracking work [13]. They mitigate this issue by continuing emulation for 50 more instructions after registers become untainted. Emulation exits only if the registers remain untainted at the end. We are presently investigating if a similar approach will suffice for us.

Tainted Data on Stack: The page containing the stack may become protected due to tainted registers that either spill onto the stack or are saved when a function call is made. A protected stack will immediately cause the thread to be emulated until the stack no longer contains tainted data. We are evaluating the performance impact of this issue and its relation to the temporal locality highlighted above. There are two ways of addressing this issue if it is a significant cause of overhead: (i) we could use a high number of watchpoints [12] if the hardware supports it to have fine-grained traps to tainted data, or (ii), we could use non-contiguous stacks [21] where tainted and untainted data are located in different pages even though they are on the stack.

False Positives: The page size on Android is 4 KB which means that page protections are coarse. Just as with the stack, a page with a single tainted byte will become protected and any access to untainted data within that page will cause unnecessary emulation. Although this is a general issue with page protections, it can take on special significance on Android. Android has a construct called the Looper [2], a message queuing system used in a multiple-producer, single-consumer manner. Each application has a single looper designated as the main looper. It is responsible for receiving events from different parts of the OS and delivering it to the application. If the page that contains the main looper's buffer becomes protected, the main event loop of the app will have to run in emulation mode. We are currently evaluating different options of addressing this issue, including the use of Dune [5].

The Trend to 64-bit ARM CPUs: We made use of memory domains, a feature of ARMv7, in our preliminary work. The ARMv7 ISA is used on 32-bit ARM CPUs. Unfortunately, the ARMv8 ISA, used on 64-bit ARM CPUs, no longer has support for memory domains. Given that newer smartphones are transitioning to 64-bit ARM CPUs [14], using memory domains is not a future-proof solution. This raises the urgency of using the other techniques discussed in Section 4 to allow the emulator to read tainted data.

6. LIFE WITHOUT DALVIK

In newer versions of Android, apps are still written in Java and compiled to Dalvik bytecode for distribution. However, the Dalvik VM is deprecated and is no longer used to interpret the app's bytecode. Instead, when an app is downloaded onto a phone, it is compiled into native code before execution. The absence of the Dalvik VM means TaintDroid will no longer work.

That said, the fact that apps are still distributed as bytecode provides us with an opportunity. We can rewrite its bytecodes and instrument them so that when the app is subsequently compiled, it will have taint tracking "baked in." This approach was first taken by Bell et al. in Phosphor [6], where tracking logic was added to Java applications running on the JVM by rewriting their bytecode. However, for performance reasons, we may not directly use their approach since in Android, the Dalvik bytecode will be further compiled into ARM assembly prior to execution. Instead of an always-on taint tracking scheme, as per Phosphor, we still need thread-local emulation.

To provide thread-local emulation we could first define a taint label for each class field. Second, we could set all class fields private and rewrite all direct field accesses as getter- and setter-method invocations. The getter for a field checks the field's taint label. If it is not tainted, then the field is returned. Otherwise, the getter raises a taint exception and passes the field's value in the exception object. This means that all getter invocations will be surrounded by a `try`/`catch` block. If the getter raises a taint exception, method execution continues in the catch block which contains the rest of the method together with the taint-propagation logic.

It is important to note that adding taint-tracking logic to the bytecode only replaces TaintDroid's functionality. It does not handle the cases in which apps may use native libraries via the JNI.

7. RELATED WORK

Taint tracking on mobile platforms is an ongoing research topic. Qian et al. proposed NDroid [17], a virtualized environment based on QEMU to run Android apps and track taints when they use native code libraries. NDroid relies on TaintDroid to perform taint propagation at the bytecode level. It uses software hooks implemented in QEMU to capture an app's use of JNI and run native taint tracking. Although NDroid performs native code taint tracking, it does not run on real smartphone devices, which is a key goal in our work.

In contrast to dynamic taint analysis, there has also been work on performing static taint analysis such as FlowDroid [4] and Amandroid [22]. The aim in both work is to detect malicious apps by performing static analysis on them and checking if they leak sensitive data. As stated in Section 2, we are interested in dynamic taint tracking as a general tool to solve a range of problems, instead of just malware detection. That said, these approaches complement ours. For example, static analysis may help during the byte code rewriting by highlighting the portions of the app where taint propagation logic is necessary.

Paupore et al. presented a preliminary design of a hybrid taint tracking system for mobile platforms in a recent paper [16]. They propose an always-on taint tracking system that runs with low overhead using a combination of static and dynamic taint analysis. The static analysis step runs first and adds special markers to paths in the app's managed code that uses sensitive data. When the app executes, the dynamic taint analysis system uses the markers to perform taint propagation. The dynamic taint tracker uses the *Embedded Trace Macrocell* (ETM), a hardware feature available on modern ARM processors, to improve performance. This feature allows a core to collect execution traces of a running thread and send it to another core, where it can be analyzed. The use of ETM allows app execution and taint propagation to run in parallel, as they are each done on separate cores. As with FlowDroid and Amandroid, the techniques used in this work complement our approach.

8. CONCLUSION

In this paper, we described *thread-local emulation*, a refinement of selective taint tracking. In thread-local emulation, only the threads that handle tainted data are emulated to perform dynamic taint tracking; all other threads run with minimal overhead. The goal of thread-local emulation is to make dynamic taint tracking practical in mobile systems dominated by native code by only performing taint tracking when necessary. Our preliminary work on implementing thread-local emulation on Android shows good promise. However, plenty of challenges lie ahead, especially achieving good performance on recent versions of Android.

9. ACKNOWLEDGMENTS

We would like to thank the anonymous reviewers and our shepherd, Andrew Rice, for their insightful feedback. This work was partially funded by the National Science Foundation under awards CCF-1335443 and CNS-0747283.

10. REFERENCES

[1] Google I/O 2014 - The ART runtime. https://www.youtube.com/watch?v=EBlTzQsUoOw?t=37m25s.

[2] Android Developers Documentation. Looper. http://developer.android.com/reference/android/os/Looper.html.

[3] A. Appel and K. Li. Virtual Memory Primitives for User Programs. In *Proceedings of ASPLOS '91*, April 1991.

[4] S. Arzt, S. Rasthofer, C. Fritz, E. Bodden, A. Bartel, J. Klein, Y. le Traon, D. Octeau, and P. McDaniel. FlowDroid: Precice Context, Flow, Field, Object-sensitive and Lifecycle-aware Taint Analysis for Android Apps. In *Proceedings of PLDI '14*, June 2014.

[5] A. Belay, A. Bittau, A. Mashtizadeh, D. Terei, D. Mazières, and C. Kozyrakis. Dune: Safe User-level Access to Privileged CPU Features. In *Proceedings of OSDI '12*, October 2012.

[6] J. Bell and G. Kaiser. Phosphor: Illuminating Dynamic Data Flow in Commodity JVMs. In *Proceedings of OOPSLA '14*, October 2014.

[7] J. Clause, W. Li, and A. Orso. Dytan: A Generic Dynamic Taint Analysis Framework. In *Proceedings of ISSTA '07*, July 2007.

[8] L. P. Cox, P. Gilbert, G. Lawler, V. Pistol, A. Razeen, B. Wu, and S. Cheemalapati. SpanDex: Secure Password Tracking for Android. In *Proceedings of USENIX Security '14*, August 2014.

[9] W. Enck, P. Gilbert, B.-G. Chun, L. P. Cox, J. Jung, P. McDaniel, and A. N. Sheth. TaintDroid: An Information-Flow Tracking system for Realtime Privacy Monitoring on Smartphones. In *Proceedings of OSDI '10*, October 2010.

[10] W. Frisby, B. Moench, B. Recht, and T. Ristenpart. Security Analysis of Smartphone Point-of-Sale Systems. In *Proceedings of WOOT '12*, August 2012.

[11] P. Gilbert, J. Jung, K. Lee, H. Qin, D. Sharkey, A. Sheth, and L. P. Cox. YouProve: Authenticity and Fidelity in Mobile Sensing . In *Proceedings of SenSys '11*, November 2011.

[12] J. L. Greathouse, H. Xin, Y. Luo, and T. Austin. A Case for Unlimited Watchpoints. In *Proceedings of ASPLOS '12*, March 2012.

[13] A. Ho, M. Fetterman, C. Clark, A. Warfield, and S. Hand. Practical Taint-Based Protection using Demand Emulation. In *Proceedings of EuroSys '06*, April 2006.

[14] Jerry Hildenbrand, AndroidCentral. Why 64-bit processors really matter for Android. http://www.androidcentral.com/why-64-bit-processors-really-matter-android.

[15] J. Newsome and D. Song. Dynamic Taint Analysis for Automatic Detection, Analysis, and Signature Generation of Exploits on Commodity Software. In *Proceedings of NDSS '05*, February 2005.

[16] J. Paupore, E. Fernandes, A. Prakash, S. Roy, and X. Ou. Practical Always-On Taint Tracking on Mobile Devices. In *Proceedings of HotOS '15*, May 2015.

[17] C. Qian, X. Luo, Y. Shao, and A. T. Chan. On Tracking Information Flows through JNI in Android Applications. In *Proceedings of DSN '14*, June 2014.

[18] H. Shen, A. Balasubramanian, A. LaMarca, and D. Wetherall. Enhancing Mobile Apps To Use Sensor Hubs Without Programmer Effort. In *Proceedings of UbiComp '15*, September 2015.

[19] R. Spahn, J. Bell, M. Z. Lee, S. Bhamidipati, R. Geambasu, and G. Kaiser. Pebbles: Fine-Grained Data Management Abstractions for Modern Operating Systems. In *Proceedings of OSDI '14*, October 2014.

[20] Y. Tang, P. Ames, S. Bhamidipati, A. Bijlani, R. Geambasu, and N. Sarda. Clean OS: Limiting Mobile Data Exposure with Idle Eviction. In *Proceedings of OSDI '12*, August 2012.

[21] R. von Behren, J. Condit, F. Zhou, G. C. Necula, and E. Brewer. Capriccio: Scalable Threads for Internet Services. In *Proceedings of SOSP '03*, October 2003.

[22] F. Wei, S. Roy, X. Ou, and Robby. Amandroid: A Precise and General Inter-component Data Flow Analysis Framework for Security Vetting of Android Apps. In *Proceedings of CCS '14*, November 2014.

[23] H. Yin, D. Song, M. Egele, C. Kruegel, and E. Kirda. Panorama: Capturing System-wide Information Flow for Malware Detection and Analysis. In *Proceedings of CCS '07*, October 2007.

Using a Multi-Tasking VM for Mobile Applications

Yin Yan, Chunyu Chen, Karthik Dantu, Steven Y. Ko, Lukasz Ziarek
University at Buffalo, The State University of New York
{yinyan, chunyuch, kdantu, stevko, lziarek}@buffalo.edu

ABSTRACT

This paper discusses the potential benifits of switching Android's *single VM per application* runtime environment to a multi-tasking VM environment. A multi-tasking VM is a type of a Java virtual machine with the ability to execute multiple Java applications in one memory space. It does so by isolating the applications to prevent interferences. We argue that using a multi-tasking VM for mobile systems provides better control over application lifecycle management, more flexible memory management, and faster inter-application communication. To support this argument, we discuss a preliminary design, implementation, and evaluation for an alternative to Android's communication mechanism, `Binder`, and demonstrate the benefits afforded by a multi-tasking VM.

Keywords

Mobile systems; Multi-tasking virtual machine; Runtime

1. INTRODUCTION

With the adoption in Android, Java-based runtime environments have become the most popular execution model for mobile applications. They have many characteristics ideally suited for mobile environments; for example, they use bytecode and executes it in a VM, making it portable across different ISAs; they automatically manage memory, allowing the underlying system to employ efficient memory management policies; they are also type-checked, lowering the cost of development. Due to these benefits, Android now supports countless devices, ISAs, users, and developers.

The default execution mode for Java is a *single VM per application*. This mode of execution is the default in almost all Java deployments, whether it is on a server, a desktop, or a mobile phone. However, this is not the only mode of execution available. Historically, *Multi-Tasking VM* (Multi-VM, or simply MVM) [4] has been providing the ability to run *all* applications in a single VM. MVM runs each ap-

plication in an isolation unit called a *partition* [17], but all applications run as a single process.

In this paper, we argue that the MVM mode of execution is the better choice for Android. With the increasing CPU power and massive on-board memory, it is common to run multiple cooperative applications on a single device. The latest Android release, Marshmallow, allows running more than one foreground activity from different applications at the same time. Executing all applications in a single MVM instance gives a global view of application behaviors with regards to system resources such as memory and I/O. This global view allows the MVM to better accommodate more application requests and efficiently manage available resources. Additionally, running all applications in a single process simplifies communication between applications; the VM can avoid context switches and copying data from one memory space to another.

To concretely demonstrate these benefits, we first examine an MVM architecture, and discuss the feasibility of replacing Android's VM (Dalvik/ART) with an MVM. We examine all the salient features of Android's VM and compare how an MVM can realize the same features. Our conclusion is essentially that *there is no feature that cannot be replicated* in an MVM architecture. To understand the advantages, we pick one essential sub-system (inter-application communication), and show how an MVM can implement the same feature more efficiently. Our overall findings are that (i) an MVM architecture has tangible benefits in comparison to existing Android, (ii) the changes necessary to use an MVM are only required in the framework level, and (iii) all the benefits can be made transparent to applications. Although single process execution for multiple programs itself is not a new idea (*e.g.*, Singularity [7, 8, 9]), our focus is not on designing a new OS, but on replacing a component in an existing OS to demonstrate additional benefits.

2. MULTI-TASKING VM

The use of an MVM architecture was first proposed to achieve better scalability as well as security for server style Java applications [4]. Later, MVM was also expanded to support multiple users instead of only a single user [6]. The design philosophy of MVM is similar to Singularity [7, 8, 9], a dependable and robust micro-kernel system built with a type-safe language. Singularity separates its computation units as Software Isolated Processes (SIPs)—each program, device driver, or system extension is executed in its own SIP under the same address space. The inter-process communications are enabled by typed bi-direction channels. To

HotMobile '16, February 26-27, 2016, St. Augustine, FL, USA

© 2016 ACM. ISBN 978-1-4503-4145-5/16/02. . . $15.00

DOI: http://dx.doi.org/10.1145/2873587.2873596

	Android Dalvik/ART	Multi-tasking VM
Application isolation	The access of sensitive framework APIs is controlled with manifest configuration, and file permissions and other application resources are protected per process.	An OS-like access of control unit can be implemented in MVM.
Application initialization	Forks zygote, creates a new VM instance in a new process, and loads application classes.	Creates a new partition for an application, configures a time slice for the application that runs in the newly created partition, and loads application classes.
Application context switch	Switching between processes requires to switch memory addresses, page tables and kernel resources, and flush processor caches.	Threads switching between different partitions only requires switching processor states, *e.g.*, scheduling counter or register contents, which can be done fast and efficiently.
Application termination	The exit of an application components do not terminate the process of the application. The process is killed only when its user manually kills it or the system runs low on memory. The Low Memory Killer (LMK) is responsible for selecting and killing processes.	Applications are executed in their dedicated partitions. MVM provides VM-level APIs to enforce all of the threads in one partition to exit, and reclaim their memory and other resources.
Application suspension and resume	The OS scheduler switches between processes.	The VM controller switches partitions in the same process.
Intra-app communication	Message passing constructs	Message passing constructs
Inter-app communication	Android Binder IPC	Shared memory in MVM
System service	Executed in one dedicated process, accessed via `Binder` calls	Executed in one dedicated partition, accessed via inter-application communication mechanism.
Memory Management	Virtual memory with per-app garbage collection.	A single memory address space with enforced memory boundaries and configurable garbage collection strategies for different partitions.

Table 1: Application Management Between Android's Dalvik/ART and MVM

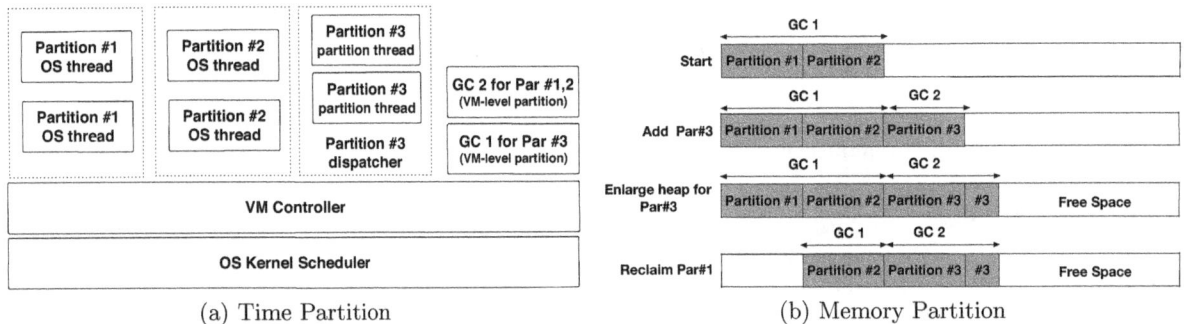

(a) Time Partition

(b) Memory Partition

Figure 1: MVM Partition Architecture

guarantee the safety and correctness, all application code is associated with manifest configurations for static validation and analysis.

Similarly, MVM has the ability to execute multiple runtime environments without interferences under one single VM instance. The spatial and temporal isolations can be achieved via class loading [3, 5] or resource partitioning [11]. In our discussion, we will focus on a resource-partitioned MVM, Fiji VM [17, 12], which isolates the interferences by partitioning applications into execution units, and enforces application lifecycle management and memory boundaries through the use of a VM controller. For the inter-application communication, MVM can develop communication primitives at the VM level over region-based memory, and higher-level protocols are more easily encoded without necessitating copying. More details will be discussed in Section 2.1 and Section 2.2. We use the term "partition" to mean the execution unit in MVM in the later sections. Compare to Singularity, MVM does not provide built-in verification tools. However, it defines sophisticated interfaces for different types of resource management. For example,

the CPU cycles and memory boundaries can be either statically configured or dynamically adjusted between partitions via the VM controller, the controller also facilitates finer-grained control for handling interrupts, task preemption, and memory reclamation.

The rest of section explores the application features that are affected by replacing Android's VM with an MVM and some of the added benefits of doing so. To explain the functional differences, we provide a side-by-side comparison of the basic features that are essential to Android's Java Runtime Environment and their analogues in MVM in Table 1. We categorize these features into three major aspects: application lifecycle management, memory management and inter-application communication.

2.1 Application Lifecycle Management

MVM manages the lifecycle of its applications by partitioning each application's tasks into separate time slots. Thus, application execution is isolated within its own temporal partition. MVM provides VM-level APIs to allow a VM controller to manipulate the initiation, suspension, and termination of the tasks in each partition with fine-grained control. Each partition can create OS level threads, which underpins Android created threads. All threads, regardless of which partition they belong to, are in the same OS process.

MVM can provide various scheduling options to manage threads that belong to different partitions, exposing the trade-off between fine-grained control and management overhead. The simplest way to manage partition threads is to directly leverage thread scheduling from the operating system; the threads of each partition are grouped and scheduled with fixed-length time slices via operating system thread scheduling. The threads in the current active partition are scheduled within partition time slices. When the current partition exceeds its time slice, the VM controller suspends all threads in this partition and resumes threads in the next partition. Figure 1a shows various scheduling options potentially available. Partition 1 and 2 are utilizing direct OS thread scheduling for their execution.

Alternatively, MVM can also provides VM-level scheduling for better control with a task dispatcher that manages a thread pool. The threads in a partition are scheduled through the dispatcher as a VM partition thread, as shown with partition 3 in Figure 1a. The VM controller can manipulate the partition lifetime via VM-level APIs to apply different scheduling policies of the task dispatcher. The execution of the task dispatcher introduces additional complexity; additional safe points [1] need to be checked during execution to allow the VM controller to safely suspend, resume, and terminate threads from the dispatcher. In a nutshell, direct OS thread scheduling is lightweight but with less control. The VM-level scheduling approach requires the execution of the dispatcher with additional safe point checking, but it provides better control. Normally, MVM supports a hybrid approach, allowing the developers to choose how their partitions are scheduled based on performance requirements.

The biggest benefit of performing application scheduling at the VM level is that context switches between applications are extremely fast. This occurs because the TLB and caches are not flushed—the cost of a context switch is simply the cost of switching between threads. In a loosely coupled, event driven system like Android, where many applications communicate, this has an additional benefit—namely a hot cache. Switching at a communication point has a good probability of retaining communication structures in the cache, yielding additional performance benefits. Singularity also enjoys fast context switching.

2.2 Application Memory Management

Although MVM provides a dynamically configurable memory management at runtime, it enforces memory boundaries for space isolation. Namely, one application cannot allocate objects or hold references to other application's heap memory. To reclaim dead objects, each application can have its own GC (typical in a partitioned MVM), but there maybe one GC that is shared by many applications (typically in an MVM that uses classloader based isolation). MVM may use a combination of GC approaches and even leverage other

automatic memory management schemes, like scoped memory [2] (typical in more specialized MVMs). The key observation is that in all MVM schemes, the applications are executed in the same address space and it is up to MVM to ensure that heap boundaries are enforced. Figure 1b demonstrates basic heap management scenarios in MVM memory management for a partitioned MVM. In this case we assume a partitioned MVM, which assigns GCs to monitor potentially more than one partition [2].

Like Android's Dalvik/ART, each partition starts with a memory quota (the application's initial heap size—this can be uniform across all applications or can be tailored based on the application's need), and the heap size can be increased at runtime, if necessary. The initiation or termination of a partition induces the allocation or reclamation of the heap memory for that partition, in much the same way as application termination on Android causes a reclamation of the host VM and its assigned heap memory.

The main benefit of an MVM GC scheme is that MVM can arbitrate memory allocation requests from different applications executing in different partitions. As a direct consequence, MVM can not only decide when, but also where to run the garbage collection. This is especially useful for managing memory on a memory constrained device. Lets consider what happens on Android when memory usage is low. In such situations, Android triggers its Low Memory Killer (LMK) to selectively kill applications. This is done via an importance metric. Crucially, the Low Memory Killer does not understand how much "garbage" a given application has resident in its heap memory. To skirt this issue, Android allows the OS to trigger GC events in a given VM. However, once the LMK is triggered, memory is reclaimed on an application level.

In MVM, the VM controller understands the memory consumption of each application. It can adjust heap boundaries between partitions to respond to shortage of memory in individual partitions. Additionally, MVM can even trigger GC on a partition whose app is currently not active and reallocate the collected memory to another partition that requires more memory. Thus, the memory requests are satisfied without sacrificing the correctness of the applications, and without resorting to drastic measures such as terminating other applications. What this means is that the system as a whole can make more *holistic* memory management decisions. We believe this will also allow for more programmatic definitions of *global* memory management schemes instead of the heuristic-based LMK mechanism. It is this global memory management that differentiates MVM from OS based solutions like Singularity.

2.3 Inter-App Communication

Android applications rely on Android's `Binder` IPC mechanism for communication and data transfer. For example, Android's messaging objects, `Intent` or `Message`, transfer their data object `Bundle` via Android's `Binder` calls. Since `Binder` calls require a data copy between the communicating applications, it is limited in the size of data it can transfer. To exchange a large chunk of data, developers have to use an external medium such as `ContentProvider` or `ashmem`.

---

[1]A safe point is a compiler injected check, to ensure GC runs periodically by suspending threads. This can be leveraged to bound the amount of time needed to suspend a thread. We note that for a given architecture, this bound can be calculated precisely, affording an added level of determinism to the system.

[2]This is useful when you may want to support different types of GC. For instances a real-time GC for applications with timing guarantees and a more throughput-oriented GC for multimedia applications.

(a) Android's `ashmem`

(b) Multi-VM Shared Memory

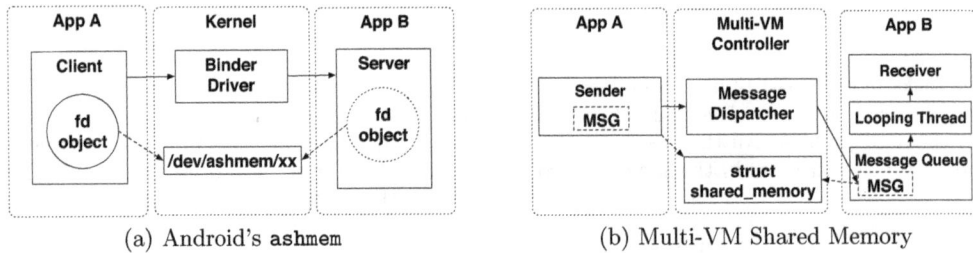

Figure 2: Communication with Shared Memory

Nevertheless, `Binder` is a building block leveraged by both `ContentProvider` and `ashmem`, not for large data transfer, but for exchanging small meta data required for data transfer.

Thus, our preliminary exploration in this paper takes a deeper look at `Binder` and replaces it with an alternative mechanism in MVM. We discuss this in more detail in the next section. Below, we briefly lay out our thoughts on how we could replace `ContentProvider` and `ashmem` in MVM.

`ContentProvider` is one of the core components of an Android application; it encapsulates data and provides standard interfaces that allows data in one process to be transferred to code running in another process. It is designed for data persistence in mind, and the access of data via `ContentProvider` interfaces requires expensive I/O operations. A `ContentProvider` implementation in MVM would look much the same as it does in Android itself. Since the primary requirement is persistence, the MVM does not provide any added benefit since the underlying file system governs the majority of the access costs. We observe, however, that typical kernel permission mechanisms need to be move to the MVM to retain the semantics that Android expects. For instance, associations between file descriptors and the process IDs would need to be maintained.

In contrast, `ashmem` is a Android Linux module that facilitates direct memory sharing between processes. As shown in Figure 2a, `ashmem` allows applications to allocate a shared memory region, map it to a physical memory address, and handle it as an file descriptor. Since the file descriptor is created via `mmap()`, it is only valid in its own process. To share the file descriptor, developers have to wrap it with an `MemoryFile` instance, and pass the `MemoryFile` object through a `Binder` call. Applications that hold the reference to the same `MemoryFile` instance have to cooperate with others explicitly via Android's communication mechanism to use the memory region abstracted by the file descriptor.

Our observation is that `ashmem`-like functionality can be implemented in an MVM very naturally, using our `Binder` replacement discussed in the next section. Our `Binder` replacement is essentially a shared memory substrate and provides a common interface that applications can leverage to communicate. We illustrate how we can build such a mechanisms in the next section and show that it can outperform kernel-based approaches for data transfer in Section 4.

3. MVM INTER-APP COMMUNICATION

To illustrate the power of MVM, we show in this section how easily we can provide an inter-application communication mechanism without crossing the process boundary between applications. Figure 2b shows one possible design that we implement to replace Android's `Binder`. The design is based on asynchronous message passing with shared memory. As Figure 2b shows, each application has a *looping thread* associated with a *message queue* in its own partition.

Other threads that have a reference to the *message queue* can send messages to the *looping thread* by synchronizing with the *message queue*. Unfortunately, MVM isolates applications in both time and space at runtime, the sender thread in one partition cannot directly refer to the *message queue* in another partition. The only way to do the inter-partition references is using native objects in a controlled manner.

Thus, our design utilizes inter-partition locks and shared memory regions as part of the functionalities in the internal MVM controller. MVM only exposes Java APIs to the application layer, encapsulating the native code. Our communication mechanism consists of three main constructs, implemented at the VM controller level: `struct shared_memory`, `Message`, and `MessageDispatcher`.

`struct shared_memory` is a shared memory object, implemented in native code. It consists of a pointer to shared data, a reference counter, *a pthread lock*, and *a conditional variable*. The lock and condition variable are used for synchronization between read and write operations from different partitions to ensure consistence of the shared data.

`Message` is a messaging object class. The instantiation of a `Message` object associates the object with the allocation of the native `struct shared_memory`. Since we do not want to expose the native object directly to developers, we decided that the `Message` instances must be instantiated and recycled via `MessageDispatcher`. Code 2 presents the primary functions of the `Message`, it has a `Pointer` field that points to the `shared_memory` variable.

`MessageDispatcher` is a Java singleton class that contains both Java and native interfaces, as shown in Code 1. It controls the initiation and reclamation of the `Message` objects, and has the references to the *message queues* in all of the partitions. `MessageDispatcher` is responsible for dispatching `Message` objects to the receiving partitions. Notice that MVM cross-partition references are forbidden, the `Message` objects from sender partition can not be directly referenced in the receiving partitions. Thus, when a sender calls `MessageDispatcher.sendMessage(msg)` function, the `MessageDispatcher` first updates the reference counter of `shared_memory`. Then, it creates a new `Message` object in each receiving partitions, and assigns the `Pointer` fields of these newly created `Message` objects. By doing this, each receiving partition has a `Message` object in its own heap memory that points to the same `shared_memory`. Then, `MessageDispatcher` can recycle the `Message` object from sender. After the receivers process the `Message` objects in the `looping thread`, they decrease the reference counter on `shared_memory`. When the reference counter is updated to zero, `shared_memory` is freed.

Since our inter-application communication is enabled via shared memory and native locks, additional care needs to be taken to insure that the native objects are recycled, and to limit their number allocated at runtime similar to kernel-

```
class MessageDispatcher {
  public static MessageDispatcher getInstance();
  ...
  public Message getMessage() { ... }
  public void recycleMessage(Message msg) { ... }
  public void sendMessage(Message msg) { ... }
  private static native void allocate_msg(Pinter msg);
  private static native void free_msg(Pointer msg);
}
```

Code 1: MessageDispatcher

```
class Message {
  Pointer shared_memory
  ...
  /*package*/ Message(){ ... }
  public Byte[] read(int s, int l) { ... }
  public void write(int s, int l, Byte[] d) { ... }
  /*package*/ static void allocate(Pointer pointer);
  /*package*/ static void free();
}
```

Code 2: Message

```
struct shared_memory {
  char* id;
  void* data;
  int ref_counter;
  pthread_mutex_t lock;
  pthread_cond_t cond;
};
typedef struct shared_memory shared_memory;
//A list holds all shared_memory variables
shared_memory* shared_memory_list;
```

Code 3: Native struct: shared_memory

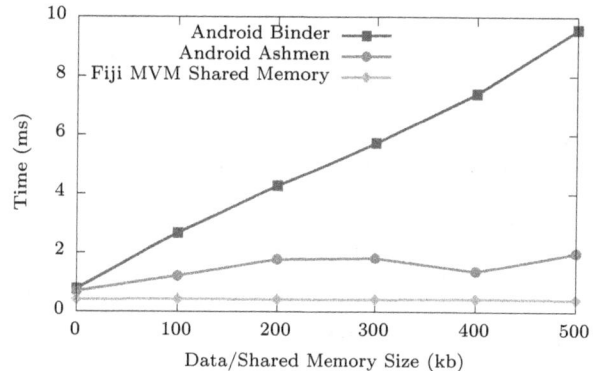

Figure 3: Communication Cost with Increasing Data Sizes

based process isolation. To achieve this, we use an object pool. This requires enforced reclamation of shared memory and native locks at the VM level, but we note that our choice of MVM supports such reclamation.

Singularity [7] provides bi-directional, two-party, typed channels that offer fast communication. More complex protocols can be implemented by using multiple channels. For instance, encoding ring-buffered communication requires the use of an intermediate channel and a thread to encode the buffer. Unfortunately, when multiple channels are leveraged, copying overhead occurs between channels. We note, however, that Singularity could be extended to support different kinds of channels (e.g., ring-buffered channels) to mitigate this, but at the cost of adding complexity to the static verification process.

4. PRELIMINARY RESULTS

To demonstrate the benefit of our proposed architecture, we have conducted preliminary experiments that measure raw communication costs. Our goal is to compare the overhead of data transfer across three mechanisms—Android's Binder, Android's ashmem, and the shared memory mechanism of an MVM. We have performed all experiments using a Google Nexus S with Android v4.1.2 (Jelly Bean) with the performance governor. For MVM experiments, we have used Fiji MVM integrated with Android v4.1.2. Our workload consists of two applications, one sender and one receiver, and we vary the amount of data transferred between these two applications. We record a timestamp before the sender sends data, and another timestamp after the receiver receives the data. We compute the communication cost as the difference of the two timestamps. We collect 500 these pairs of timestamps for each data size.

Figure 3 shows the average data transfer costs for the three mechanisms with different data sizes. Since Android's Binder transfers actual data through /dev/binder in kernel by copying the data from the sender to the receiver, it is expected that its performance increases linearly with the data size. The other two methods are more or less constant,

since there is no actual data transferred between two applications. They only involve a context switch between two applications. However, we observe that the data transfer overhead of Android's ashmem is around 5 times slower than that of Fiji MVM, because Android runs each application in a separate process with a dedicated VM instance; the context switch between two processes is generally much more expensive than switching between two threads, even if those threads reside in different partitions.

5. DISCUSSION

While MVM brings the advantages described in previous section, it has the following disadvantages compared to using a single VM per app.

Access Control Since MVM runs all applications in a single process, it needs to have its own access control mechanism for shared resources, such as hardware devices and data files. This adds runtime overhead and complexity in terms of implementation as well as access control policy definition.

Isolation MVM provides spatial and temporal isolation to avoid interferences between applications in the Java runtime. Even if an application is misbehaving or exhibits a Java-side bug, the MVM controller can tear down the malfunctioning application and its associated partition without affecting the others. However, native code requires separate mechanisms for isolation and misbehavior as discussed below.

Native Code Native code is a major concerns for an MVM. Native code provides the capabilities for direct memory access to anywhere in the memory address space, giving rise to a potential mechanism to violate the MVM isolation. Similarly, objects allocated in native code are not subject to the reclamation. Both these aspects pose challenges to the adoption of the MVM for Android.

In fact, Singularity [7, 8, 9] has the same challenges and

overcomes them with code verification. Each piece of native code in Singularity must provide a specification and be verified against this specification. In Singularity, there is a limited set of hardware-related implementations that are written in C++ and assembly as privileged instruction. Because type and memory safety assure the execution integrity of functions, Singularity can place privileged instructions, with safety checks, in trusted functions. For example, privileged instructions for accessing I/O hardware can be safely in-lined into device drivers.

For MVM, such an approach is also a viable solution. We believe this can be done by abstracting away common native functionality into libraries. As a concrete example, we are currently investigating certain communication protocols on top of more specialized MVM communication primitives. Priority rollback protocol [18] and wait free pair transaction [1] can be used for fast inter-partition communication with bounded latency and known memory bounds. We believe we can leverage both as the foundation for building Android communication primitives.

6. RELATED WORK

The canonical approach to multitasking in the Java programming language is to start each application in a new JVM [10]. This typically requires spawning a new operating system process for each application and protect the application from each other, but uses large amounts of resources (memory, CPU time) and makes inter-application communication expensive.

Android's VM is this type of a virtual machine. Dalvik VM was introduced when the first version of Android was released on 2008. It takes its own bytecode format and executes them on mobile devices. To provide isolation between applications, Android applications run in their dedicated VM instances within separate OS processes. When an application is started, the *zygote* process forks itself, creates a new VM instance, and duplicates the preloaded classes and resources in a new process for runtime. To achieve hardware-specific optimization, Google replaced Dalvik VM with Android Runtime (ART) in Android v5.0 (Lollipop). One of the major changes is that ART includes an ahead-of-time compiler (AOT) which compiles the Dex bytecode to native ELF executable. The compilation is done when the app is installed. An alternative to this model is to execute applications in one Multi-VM (MVM), which we explore in this paper.

MVMs have been adapted for real-time applications, where it is hard to preserve predictability in the presence of dynamic memory management [13]. Our prototype is built on the top of the Fiji MVM [17, 12], which provides predictable temporal isolation with real-time capabilities. Fiji MVM allows us to statically configure the memory bounds for its payloads at compile time. Similarly, KESO [14] is another MVM designed for statically configured resource-constrained embedded systems. It uses ahead-of-time knowledge to generate a Java runtime that is specifically tailored towards a given application and configures spatial isolation and memory protection statically.

7. CONCLUSION AND FUTURE WORK

In this paper, we have explored the feasibility of using MVM for Android. Unlike the existing mode of execution where an application runs within its own VM, MVM runs all applications in a single process. This architecture enables fine-grained control over application lifecycle and memory management and also reduces the context switching cost significantly as there is no real context switch happens across processes. To demonstrate these benefits, we have presented a design of an inter-application communication mechanism using an MVM. This can replace Android's `Binder` IPC mechanism. Our performance comparison shows that our design reduces the cost of communication significantly. As part of our ongoing work, we are integrating the Fiji MVM with RTDroid [16, 15] to provide a mixed-criticality environment for multiple applications.

Acknowledgments: This work has been supported in part by an NSF CAREER award, CNS-1350883.

8. REFERENCES

[1] E. Blanton and L. Ziarek. Non-Blocking Inter-Partition Communication with Wait-Free Pair Transactions. In *JTRES*, 2013.

[2] G. Bollella and K. Reinholtz. Scoped Memory. In *ISORC*, 2002.

[3] G. Czajkowski. Application Isolation in the Java Virtual Machine. In *OOPSLA*, 2000.

[4] G. Czajkowski and L. Daynés. Multitasking without Comprimise: A Virtual Machine Evolution. In *OOPSLA*, 2001.

[5] G. Czajkowski, L. Daynès, and N. Nystrom. Code Sharing among Virtual Machines. In *ECOOP*, 2002.

[6] G. Czajkowski, L. Daynès, and B. Titzer. A Multi-User Virtual Machine. In *USENIX ATC*, 2003.

[7] M. Fähndrich, M. Aiken, C. Hawblitzel, O. Hodson, G. Hunt, J. R. Larus, and S. Levi. Language Support for Fast and Reliable Message-based Communication in Singularity OS. In *EuroSys*, 2006.

[8] G. Hunt, M. Aiken, M. Fähndrich, C. Hawblitzel, O. Hodson, J. Larus, S. Levi, B. Steensgaard, D. Tarditi, and T. Wobber. Sealing OS Processes to Improve Dependability and Safety. In *EuroSys*, 2007.

[9] G. C. Hunt and J. R. Larus. Singularity: Rethinking the Software Stack. *SIGOPS Oper. Syst. Rev.*, 41(2):37–49, Apr. 2007.

[10] Java Language and Virtual Machine Specifications. https://docs.oracle.com/javase/specs/.

[11] M. Jordan. Resource Partitioning in a Java^{TM} Operating Environment. Technical report, 2006.

[12] F. Pizlo, L. Ziarek, E. Blanton, P. Maj, and J. Vitek. High-Level Programming of Embedded Hard Real-Time Devices. In *EuroSys*, 2010.

[13] M. Stilkerich, I. Thomm, C. Wawersich, and W. Schröder-Preikschat. Tailor-made JVMs for Statically Configured Embedded Systems. *Concurr. Comput. : Pract. Exper.*, 24(8):789–812, June 2012.

[14] I. Thomm, M. Stilkerich, C. Wawersich, and W. Schröder-Preikschat. KESO: An Open-source multi-JVM for Deeply Embedded Systems. In *JTRES*, 2010.

[15] Y. Yan, S. H. Konduri, A. Kulkarni, V. Anand, S. Ko, and L. Ziarek. RTDroid: A Design for Real-Time Android. In *JTRES*, 2013.

[16] Y. Yan, S. H. Konduri, A. Kulkarni, V. Anand, S. Ko, and L. Ziarek. Real-Time Android with RTDroid. In *MobiSys*, 2014.

[17] L. Ziarek, , and E. Blanton. The Fiji MultiVM Architecture. In *JTRES*, 2015.

[18] L. Ziarek. PRP: Priority Rollback Protocol – a PIP Extension for Mixed Criticality Systems: Short Paper. In *JTRES*, 2010.

Uncovering Privacy Leakage in BLE Network Traffic of Wearable Fitness Trackers

Aveek K. Das, Parth H. Pathak, Chen-Nee Chuah, Prasant Mohapatra
University of California, Davis, CA, USA.
Email: {akdas, phpathak, chuah, pmohapatra}@ucdavis.edu

ABSTRACT

There has been a tremendous increase in popularity and adoption of wearable fitness trackers. These fitness trackers predominantly use Bluetooth Low Energy (BLE) for communicating and syncing the data with user's smartphone. This paper presents a measurement-driven study of possible privacy leakage from BLE communication between the fitness tracker and the smartphone. Using real BLE traffic traces collected in the wild and in controlled experiments, we show that majority of the fitness trackers use unchanged BLE address while advertising, making it feasible to track them. The BLE traffic of the fitness trackers is found to be correlated with the intensity of user's activity, making it possible for an eavesdropper to determine user's current activity (walking, sitting, idle or running) through BLE traffic analysis. Furthermore, we also demonstrate that the BLE traffic can represent user's gait which is known to be distinct from user to user. This makes it possible to identify a person (from a small group of users) based on the BLE traffic of her fitness tracker. As BLE-based wearable fitness trackers become widely adopted, our aim is to identify important privacy implications of their usage and discuss prevention strategies.

1. INTRODUCTION

The number of wearable devices shipped worldwide has had a growth of 200% from 2014 to 2015 [1]. Fitness trackers are by far the most popular wearable devices due to ever-increasing interest in the notion of *quantified-self* where users are able to track their daily activities (e.g. walking, physical workout, vital signs) with very high accuracy. The fitness trackers connect to user's smartphone using a short-range wireless communication like Bluetooth Low Energy (BLE). Due to substantial reduction in energy consumption, BLE has become the dominant standard for the fitness trackers to connect and communicate with smartphones.

Although the fitness trackers and BLE are becoming widely used, the private information that leaks through the BLE communication has largely remained unexplored. In a recent study [2], it is shown that motion sensors on wrist-worn devices (like fitness trackers) can leak the information about what a user is typing. Different from this, we explore how private information about the user can

HotMobile '16, February 26-27, 2016, St. Augustine, FL, USA

© 2016 ACM. ISBN 978-1-4503-4145-5/16/02. . . $15.00

DOI: http://dx.doi.org/10.1145/2873587.2873594

be leaked by eavesdropping on BLE communication between the fitness trackers and the smartphone. As BLE becomes pervasive with its adoption for Internet of Things and proximity sensing services like iBeacons in public places, eavesdropping BLE communication can be easier than ever before, making it imperative to protect user's privacy. In this paper, we present a measurement study by collecting BLE traffic between fitness trackers and smartphones, and discover the following privacy leakage -

(1) User Tracking: We show that almost all fitness tracker devices utilize unchanged BLE addresses, making the user vulnerable to tracking. Specifically, fitness tracker and smartphone only periodically connect to each other for exchanging data, leaving the fitness tracker in disconnected advertising mode most of the time where it constantly announces its presence by broadcasting advertising packets. This continuous advertising by the fitness trackers using unchanged BLE addresses can be combined with additional information (e.g. video monitoring) by an attacker to track the owner of the BLE device. Using traces collected in a gymnasium as well as in controlled experiments, we find that the issue prevails in over 90% of observed devices including top five leading fitness tracker manufacturers, namely Fitbit, Jawbone, Polar, Garmin and Misfit. BLE standard [3] outlines the use of randomized addresses for prevent tracking, however, it is optional and we find that majority of the fitness tracker manufacturers do not follow them in practice. Compared to tracking through WiFi MAC address (recently addressed in [4]), BLE tracking can provide more fine-grained location of user due to its smaller range and is also feasible even when user's smartphone is connected to a cellular network.

(2) User Activity Detection and Person Identification: We find that the BLE data traffic between a fitness tracker and a smartphone is correlated to the intensity of user's activity. This means that simply by observing and analyzing the BLE traffic, an eavesdropper can detect user's current activity such as walking, sitting, running etc. For example, a employer can track the activities of employees by deploying sniffers in the office space. Our evaluation shows that the activity recognition is feasible with 97.6% for 10 users.

Furthermore, we show that there is a strong correlation between the motion sensor (accelerometer) readings of wrist-worn fitness tracker and the patterns of its BLE traffic to the smartphone. Based on the fact that different users walk with distinct gait, an eavesdropper can analyze the BLE traffic and uniquely identify the user from a small group of users. This means that a fitness tracker user can be identified through BLE traffic analysis even when the fitness tracker randomizes its BLE address. We derive the necessary BLE traffic attributes and show that person identification is feasible with an accuracy of 89% for groups of 5 people. Compared to address-based device tracking where a person can be tracked anywhere, identification of a person is only possible from a small group of fixed

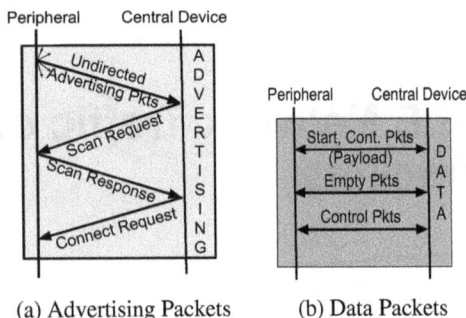

Figure 1: BLE Communication - Advertising & Data

users, making it a privacy risk in cases like homes, offices etc.

2. BLE OVERVIEW AND SNIFFING

In this section, we provide an overview of BLE communication. We focus on the aspects necessary in understanding the BLE privacy leakage. We also discuss the challenges related to sniffing BLE traffic and our data collection methodology.

2.1 BLE Background

2.1.1 BLE Communication

BLE operates in the 2.4 GHz ISM band and utilizes 40 RF channels with 2 MHz spacing. The BLE communication is divided in two phases - advertising and data communication.

Advertising: This phase is responsible for device advertisement, device discovery and establishing a connection. Packets in the advertising phase are sent out in the 3 dedicated channels. A BLE peripheral device (e.g. a fitness tracker) transmits advertisement packets to announce its presence to the master device (e.g. a smartphone). In BLE communication, each packet is associated with an access address which uniquely identifies a connection between two devices. The flow diagram of the advertising packets is shown in Fig. 1a. As we will discuss later, fitness tracking devices commonly use *Undirected Connectable Advertising Packets* in order to allow any master device to connect to it. The advertising packets contain information like MAC address, connectability modes and TX(transmission) power level. A master device upon receiving an advertising packet, if interested in initiating a connection, can send a *Scan Request* to the peripheral requesting additional information such as device local name, supported profiles, etc. The peripheral responds with a *Scan Response* which contains these additional information not included in the initial advertising packet. The master device then establishes a connection using a *Connect Request* along with further exchange of information (e.g. sharing of keys for secure connection). Other types of advertising packets are *Connectable Directed, Non-Connectable Undirected and Scannable Undirected* - used by devices to establish a quick connection or by devices which act just as transmitters.

Data Communication: Once a BLE peripheral is connected to a master device, the communication is carried out over the 37 data channels using adaptive frequency hopping. In the data communication phase, a new access address is used every time the master and peripheral reconnect. Most of the data communication (transfer of data payload) in BLE happens through the use of *Start* and *Continuation* packets. When new data is being exchanged between the devices, a start packet is used which is then followed by one or more continuation packets if more bytes are needed to be transferred. When two devices are connected, meaningful data is normally sent out in bursts (in order to save energy). On the other hand, the devices hop from one frequency to another in very short intervals. During each hop, if no meaningful data is to be transmit-

ted, empty packets are exchanged before the devices hop to a new channel. These packets have no payload and just consist of packet headers. In addition, we also see *Control* packets which are used for updating of connection parameters (like hop interval, access address, etc.) and for connection termination.

2.1.2 Private advertising addresses in BLE

Compared to Bluetooth classic, BLE introduces the use of random addresses, whereby the real address (i.e. MAC address) of a BLE device is hidden and a random address (which changes frequently) is advertised. BLE devices can use manufacturer provided fixed MAC address as its address or optionally choose one of three types of random addressed described below [3].
1) Static address: A BLE device uses a randomly generated address that either changes only at bootup or always remains unchanged. This type provides the least privacy against device tracking, especially if the address remains unchanged.
2) Non-resolvable Private address: The address changes periodically and provides better privacy compared to the static addresses.
3) Resolvable Private address: It is generated using a Identity Resolving Key (IRK) and a random number. The advantage of this type of address over non-resolvable is that it can be resolved using the shared IRK to uniquely identify a device.
The type of random address can be detected by looking at two Most Significant Bits (MSB) of an address (11 - static address, 00 - nonresolvable private address and 10 - resolvable private address).

2.2 BLE Network Traffic Sniffing

There are two main challenges in sniffing BLE traffic. First, when a BLE peripheral is in advertising phase, the advertising packets are transmitted on all three advertising channels by periodically switching between them. Since the connection can be established on any of the three channels, it is necessary to sniff all three advertising channels in parallel. Second, once the connection is established, the sniffer should be able to follow the hopping sequence (channel map) of the connection to sniff each data packet on 37 data channels. We use ComProbe Bluetooth Protocol Analyzer (BPA) 600 [5] for sniffing. It can capture BLE advertising packets on all 3 channels and can follow a connection over data channels after the connection is established. The analyzer software (shown in Fig. 2a) allows us to investigate each filed of BLE packets. We note that popular open-source BLE sniffing platform - Ubertooth [6] - can also be used, however, it is limited to sniffing only one advertising channel at a time and provides very few dissectors for traffic analysis.

3. DEVICE TRACKING USING ADVERTISING PACKETS

In this section, we investigate the private information leaked about the user from the advertising packets of her fitness tracker. We study how the information leakage can lead to tracking of the user.

3.1 BLE Dataset

In order to study the privacy leakage from advertising packets, we collect network traffic traces in the form of two datasets -

Gym Dataset: For understanding BLE traffic in the wild, we collect traffic traces in a gymnasium where there are likely to be more users with fitness trackers. We collect the network traffic traces by sniffing the packets in the air using the ComProbe BPA 600. We only capture the packets for BLE (and not Bluetooth Classic) as most of the fitness trackers use BLE for communicating with smartphone. We primarily focus on collecting advertising packets

100

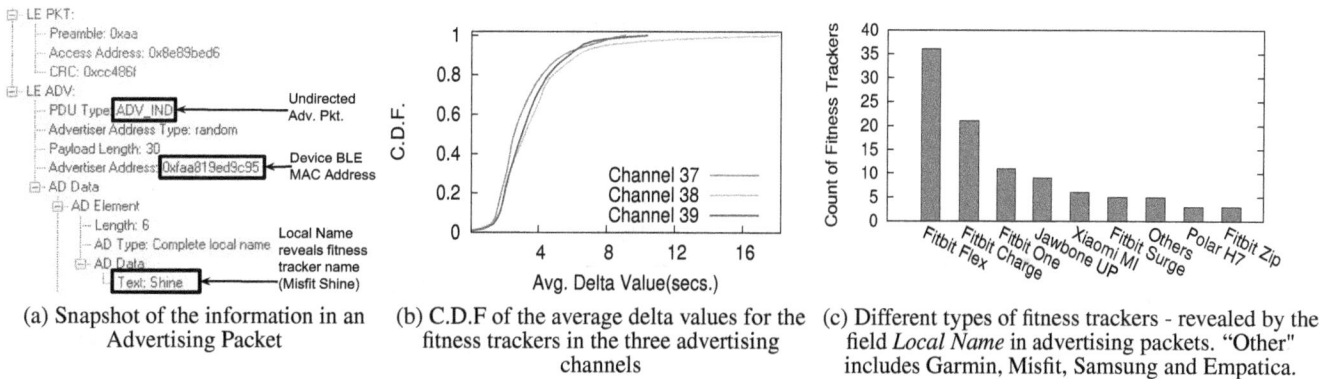

(a) Snapshot of the information in an Advertising Packet

(b) C.D.F of the average delta values for the fitness trackers in the three advertising channels

(c) Different types of fitness trackers - revealed by the field *Local Name* in advertising packets. "Other" includes Garmin, Misfit, Samsung and Empatica.

Figure 2: BLE Dataset: Snapshot of Packet in Data Collected, Packet intervals distributions , Fitness Trackers in the Dataset

in this data collection. The traces were collected for 8 consecutive days, with each trace being two hours in duration. Overall, the dataset contained a total of around 7.5 million packets with the total size of traces being 3.5 GB. Table 1 shows the number of advertising packets and devices for each day, and average packets per second. Fig. 2b represents how frequently the advertising packets are sent out by showing the C.D.F. of the mean value of time interval between two consecutive packets in the same channel for each device. We note here, that in each interval calculated, there are two more packets being sent out in the other two advertising channels. As per BLE standard, the duration between two advertising packets should vary between 20 ms and 10.24 seconds. We observe that most values of the this interval (about 95%) are less than 8 seconds, proving that these devices transmit advertising packets continuously.

Apart from the BLE MAC addresses, which we anonymize, the collected BLE traffic contains no user-identifiable information (such as user names or email addresses). An attacker can associate a MAC address to a specific user over a period of time with the use of auxiliary information about user's presence (such as video recording). We do not acquire an IRB approval because we do not collect any such additional information in our dataset and only rely on passively monitoring network packets without direct user involvement.

Controlled Dataset: For controlled experiments, we use 6 popular fitness trackers (Fitbit Flex, Fitbit Charge, Jawbone UP, Garmin vivosmart, Misfit Shine and Polar Heart Rate Sensor) and collect its BLE traffic over multiple days in a controlled setup using the ComProbe BPA 600 when these fitness trackers are connected to an iPhone 6 and a Nexus 6.

We empirically evaluate the range of the sniffer to be approximately between 20 to 25 meters. Fig. 2a shows a sample advertising packet and its fields such as device's advertised address, access address (fixed for advertising) and "Complete Local Name".

3.2 Consistent Advertising and Static BLE Addresses

For the gym dataset, we first determine if the advertising BLE device is a fitness tracker using the "Shortened Local Name" or "Complete Local Name" field. We observe that the local name field reveals the device name in plain-text. For example, a fitness tracker "Fitbit Flex" has the "Shortened Local Name" of *Flex* in the advertising packet. In Fig. 2a we see the complete local name *Shine* as a part of the packet - which indicates that the device is a "Misfit Shine". Using this information, we determine that there are 99 distinct fitness trackers in the collected traces. Fig. 2c shows the manufacturer and model of the fitness trackers in our dataset as determined from the complete local name. Note that there can be many other fitness trackers that do not reveal their name in the advertising packets. The other types of BLE devices observed in the traces, that

Trace	Advertising Packets (millions)	Advertising Devices	Fitness Trackers	Avg. Pkts. per sec.
A	0.504	189	12	69.1
B	.41	147	7	60.2
C	0.76	200	12	99.7
D	1.07	182	18	145.2
E	1.40	207	24	196.8
F	1.28	226	21	172.6
G	1.09	277	21	125.7
H	.99	188	12	147.3

Table 1: BLE Packet Traces collected from Gymnasium

are not fitness trackers, primarily include gym equipment like body scales and treadmills. In our traces, we do not find any devices which we could identify as a smartwatch. We also observe that the smartphones (both iOS and Android), being master devices, do not advertise continuously and also change their addresses (which is observed in *Connect Request*). The only devices, apart from fitness trackers, which have a "Local Name" in our dataset are gym equipment.

Why fitness trackers constantly advertise? The high frequency of advertising packets by almost all fitness trackers raise an important question - why the fitness trackers consistently advertise even when they are in close proximity of owner user's smartphone? Through the controlled dataset, we observe that the frequent advertising is due to the fact that the master device (i.e. smartphone) frequently disconnect the fitness trackers in order to reduce its own energy consumption. The fitness trackers are only connected to the smartphone when the corresponding smartphone application on the smartphone is running (foreground). When the app is running, the tracker actively communicates and synchronizes the activity data (e.g. steps, calories etc.). When the app is not running, the connection is terminated, leaving the fitness tracker in advertising state. This behavior was observed in all six fitness trackers in the controlled dataset.

The constant advertising of BLE fitness trackers make them vulnerable to tracking. This means that an attacker can sniff the BLE traffic and track the users' visits as they move around in public places such as shopping malls, gymnasiums, cafeterias etc. As discussed in Section 2.1.2, the BLE devices can choose to change their address in order to avoid tracking. However, as we discuss next, majority of the BLE fitness trackers do not use the random addresses, leading to a severe privacy implication of user tracking through fitness trackers.

Unchanged BLE Addresses: Through our controlled experiments, we observe that none of the six fitness trackers change their BLE address. We power-cycle the devices multiple times by draining their battery and find that the addresses do not change after reboot. We also observe that the advertised address do not have the

Trace	A	B	C	D	E	F	G	H
A	-	1	2	0	2	0	0	1
B	1	-	1	1	0	0	0	0
C	2	1	-	0	1	0	1	1
D	0	1	0	-	1	1	2	1
E	2	0	1	1	-	4	2	0
F	0	0	0	1	4	-	4	2
G	0	0	1	2	2	4	-	4
H	1	0	1	1	0	2	4	-
Total	5	3	4	6	8	9	10	7

(a) Reappearing Fitness Trackers

Trace	A	B	C	D	E	F	G	H
A	-	3	9	2	16	1	3	4
B	3	-	5	4	1	16	1	2
C	9	5	-	0	3	2	3	2
D	2	4	0	-	5	4	21	2
E	16	1	3	5	-	6	8	4
F	1	16	2	4	6	-	13	8
G	3	1	3	21	8	13	-	9
H	4	2	2	2	4	8	9	-
Total	30	27	15	32	34	40	45	21

(b) Reappearing BLE Devices

Table 2: Reappearing Device Count Matrix - Each element of the matrix is the number of BLE devices that are common between two traces.

Address Type	MSB	% Fitness Trackers
Non-resolvable Private Address	00	0
Resolvable Private Address	10	11
Static Address	11	89

Table 3: Fitness Trackers and their different address types

MSB of 00 or 10 (Section 2.1.2) - the recommended standard for private addresses. Thus, we conclude that these devices never alter their address. With additional information which can map a specific device to a specific user, the unchanged BLE addresses make the users carrying these devices trackable.

To further confirm our observation about unchanged device addresses in the controlled experiments, we analyze the gym dataset. Table 3 shows the MSB of the observed fitness trackers in our dataset where we see that majority (89%) of them use static address with MSB of 11. Furthermore, Table 2 shows a matrix where each element is the number of common devices (same advertising address) across the two traces. We show the matrix for all BLE devices and the ones which we know are fitness trackers based on their advertised names. We find that -

(1) 113 devices out of a total of 1485 BLE devices have appeared in more than one trace.

(2) 24 out of the total 99 fitness trackers have appeared in more than one trace. This is number is noticeably high (almost 25%) given that the traces were only collected on different days for only two hours per day.

(3) The highest overlap in advertising devices between two traces is 21, whereas the highest for fitness trackers is 4.

The number of reappearing devices proves our hypothesis inferred from the controlled experiments - that the BLE devices do not alter their advertising addresses - making its users vulnerable to tracking through the use of auxiliary information which can map a specific device to its user.

4. ACTIVITY AND PERSON IDENTIFICATION USING DATA PACKETS

As described in Section 2, once the advertising device (fitness tracker) receives a connection request from the master device (smartphone), the data transfer phase starts and data is transferred on all 37 channels. BLE utilizes AES-CCM encryption method and it is difficult to decrypt the payload without intercepting packets in initial key exchange phase [7]. In this section, we show how statistical traffic pattern analysis over the encrypted traffic can be used to detect user's activity. In scenarios, when the BLE devices actually use the private address techniques and alter their advertising addresses regularly, this method can also be used to identify an individual from a small user group. Since Fitbit fitness trackers are by far the most widely adopted devices (from [1] and Fig. 2c), we only focus on Fitbit devices (specifically, Flex) in this section.

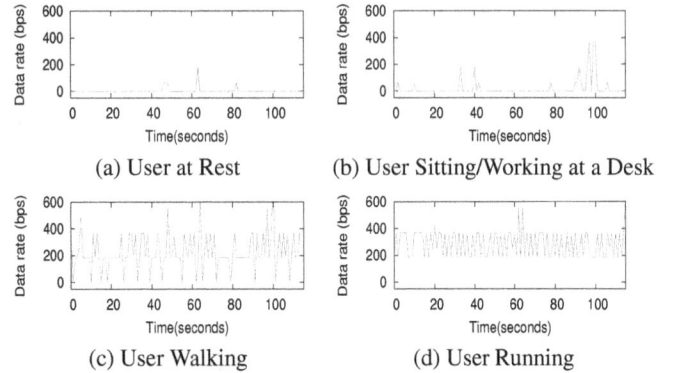

(a) User at Rest (b) User Sitting/Working at a Desk

(c) User Walking (d) User Running

Figure 3: Data Rate for different User Activities

Experimental Setup: We conduct experiments with 10 volunteers who wear a Fitbit on their non-dominant wrist and walk in their natural gait. We also attach a smartphone (Nexus 6) close to the Fitbit on user's wrist to collect raw accelerometer signals at 20Hz sampling rate. The BLE traffic between the Fitbit and user's smartphone is sniffed using ComProbe BPA 600. Each experiment lasts for 150 seconds and is repeated 10 times per user. The data is collected while the Fitbit app is open in the foreground on an iPhone 6. In addition to the walking experiments, we collect the accelerometer and BLE traffic data while the user is at rest, working at a desk and running.

4.1 Activity Detection

When the smartphone application of Fitbit is open and running in foreground, the Fitbit and the smartphone actively exchange data packets. The data communication stops when the smartphone application is closed. We observe that the amount of BLE data traffic between the Fitbit and the smartphone is proportional to the (motion) intensity of user's activity. For example, when the user is sitting with some sporadic low-intensity motion (desk-bound or sedentary), the BLE traffic consists of a large number of empty packets and only a small number of start or continuation packets. This means that the size of data being transferred is much relatively smaller in size. In comparison, when the user is walking, the data to be transferred increases, resulting in more number of start packets. We observe that even though the packets are encrypted, the volume of the data is a definite indicator of the user's activity. The privacy implication is that an attacker can sniff the BLE traffic and infer user's current activity. For example, an employer can track and monitor the activities (e.g. sitting on desk, walking etc.) of employees at workplace, and if the fitness trackers also don't change their device address, the employer can even track employee's walking trajectories using multiple sniffers. In a gymnasium, an attacker can monitor the amount of time a user sits, walks or runs everyday.

In BLE data communication, meaningful data is transmitted in *Start* and *Continuation* packets. We refer to the data transmitted in these packets (without their header) as the BLE payload. Fig. 3

102

Accelerometer	Mean and Max Acceleration Zero-Crossings, Absolute Area Sum of Absolute Acceleration
BLE Data	Start Pkts., Empty Pkts., Payload Size Payload Datarate, Time b/w Start Pkts. Empty Pkts. b/w Start Pkts

Table 4: Feature Set : Accelerometer Features for Correlation, each measured on each of the 3 axis (X,Y,Z). BLE Data features for person identification. We calculate min, max, mean and standard deviation for the last two BLE Data features.

BLE Data Feature	Correlation
Empty Pkts.	0.705
Payload Datarate	0.699
Start Pkts.	0.684
Payload Size	0.676
Time b/w Start Pkts.	0.647
Pkts b/w Start Pkts.	0.634

Table 5: Correlation between predicted values of BLE Data feature, calculated using linear regression on accelerometer values, and the actual value of the feature.

shows the payload data-rate in bits per second for four different user activities, namely, stationary (at rest or sleeping), sitting (or working at a desk), walking and running. We observe that the data rate of the Bluetooth communication is different from when the user is at rest or in motion. A comparison of Figs. 3a and 3b shows that when a user is working, the data rate for most parts is similar to a stationary user apart from when the user moves her hands which results in spikes in data transmission, as seen in the later part of the Fig. 3b. Since, Fitbit is not just a step-counting device, we note here that these spikes are not necessarily due to a step being reported, but also due to the update of other information (like calories). Comparing the data rates of walking and running, we observe that the data rate does not fall to *zero* for the running case Fig. 3d, confirming the proportionality with the intensity of activity.

We further validate the claims of activity detection through BLE traffic analysis using the data collected from 10 volunteers. Using the collected data we calculate a feature vector for time windows of 20 seconds. The feature vector includes (1) payload data rate, (2) number of empty packets and (3) number of start packets. Using the feature vector, a decision tree classifier can classify the 4 activities with an accuracy of 97.6%.

4.2 Person Identification

Wearable fitness trackers calculate a number of useful health-related statistics like number of steps walked, total calories burnt, total distance covered, flights of stairs climbed etc. When the smartphone app is running in the foreground, these information is sent from the Fitbit to the smartphone, which in-turn updates the user interface on the app. In the previous subsection, we observed that the intensity of a user activity is related to the data-rate of the Bluetooth connection. In this section, we show that the BLE data exhibits different patterns when different users are walking, making it possible to uniquely identify a user from a small group of users.

Correlation with Accelerometer Data: Fitbit Flex utilizes a 3-axis accelerometer to monitor user movements (frequency, duration and patterns) and derive necessary statistics [8]. A later model of Fitbit (Surge) also has a gyroscope, compass and ambient light sensor, but for our experiments we just focus on the accelerometer readings. Since the actual algorithms used by Fitbit to monitor user activities are unknown, we conjecture that there is a strong correlation between the observed accelerometer signal and corresponding BLE traffic. If this correlation is indeed strong, the BLE traffic can be used by an attacker to detect user's walking speed and gait. As we know from past research [9] that user's gait can uniquely identify the user with high accuracy (especially in a small group of users), the BLE traffic can also be misused for user identification.

Using the collected accelerometer and BLE data for walking activity of 10 volunteers, we calculate the statistical features listed in Table 4 for 20 seconds time windows. The accelerometer features we use are found to be useful in detecting human physical activities in [10]. We then build separate linear regression models which use these accelerometer features as input to predict each of the BLE network features. We compute the correlation coefficient between the calculated values of the BLE network features (using

regression) and the actual values obtained from the captured data. The correlation coefficients for different BLE traffic features are listed in Table 5. We observe a correlation of approximately 70% for payload datarate and empty packet count. This shows that the BLE traffic is correlated to the observed accelerometer data.

Person Identification using BLE Traffic: Because of the correlation of BLE traffic pattern with the accelerometer data, it represents user's gait while walking and thereby can be used to uniquely identify the user. Based on the BLE network data collected for 10 users, we calculate the features shown in Table 4 for 20 second windows. Fig. 4a shows two features - payload data rate and average number of empty packets between two start packets - for 5 users. We observe that for each user there is a non-overlapping cluster signifying the two BLE features can distinguish the 5 users. We also represent the BLE payload data rate for two representative users in 4b and see the variation is very distinct. Thus, the features extracted can be considered useful for uniquely identifying a user. We use the BLE features and build a person identification classifier using decision tree. Fig. 4c show the average accuracy of person identification using the BLE traffic features. We consider all possible combinations of users when the person identification classifier is built for less than 10 users. The standard deviation of accuracy for different user sets are also shown in Fig. 4c. The false positive rate for all the different user sets was less than 5%. The classification accuracy decreases with increase in number of users because dissimilarities in gait reduces as user population increases.

Person identification through BLE traffic analysis is a major privacy concern as it can enable an attacker to track a user using her fitness tracker even when it changes its BLE address. The person identification works when a classifier is pre-trained for the walking pattern of a known set of users. In many cases such as office buildings or gymnasiums where the same set of users reappear frequently, the collected data can be used to train an accurate model. It is to be noted here that the attack model we discuss works when the Fitbit app is open in the foreground. However in the case of certain trackers, like Garmin, the attack is possible even when the app is not running in the foreground, as long as the phone and the BLE device has been previously paired.

5. RELATED WORK

In recent years, there has been a number of research works on the leakage user's activity through wireless signal analysis. Keystroke recognition [11] and human activity recognition [12] has become possible through changes in the Channel State Information(CSI) as a user moves or types on her keyboard. [13] shows how the accelerometer and gyroscope sensors in smartwatches can be used to uniquely identify finger movements, hand and forearm motion of users on the basis of some essential features extracted from these sensors' data. This paper also shows that finger-writing on a surface or on the air can be detected from these sensors, whereas [2] shows that when a user is typing on the keyboard the motion sensors on a smartwatch can predict the word typed out with a certain level of confidence. Our work differs from these, as we focus on device tracking and user activity detection just from the point of

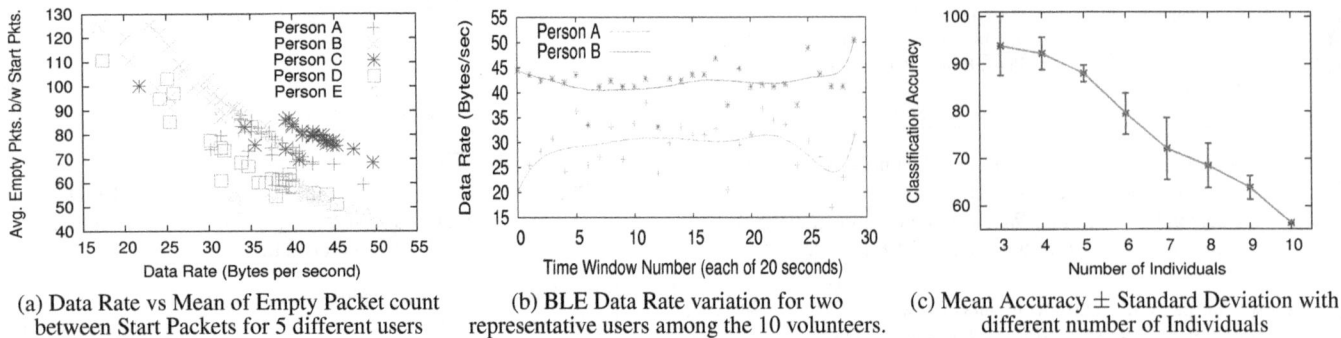

(a) Data Rate vs Mean of Empty Packet count between Start Packets for 5 different users

(b) BLE Data Rate variation for two representative users among the 10 volunteers.

(c) Mean Accuracy ± Standard Deviation with different number of Individuals

Figure 4: BLE Person Identification Results

view of the network data created by the devices (and not based on the sensor values themselves).

In mobile telephony, temporary and contextual user identifiers have been proposed instead of the permanent ones to prevent tracking but some of these techniques have not been very successful in providing privacy [14]. From the point of view of Bluetooth traffic, a Man-in-the-Middle attack on a Bluetooth keyboard allows an attacker to access all keystrokes on a keyboard and lead to serious security leaks. Similar attacks has been executed using data from wireless mouse to reconstruct mouse cursor trajectory and infer private user information [15]. Some researchers proposed the use of the device clocks (time interval among advertising packets) to fingerprint different Bluetooth devices and prevent address forging. There has been recent some research which looks at how BLE data communication security can be broken by capturing the necessary keys during the connection-establishment phase [7]. Compared to this, our work does not attempt to decrypt the encrypted BLE traffic but focuses entirely on feasibility of mining already encrypted BLE data from the point of view of activity and person identification.

6. DISCUSSION AND CONCLUSION

The advertising and data communication phases of BLE network traffic cause concerns from the point of view of user privacy. The detection of activity is possible due to the fact that sending of BLE data (payload) is triggered only by user activity. This can be prevented by sending out artificial traffic (or chaff) [16]. In this solution, we can insert artificial data packets (start and continuation) in our BLE network so that activity recognition from the payload pattern becomes more complex and circumvent traffic analysis. However, one drawback of this is that the energy consumption would increase as a result of transmitting more packets than required. Thus, a balance has to be maintained between sending out artificial traffic at certain intervals so as to prevent detection but not at the expense of high energy consumption.

To prevent user tracking based on advertising packets one potential solution is to randomize the advertised address, a topic that has recently been brought to light for WiFi communication, with the recent versions of iOS randomizing the MAC address while broadcasting to prevent tracking at public places. There has also been efforts in terms of mobile telephony to use temporary identifiers instead of long term permanent identifiers to prevent third-party tracking. However, usage of randomized addresses can lead to the smartphone not being able to identify the BLE fitness tracker to which is has already been paired and might need the tracker to pair again - leading to a disruption in user experience. Also, randomized addresses can still be used to track a user based on the user activity determined using data packets. Another solution is not to advertise continuously and instead, use direct advertising packets from the fitness trackers directly to the user's smartphone (to

which the tracker has been previously synced), when the smartphone switches on the fitness tracker app. With the ever increasing popularity of smartwatches and corresponding applications on these devices, BLE communication privacy is even more critical in the near future. In our future work, we will analyze BLE network data generated by different applications in smartwatches from the point of view of user privacy.

7. REFERENCES

[1] "IDC Worldwide Quarterly Wearable Tracker, June 2, 2015." http://www.idc.com/getdoc.jsp?containerId=prUS25658315.

[2] H. Wang, T. T.-T. Lai, and R. Roy Choudhury, "Mole: Motion leaks through smartwatch sensors," ACM MobiCom '15.

[3] "Bluetooth Low Energy 4.1 Standard," Bluetooth SIG., Inc. Specification of the Bluetooth System, 2013.

[4] "Randomized Wi-Fi addresses." http://www.apple.com/lae/privacy/privacy-built-in/.

[5] "ComProbe BPA 600." http://www.fte.com/products/BPA600.aspx.

[6] "Project Ubertooth." http://ubertooth.sourceforge.net/.

[7] M. Ryan, "Bluetooth: With low energy comes low security," in 7th USENIX Workshop on Offensive Technologies, 2013.

[8] "Fitbit Help: How does my tracker count steps?." http://help.fitbit.com/articles/en_US/Help_article/How-does-my-tracker-count-steps.

[9] L. Rong, D. Zhiguo, Z. Jianzhong, and L. Ming, "Identification of individual walking patterns using gait acceleration," in ICBBE 2007.

[10] E. Munguia Tapia, Using machine learning for real-time activity recognition and estimation of energy expenditure. PhD thesis, MIT, 2008.

[11] K. Ali, A. X. Liu, W. Wang, and M. Shahzad, "Keystroke recognition using wifi signals," ACM MobiCom '15.

[12] W. Wang, A. X. Liu, M. Shahzad, K. Ling, and S. Lu, "Understanding and modeling of wifi signal based human activity recognition," ACM MobiCom '15.

[13] C. Xu, P. H. Pathak, and P. Mohapatra, "Finger-writing with smartwatch: A case for finger and hand gesture recognition using smartwatch," ACM HotMobile '15.

[14] M. Arapinis, L. Mancini, E. Ritter, and M. Ryan, "Privacy through pseudonymity in mobile telephony systems," NDSS '14.

[15] X. Pan, Z. Ling, A. Pingley, W. Yu, N. Zhang, and X. Fu, "How privacy leaks from bluetooth mouse?," ACM CCS '12.

[16] S. Le Blond, D. Choffnes, W. Zhou, P. Druschel, H. Ballani, and P. Francis, "Towards efficient traffic-analysis resistant anonymity networks," ACM SIGCOMM '13.

Identifying and Analyzing the Privacy of Apps for Kids

Minxing Liu[1*], Haoyu Wang[1], Yao Guo[1], Jason Hong[2]
[1]Peking University
[2]Carnegie Mellon University
{liuminxing, howiepku, yaoguo}@pku.edu.cn, jasonh@cs.cmu.edu

ABSTRACT

One aspect of privacy that has not been well explored is privacy for children. We present the design and evaluation of a machine learning model for predicting whether a mobile app is designed for children, which is an important step in helping to enforce the Children's Online Privacy Protection Act (COPPA). We evaluated our model on 1,728 apps from Google Play and achieved 95% accuracy. We also applied our model on a set of nearly 1 million free apps from Google Play, and identified almost 68,000 apps for kids. We then conducted a privacy analysis of the usage of third-party libraries for each app, which can help us understand some of the app's privacy-related behaviors. We believe this list can serve as a good start point for further fine-grained privacy analysis on mobile apps for children.

Keywords

mobile applications; children's privacy; Android

1. INTRODUCTION

Mobile apps have seen widespread adoption, with over one million apps available on each of Google Play and the Apple App Store. These apps can use the rich capabilities of smartphones, including personal data (e.g., contact lists, emails, photos, and call logs) and sensor data (e.g., GPS, camera, and microphone), enabling many new kinds of user experiences and functionality. However, these same capabilities have led to many new kinds of privacy concerns and intrusions. Previous work has investigated a wide range of privacy issues with respect to mobile apps, for example finding potential leaks of sensitive information [16] or wisdom of crowds approaches to making decisions about sharing data [7, 22, 21]. However, one area that is relatively unexplored is privacy for children.

*Most of this work was done when Minxing was a visiting student at CMU.

HotMobile '16, February 26-27, 2016, St. Augustine, FL, USA

© 2016 ACM. ISBN 978-1-4503-4145-5/16/02...$15.00

DOI: http://dx.doi.org/10.1145/2873587.2873597

According to a 2013 survey, 75% of children under age 8 are using mobile devices [18]. In the United States, privacy protection for children is especially important due to the Children's Online Privacy Protection Act [1], or COPPA. Passed in 1998, COPPA regulates actions of operators of online services (thus including mobile apps) that are targeted at children under age 13. COPPA requires operators to only collect necessary information from children, offer a clear description of what information will be collected and for what purpose, and obtain consent from parents. Furthermore, any collected information should not be made publicly available in an identifiable form.

Currently, the task of enforcing COPPA falls mainly to the Federal Trade Commission (FTC), which has levied several warnings and fines for violations [3]. The FTC has also published two reports examining app privacy in the context of children in 2012 [13, 14]. In the first report, the FTC manually checked 200 apps from Google Play and the Apple App Store respectively, and found that there was little or no information available to parents about the privacy of apps on the product detail pages[1]. In a follow-up report six months later, the FTC found little improvement to privacy information. The FTC also downloaded and tested apps and found that many apps shared kids' information with third parties without disclosing these practices to parents.

These two FTC reports offer insights into some of the privacy issues with respect to smartphone apps for kids. However, a major limitation is that, today, there is no automated way of identifying and analyzing the privacy-related behaviors of apps that target children. To underscore this point, the FTC used a manual and highly labor-intensive process for their reports. First, FTC employees gathered a set of apps by searching for "kids". Second, FTC employees examined each app's description to identify whether an app actually targets kids or not. The reports found that about 25% of apps collected were actually not directed at children [13]. Third, FTC employees manually downloaded and checked if a given app linked to any social media, allowed in-app purchases, or used advertising. Fourth, FTC employees intercepted Internet traffic for a given app to see if it transmitted device ID, phone number, and geolocation information.

While the FTC's approach was fairly comprehensive, the amount of labor involved severely limits how many apps can be inspected, and how often. For example, the FTC was

[1]The webpage that includes all detailed information of an app, e.g., description, icon, screenshots, etc.

able to only inspect 400 apps, and has not repeated their work since 2012. As such, our long-term goal is to improve the speed, accuracy and scalability of inspecting apps for kids by introducing a series of automated methods. In this paper, we present some of our initial results.

A general pipeline for identifying potentially problematic apps can be derived from the method used by the FTC: (1) gather a set of apps, (2) identify which apps likely target children, (3) analyze the apps to see which ones use social media, in-app purchases, or advertising, and (4) apply static and dynamic analysis techniques to see which apps transmit potentially sensitive data. The work presented in this paper focuses on the first three steps. More specifically, we developed a machine learning classifier that uses several text-based and image-based features to identify apps designed for kids, which achieved 95% accuracy. We also ran our classifier on almost 1 million apps from Google Play, and for each app classified as being for kids, we retrieved a privacy grade from *privacygrade.org* [5] and applied simple static analysis techniques to see if it used social media, in-app purchases, or advertising.

Our work has at least three potential applications. The first is to help regulators like the FTC and their equivalent in other countries. Regulators can use our tool to get a list of potentially problematic apps, which can then be used to prioritize which apps they will manually inspect further (e.g. the most popular and problematic apps for kids). Given that regulators often have limited resources, this approach can help them in making their work more comprehensive and ongoing. The second is to help parents. For example, third parties, such as *Consumer Reports* or *privacygrade.org*, could make the results of these analysis easily browsable and searchable by the general public, making it easy for parents to understand what potential problems there might be before downloading an app. The third is to help app store administrators, who can use the information to better label which apps are for kids, help flag apps for further inspection, or nudge developers to be aware of potential legal issues they may be violating when they upload apps.

This paper makes the following research contributions:

- We present the design of a machine learning classifier that can identify whether a mobile app is directed towards children. Our classifier uses both text-based and image-based features extracted from an app's product detail page. To the best of our knowledge, we are the first to build a classifier to recognize mobile apps for kids.

- We evaluate our approach on 1,728 apps. The results of 10-fold cross validation yield an accuracy of about 95% and over 91% for both precision and recall. We also discuss which features are the most effective in predicting whether an app is directed to kids.

- We also apply our classifier on nearly 1 million apps, and analyze the privacy-related behaviors of apps targeting kids. Our results can serve as a good start point for further fine-grained analysis.

2. RELATED WORK

There are two major lines of related work. The first are studies that use data mining to analyze mobile app markets [17, 15, 26, 10]. Examples include analyzing correlations between apps' technical, customer, and business aspects, e.g. relation between download volume and price [17], detecting ranking fraud [26], or detecting similar apps [10]. Some past work here also looked at privacy of apps, though not in the context of children. For example, WHYPER [23] leveraged natural language processing (NLP) techniques to infer the usage of sensitive data from app descriptions. They then detected the inconsistencies between the description and real app behaviors related to fetching private data to determine the privacy performance of an app. Wang et al. [24] utilized text-mining skills on the package/class/variable names used in the custom code to infer the purpose of privacy-related behaviors of an app.

Another line of work focuses on potential risks of online services directed to children. As mentioned above, the FTC released two reports inspecting privacy issues in mobile apps designed for children in 2012 [13, 14]. Liccardi et al. [20] developed a new framework to help mobile app developers comply with COPPA. Specifically, they provided a simple and efficient interface for developers to state their usage of personal data so that parents could understand potential privacy risks. Chen et al. [12] and Bhoraskar et al. [8] both focus on in-app advertisements of "kids' apps" and check if they include inappropriate content for children or if they attempt to collect personal information.

The closest research is Chen et al. [11] and Hu et al. [19], which focus on unreliable content rating of apps. They proposed algorithms to detect mature content in an app and assigned it an accurate maturity level. Our work differs as the content rating of an app does not necessarily denote its intended users. For example, while apps with "High Maturity" are usually not designed for children, apps with content rating "Everyone" does not mean it is designed for children. Thus, their work might assist us in improving the accuracy, but we focus on a different goal.

3. IDENTIFYING APPS FOR KIDS

3.1 Overview

In this section, we present the design of our machine learning classifier for identifying mobile apps directed to children. The classifier accepts a feature vector based on content extracted from an app's product detail page. We use manually labeled data from Google Play to train the classifier.

3.2 Feature Extraction

We want features that are relatively simple and fast to calculate (to help with scalability), and general enough for different app markets (e.g. Apple App Store). After manually examining several popular apps for kids, we chose 171 features, summarized in Table 1 and described below.

3.2.1 Meta Features

This set of features describes basic metadata about an app. Here we extracted 2 features. The first is **Category**, which is a binary value indicating whether or not the app belongs to a common category for "kids' apps", namely *Education, Games, Comics, and Entertainment.* Intuitively, this feature should be effective in identifying apps for kids, but should also have many false positives since many apps in these categories also target adults.

Table 1: The features used in our classification model.

Category	Feature Description	Details
App Category	Category of an app	A binary value, which represents whether the app belongs to a relevant category where most "kids' apps" are classified (Education, Games, Comics, or Entertainment).
Content Rating	Content rating of an app	An ordinal value, which represents corresponding content rating of the app.
Title	Frequency and importance of key words from the title	A 5 dimension vector, each value representing the TF-IDF value of five key words, namely "children", "fun", "game", "kid" and "toddler".
Description	Frequency and importance of key words extracted from app description	A 10 dimension vector, each value representing the TF-IDF value of ten key words, namely "animal", "children", "education", "fun", "game", "kid", "learn", "play", "preschool" and "toddler".
Readability of the description	Readability score	A value that represents the readability of the description using the Flesch-Kincaid readability test [2].
Picture Resources	Color distribution and usage of the icon and screenshots	A 49 dimension vector for each picture resource, and a total of 147 (49×3) dimensions (icon+two screenshots). Features of a picture resource include the color histogram, average hue, average saturation, average brightness value, and number of colors used.
Strings on Screenshots	Frequency and importance of key words extracted from strings in screenshots	A 6 dimension vector. The first five represent TF-IDF values of key words selected, specifically "baby", "children", "fun", "kid" and "play". The last one represents the length of strings on the screenshots.

The second is **Content Rating**. There are five different content ratings on Google Play: *Everyone, Low Maturity, Medium Maturity, High Maturity* and *Unrated*. Usually, apps for kids are tagged with *Everyone* or *Low Maturity*. Similar to the category feature, content ratings should identify many "kids' apps" but also have many false positives. For example, many calculator apps are rated "Everyone". We mapped the 5 different ratings to a corresponding numerical value (1-5).

3.2.2 Title and Description

This set of features focuses on the text describing an app. For both title and description, we first split the text into a bag of words, filtering out non-ascii words, punctuation, and stop words like "the". Then we used the Porter stemming algorithm [4] to identify the root of a word, combining singular forms and plural forms of words, such as "kid" and "kids". Next, we calculated a TF-IDF value for each word to denote its importance. Common words within a document (Term Frequency) but relatively rare in other documents (Inverse Document Frequency) will have high scores. Each value is in the range of [0.0, 1.0]. To calculate TF, we counted the number of times each word occurs in a given text. To calculate IDF, we used our entire training corpus, which contains 1,728 labeled apps from Google Play. Note that we completed the process above separately when extracting features from the title and from the description.

To optimize, we reduced the number of dimensions using the Chi-square test to select words that are the most efficient for classification, and only calculating TF-IDF values for these key words as features. This technique was first proposed by Yang *et al.* [25], who found that preserving just the most representative key words will generally obtain similar or even improved average accuracy. The key words for titles and descriptions are described in Table 1.

3.2.3 Readability of App Description

Intuitively, apps for kids are more likely to have descriptions that are easier to read and understand. To represent this feature, we ran the Flesch-Kincaid readability test [2] on the description and generate a score based on the total number of sentences, words, and syllables (with lower scores meaning easier to read).

3.2.4 Color Features from Icon and Screenshots

In our initial investigations, we found that the picture resources of "kids' apps" often use bright primary colors with colorful backgrounds. In contrast, many apps not targeting kids tend to use colors from a wider palette of colors, and few seem to use highly saturated colors.

To extract color-related information, we represented each picture in hue, saturation, and brightness value (HSV) format. Concretely, we calculated 49 features for the app icon and associated screenshots. Google Play requires each app to upload at least two screenshots. We only use the first two screenshots if there are more than two. Thus we have a total of 147 (49×3) features.

We have three features representing the average values for each of hue, saturation, and brightness value, and one more for the total number of colors used. The remaining features represent the HSV histogram. There is a tradeoff here between fidelity of the histogram and dimensionality. A fine-grained histogram might better capture the distribution of colors, but will also lead to a high-dimensional set of features with relatively sparse data. After trying a variety of groupings on a small set of apps, we chose to represent the histogram with a granularity of 3 hues, 3 saturations, and 5 brightness values, leading to 3×3×5 or 45 "color groups". We then calculated the relative proportion of each color group for the icon and screenshots, each ranging between [0.0, 1.0].

3.2.5 Text in Screenshots

We also extracted text from screenshots using Tesseract-OCR [6], an open source OCR library. We conjectured that the words used in an app could help with identifying if it were for kids. We extracted text from all screenshots and aggregated them into a single string. Then, similar to the processing for title and description, we applied TF-IDF and used the top 5 key words as features.

We also used the average length of the string in all screenshots as a feature. In our initial explorations, we found that the length tends to be shorter for "kids' apps". A possible explanation is that these apps have fewer words. An alternative is that "kids' apps" tend to use colorful and exaggerated fonts that the OCR library fails to recognize.

3.2.6 Features from APK File

We also extracted features from the Android Application

Package (APK) file, including strings and picture resources stored in the APK file. We used similar text and picture analysis techniques to extract the features. However, in practice, we found that these features offered marginal improvement to the overall accuracy. Therefore, we chose not to integrate APK level features in our current classifier and the details will be omitted in this paper.

4. EVALUATION

4.1 Data Collection

To gather our data set, we chose to use sites that reviewed apps for kids, so as to minimize subjective judgement on our part in terms of what keywords to search for on Google Play, as well as identifying which apps are targeted at children. More concretely, we selected a set of key words to search for on the Google search engine, e.g. "Android apps for kids" or "Android apps for preschool". The key words we used came from the FTC report [13], all of which are variants of the word "children". Among the search results (using just the first three pages to ensure relevance), we looked for review websites and recommendation lists, which often had titles like "The best Android apps for your kids". Finally, we downloaded each app mentioned in those lists and eliminated duplicate apps and apps not available on Google Play. Using this method, we downloaded 576 apps directed towards children, or "positive examples".

We also collected apps not targeting children as counter-examples. We collected 12 key words such as "men", "women", "college students", and other key words from the FTC report. Using the same method as above, we downloaded a total of 804 apps. We also used a list of key words from the same FTC report describing categories of apps, such as "Educational", "Game", "Animal-related", and "Math". We then combined them with the previous 12 key words and made new search queries, e.g., "Android math apps for college students" and used the same method to collect 348 more apps. This approach gave us a wide range of apps and should help prevent overfitting. For example, we do not want our classifier to simply predict an app to be for kids because it contains the word "Math" in its title. The total number of negative examples in our dataset is 1,152 (804+348).

4.2 Evaluation Method

We first normalized the value range of our features to [0.0, 1.0], and then used LibSVM [9] to train our classifier. We did a grid search of models and parameters, and chose the *radial basis function* kernel and best parameters (cost=1.0, gamma=0.125, degree=3) for our classifier. We then used 10-fold cross validation to test the performance of our classifier. Concretely, we measured true positives (TP), false positives (FP), true negatives (TN), and false negatives(FN), and then calculated accuracy, precision, recall, F-measure, and Area under the ROC curve.

4.3 Results and Analysis.

Overall Result. Our classifier achieved an overall accuracy of 95%, with 93% precision and 91% recall. Table 2 presents detailed results of different evaluation metrics.

Compared with baselines. Table 3 compares our

Table 2: Performance Overview.

Precision	Recall	F-measure	AUC	Accuracy
0.933	0.915	0.924	0.983	94.97%

Table 3: Comparison of our classifier to baselines.

Baseline description	Precision	Recall
Use app category as the only feature	0.624	0.945
Use content rating as the only feature	0.460	0.815
FTC search on app market	0.757	N/A
"Family" tag of Google Play	0.988	0.436

results with four selected baselines. Overall, our classifier has better performance than these baselines.

The first baseline uses the App Category. Specifically, we removed all the other features and trained a new model using the same algorithm (LibSVM). It achieves good recall because most apps for kids fall into the Education or Games category. However, these categories also contain many apps not targeting kids, e.g., educational apps for college students or adults, thus leading to relatively low precision.

The second baseline uses Content Rating and its precision and recall are both significantly lower than ours.

Then we compared against the search results of Google Play, referring to the results from the FTC report [13]. This is not an actual algorithm, but we compare their precision results against ours. The FTC staff searched for "kid", and after manual checks found that 24.25% of apps did not actually target kids, but rather parents or teachers[2]. Compared to them, only 7% of apps predicted as "kids app" by us are actually not targeted at kids.

For our fourth baseline, we used Google Play's "Family" category[3], which is a special category that draws on apps from other categories. It even has subcategories specifying different age groups of kids, like "kids 6-8". We looked at our training data and found that only 254 apps in our data set were in the Family category, with 251 positive examples and 3 negative ones (which targeted parents). It seems that the Family category is done manually, and so can achieve high precision but lacks scalability, causing low recall.

Error Analysis. Here, we examine misclassified apps, including false positives (apps incorrectly classified as "kids app") and false negatives (apps targeted at kids not recognized).

For false positives, most are borderline cases, typically games for both kids and adults but not specifically targeting kids. These apps often include colorful pictures to attract users. Some games, e.g., "ca.samsstuff.samstictactoe", also include words like "children" in its description. As such, the features extracted from these apps resemble apps specifically targeting kids.

For false negatives, most cases come from the apps whose title and description do not include common keywords. For example, "kr.co.smartstudy.cartown_android_googlemarket" is an app where you can "sing, drive and play with your favorite cars," but does not have any of our keywords as listed in Table 1. This finding suggests a need for improving the analysis for Title and Description.

---

[2]The report claimed that some of these apps are also for kids too. In our paper, we aim to find apps that are designed primarily for kids. Thus, we regard all of these apps as wrongly classified.

[3]The special Family category was created from June 2015.

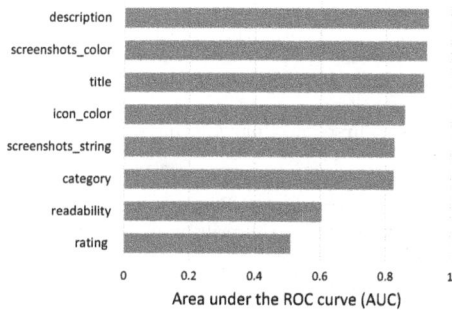

Figure 1: Area under the ROC curve (AUC) of different features used by our classifier.

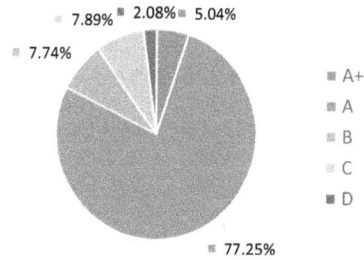

Figure 2: Distribution of Privacy Grades

Most Important Features. Figure 1 shows the relative importance of features using Area Under the ROC Curve (AUC), with higher AUC values being better. Some features stand out, including *text-based information from title and description*, and *color-related information from icon and screenshots*. Apart from the title and the description, features from image resources are also effective. Another image-based feature, OCR strings from screenshots, works surprisingly well at about 0.83 AUC.

As for other features, "Category" is a good indicator. Contrary to our expectations, "Readability" is not quite effective, perhaps because developers typically write for parents and also it is dependent on developers' own writing style. "Rating" is not effective either, partly because the inefficient rating system of Google Play [11, 19].

5. PRIVACY ANALYSIS

We applied our classifier on a large set of free apps from Google Play and conducted a preliminary privacy analysis. The use case is to find the most egregious apps in the context of COPPA, which can help regulators focus their resources on ones that should be further investigated manually.

List Generation. We collected 977,948 free apps from Google Play ending around April 2015, including their meta information, titles, descriptions and picture resources. For each app, we extracted features as described in Section 3 and fed them into our classifier. Our classifier identified a total of 67,778 apps targeting kids (∼6.9% of the data set).

Privacy Analysis. For each identified "kids' app", we analyzed three potential privacy issues. First, we examined its privacy grade, as retrieved from *privacygrade.org* [5]. Each app is assigned a privacy grade, one of A+, A, B, C and D, as calculated by a machine learning model trained on labeled training data collected from crowdsourcing. More details can be found in previous work [21, 22].

Second, we examined three behaviors of interest to the FTC [13], namely (1) whether the app uses targeted advertising, (2) whether the app can connect with a social network (e.g., has "share to Facebook" option), and (3) whether the app offers in-app purchases. For targeted advertising and social network, we compared the package names of libraries in the app with a list of third-party libraries known to be relevant with targeted ads or social networking, using results previously compiled by *privacygrade.org*. For in-app purchases, this feature must be declared in the app's manifest file. We simply decompiled each app and looked for that. Note that just

because the app contains a given library or permission does not mean that it actually uses it. However, for our given use case, we can expect a person to manually inspect the app to verify.

Third, we examined the app's popularity. We used the download volume as the popularity of an app, which can be found on its detail page. Generally, an app with more downloads should be paid more attention.

We generated a table of 67,778 rows with the above information. The distribution of privacy grades of these apps is shown in Figure 2. About 82% of apps get an A or A+, which means that these apps use few permissions for unusual purposes. In contrast, about 10% get a C or D, which could warrant more attention.

Table 4 shows the usage of three interactive behaviors discussed above. About 53% of the apps include targeted ads. This high percentage can partly be attributed to the fact that we have only analyzed free apps, which typically use ads to make money. About 20% of the apps use social networks, and another 22% have in-app purchases. Again, these behaviors alone are not necessarily violations of COPPA, but may suggest further attention.

6. DISCUSSION

6.1 Limitations

Incomplete or wrong information on app markets. Currently, we extract features from the detail page of Google Play for each app. We selected features that should also be available in other app markets, e.g., description, icon, screenshots, etc. However, our approach assumes that developers do not provide misleading information, which would clearly impact our approach. As such, it may be helpful to extract features from the APK file, since it represents the actual behavior of each Android app. Although adding APK features cannot improve the current results, they might be used as an alternative or as a complementary approach if developers start to deliberately put misleading data on app markets.

Data collection. Our data set is based on review websites. This approach minimizes certain kinds of biases but may introduce others. For example, most review sites do not look at the long tail of apps.

App coverage. Currently, our work focuses on apps that specifically target kids, but the FTC has also fined

Table 4: Usage of interactive behaviors in the app.

Category	Targeted Ads	Social network	In-app purchase
Percentage	53.0%	19.6%	22.5%

other kinds of apps that collect data from children under the age of 13. For example, neither Yelp nor Path specifically target children, but they were fined by the FTC since they explicitly asked users for their age and still collected data from people who stated they were under the age of 13. Our approach does not address this problem.

Future privacy analysis. We presented an initial privacy analysis in Section 5 using fairly general approaches. For future work, we would like to develop automated techniques to address issues more specific to children and their parents. For example, COPPA requires app developers to provide notice on the product detail page about what information will be collected from children. Program analysis can be used to identify what information will be collected by the app at runtime. These results can then be cross-checked using NLP techniques on app descriptions or terms & conditions page. As another example, we can develop algorithms to detect if parents are involved at any point in data collection, e.g. looking for certain kinds of dialog boxes.

6.2 Further Implications for Privacy

In general, privacy for kids is less ambiguous and contentious than privacy for adults, given widespread agreement that children are a vulnerable population, the detailed laws, and clear enforcement mechanisms by regulators. While improving privacy for children is a useful goal in itself, it might also be a potentially powerful leverage point for advancing privacy for all people in general. For example, some developers might not want to collect certain kinds of personal information due to the challenge of identifying children and the increased risk of enforcement. As another example, app stores might compel developers to do better with respect to privacy for kids before uploading their apps, which could in turn help educate developers about other best practices for privacy.

7. CONCLUSION

We presented the design and evaluation of a classifier to predict whether an app is designed primarily for kids. We extracted several features from the detail page of an app and evaluated the classifier on a set of 1,728 labeled apps, achieving an accuracy of 95%. We also ran our classifier on a large set of apps to generate a list of apps for children and conducted some privacy analysis on them. Our method and results can benefit regulators, parents, third-parties, and app stores in understanding and improving privacy.

8. ACKNOWLEDGMENTS

This paper is supported in part by National Science Foundation (CNS1228813), the Air Force Research Laboratory (FA8750-15-2-0281), the National Basic Research Program of China (973) under Grant No. 2015CB352201, and the National Natural Science Foundation of China under Grant No. 61421091, 61103026.

9. REFERENCES

[1] COPPA - Children's Online Privacy Protection Act. http://www.coppa.org/coppa.htm.

[2] Flesch-Kincaid readability test. https://en.wikipedia.org/wiki/Flesch%E2%80%93Kincaid_readability_tests.

[3] FTC's first fines for violating online kids' privacy law. http://www.computerworld.com/article/2592253/government-it/ftc-assesses-first-fines-for-violating-online-kids–privacy-law.html.

[4] The porter stemming algorithm. http://tartarus.org/martin/PorterStemmer/.

[5] Privacygrade: Grading the privacy of smartphone apps. http://privacygrade.org/.

[6] Tesseract-ocr. https://github.com/tesseract-ocr.

[7] Y. Agarwal and M. Hall. ProtectMyPrivacy: detecting and mitigating privacy leaks on iOS devices using crowdsourcing. In *MobiSys*, 2013.

[8] R. Bhoraskar, S. Han, J. Jeon, T. Azim, S. Chen, J. Jung, S. Nath, R. Wang, and D. Wetherall. Brahmastra: Driving apps to test the security of third-party components. In *USENIX Security Symposium*, 2014.

[9] C.-C. Chang and C.-J. Lin. LIBSVM: A library for support vector machines. *ACM Transactions on Intelligent Systems and Technology*, 2011. Software available at http://www.csie.ntu.edu.tw/%7Ecjlin/libsvm.

[10] N. Chen, S. C. Hoi, S. Li, and X. Xiao. SimApp: A framework for detecting similar mobile applications by online kernel learning. In *WSDM*, 2015.

[11] Y. Chen, H. Xu, Y. Zhou, and S. Zhu. Is this app safe for children?: A comparison study of maturity ratings on Android and iOS applications. In *WWW*, 2013.

[12] Y. Chen, S. Zhu, H. Xu, and Y. Zhou. Children's exposure to mobile in-app advertising: An analysis of content appropriateness. In *SocialCom*, 2013.

[13] F. T. Commission et al. Mobile apps for kids: current privacy disclosures are disappointing, 2012.

[14] F. T. Commission et al. Mobile apps for kids: Disclosures still not making the grade, 2012.

[15] B. Fu, J. Lin, L. Li, C. Faloutsos, J. Hong, and N. Sadeh. Why people hate your app: Making sense of user feedback in a mobile app store. In *KDD*, 2013.

[16] C. Gibler, J. Crussell, J. Erickson, and H. Chen. Androidleaks: Automatically detecting potential privacy leaks in Android applications on a large scale. In *TRUST*, 2012.

[17] M. Harman, Y. Jia, and Y. Zhang. App store mining and analysis: MSR for app stores. In *MSR*, 2012.

[18] D. Holloway, L. Green, and S. Livingstone. Zero to eight: Young children and their internet use. *LSE London, EU Kids Online*, 2013.

[19] B. Hu, B. Liu, N. Z. Gong, D. Kong, and H. Jin. Protecting your children from inappropriate content in mobile apps: An automatic maturity rating framework. In *CIKM*, 2015.

[20] I. Liccardi, M. Bulger, H. Abelson, D. Weitzner, and W. Mackay. Can apps play by the COPPA rules? In *PST*, 2014.

[21] J. Lin, S. Amini, J. I. Hong, N. Sadeh, J. Lindqvist, and J. Zhang. Expectation and purpose: Understanding users' mental models of mobile app privacy through crowdsourcing. In *UbiComp*, 2012.

[22] J. Lin, B. Liu, N. Sadeh, and J. I. Hong. Modeling users' mobile app privacy preferences: Restoring usability in a sea of permission settings. In *SOUPS*, 2014.

[23] R. Pandita, X. Xiao, W. Yang, W. Enck, and T. Xie. WHYPER: Towards automating risk assessment of mobile applications. In *USENIX Security Symposium*, 2013.

[24] H. Wang, J. I. Hong, and Y. Guo. Using text mining to infer the purpose of permission use in mobile apps. In *UbiComp*, 2015.

[25] Y. Yang and J. O. Pedersen. A comparative study on feature selection in text categorization. In *ICML*, 1997.

[26] H. Zhu, H. Xiong, Y. Ge, and E. Chen. Ranking fraud detection for mobile apps: A holistic view. In *CIKM*, 2013.

Author Index